Progress in Psychology of Personality

XXIInd International Congress of Psychology
Leipzig GDR July 6–12, 1980

Selected Revised Papers

Progress in Psychology of Personality

Edited by
Adolf Kossakowski and Kazimierz Obuchowski

1982

North-Holland Publishing Company
Amsterdam · New York · Oxford

ISBN: 0444 86347 8

Publishers:

NORTH-HOLLAND PUBLISHING COMPANY
AMSTERDAM · NEW YORK · OXFORD

Sole distributors for the U.S.A. and Canada:
ELSEVIER NORTH-HOLLAND, INC.
52 VANDERBILT AVENUE
NEW YORK, N.Y. 10017

PRINTED IN THE GERMAN DEMOCRATIC REPUBLIC

Contents

Introduction

Problems of personality psychology played a remarkable role at the 22nd International Congress. Symposia and thematic sessions served to introduce and discuss the results of investigations centred on personality psychology. This is, no doubt, connected with a development trend in our science, namely to integrate the results of increasingly specialized studies into general conceptions and to elucidate the mutual relations between cognitive, emotional, motivational and volitional processes in the process of interaction between personality and environment and of its integrative development in the ontogenesis.

The editors were anxious to select from the abundance of papers presented at the Congress those which seemed to them particularly important for the further development of theoretical fundamentals of personality psychology and which introduced new analytic strategies for the study of different personality variables as well as for the analysis of courses and determinants of their ontogenesis.

In this connection such papers were selected which placed special emphasis on the theoretical analyses and empirical investigations which were based on action-psychologyoriented models of the interpretation of the structure, function and development of the personality.

Part I of the book covers papers which deal predominantly, apart from methodological problems of the research and the development of theories in the sphere of personality psychology, with theoretical and empirical analyses of the organization and function of the specific structural components of the personality. A general concern of these contributions consists in making clear the change from a naturalistic and egocentric personality psychology to an analysis of the personality which is based on the interaction between individual and environment. Personality is understood as a socially determined subject of conscious activity (of the interaction between individual and environment), whose psychic structure is determined by the psychic components which regulate the conscious activity. This activityoriented approach becomes evident also in part II of the book, which emphasizes the aspects of the development of the personality in the ontogenesis, of the courses and determinants of the psychic development. Psychic development of a personality is understood as the development of integrated and connected structures of cognitive, emotional and motivational-volitional psychic components which enable the developing individual to regulate the activity in an increasingly independent and reflecting manner which is adapted to the requirements of the environment (situation) or induces a change of the environment.

It is shown that, in the course of the ontogenesis, qualitatively differing regulating structures and, consequently, personality structures emerge which are related either to the psychic regulating components as a whole or, in a pronounced manner, to cognitive or motivational structures. The quality of the developing regulating or personality structures is consistently described as a function of the internal and external conditions of interaction, and the effectiveness of social development conditions, e.g. of the economic and socio-cultural conditions, is proved by various studies.

Part III introduces, apart from methodological problems of empirical research in personality psychology, some recent empirical research methods and methods of personality diagnostics.

By publishing these papers the editors hope to throw some light on current problems involved in the development of theories of, and the research in, personality psychology.

A. Kossakowski

K. Obuchowski

The Application of Dialectics to the Theory of Personality

CARL SHAMES

The scientific study of the human individual has made tremendous progress in the century following the pioneering work of Wilhelm Wundt, and yet the dream of a coherent, mature science, freed from its origin in speculative philosophy, is more elusive today than ever before. The deepening sophistication of psychological science has, in fact, led to the opposite circumstance: from the scientific advances themselves, questions have emerged that call for philosophical intervention.

Scientific psychology has responded to the revolutionary advances in science, technology and in social life itself, with increasingly sophisticated techniques of investigation and a broad elaboration of concrete data. From these advances have emerged questions of the overall coherence and subject matter of psychological science, and the specificity of the psychological level of phenomena in relation to the social and biological levels. The integrity of the individual psychological subject, the coherence of the personality, has recently come to be seen as an issue that requires theoretical analysis. The nature of consciousness and the origins of motivation, remain as unsolved problems. The advances in psychology have called for the philosophical understanding of epistemology, the relation of conceptual models to objective reality, and the nature of causality and development.

A central question, one to which the others are in a sense secondary, is, what, precisely, is the meaning of 'human'? What is the specificity of human phenomena in relation to biological and technological phenomena? Ironically, the advances in technology and biological science have led to theories that model human processes on the basis of technological and biological processes. This tendency neglects the fact that it is the advance of human power itself that has led to the technological and scientific progress, and that this progress, far from negating the 'human factor', calls it forth as an issue demanding theoretical attention. Such models, while serving a transitory descriptive function, cannot address the pressing issues of our time in which psychology occupies a central role. The increased potential for conscious control over human processes, humanity's social conditions of existence, requires a psychological science based on the objective historical development of specifically human processes.

In the following pages, I will review various facets of this philosophical conjuncture of contemporary psychology, and, in particular, discuss the contributions to this discussion, of the late Soviet psychologist A. N. Leontiev and the French Marxist philosopher, Lucien Sève. The particular focus will be the contribution of dialectical methodology to the solution of these problems.

The tradition of naturalism

From the time of Wundt, psychology has been based upon what may be termed naturalism. That is, psychological processes have been seen as faculties of the biological human individual. This idea, that psychological processes are constructed upon the biological individual and that the latter is the proper unit and starting point of analysis, has not only rarely come under question, but has been definitive of the science itself. Psychologists have dutifully followed the Aristotelean methodology of observing the functioning of this individual, abstracting from data to form generalizations, and then positing these generalizations as laws that govern the functioning of the individual. Psychological processes have therefore been theorized as at least, homologous with biological processes, based, in one way or another, upon the life of the *homo sapiens* organism.

It has been understood that psychological science would be coherent and unified when all the aspects of the functioning of this human individual are understood in some organized way. But this goal has proven to be more elusive than it first seemed. The problem of how to organize psychological data into a coherent theoretical whole became an explicit issue at the time of the pioneering work of Vygotsky, Lewin and Piaget. Vygotsky, in particular, was interested in the question of understanding the integral human individual within a total historical social process. Behaviorism, psychoanalysis and anthropology all tried their hand at this particular problem but they all were content with generalizing a theory or methodology from their specific area of analysis, to those remaining. This tendency remains in strength today in sociobiology, and, as we shall see, in systems theory. A key problem in the formulation of a coherent understanding of the human subject and the subject matter of psychology, therefore, has to do with the specificity of human psychological laws, and their relation to processes at the biological and social levels.

A. N. Leontiev (1978), in the last decade of his life, came to see the source of the perennial methodological crisis of psychology in its most fundamental assumption: the pre-existing psychological individuality of the *homo sapiens* organism, and correspondingly, the naturalism that takes the split between subject and object as given and not itself requiring theoretical scrutiny. Leontiev's final work was devoted to an analysis of this problem, and to laying what he saw as the groundwork for a "reformulation of the entire conceptual apparatus" of psychology. This juncture of present-day psychology bears many similarities to that of the physical sciences in the early part of the century. As investigation penetrated more deeply into reality, the notion of a pre-existing *element* as a building block of *matter* was forced to yield to theories based upon motion, time, relation and transformation. Similarly, according to Leontiev, the concept of a pre-existing natural psychological individual has become untenable as the unit of psychological theory.

The principle of activity

Psychology, then, has not eliminated philosophical questions, but has called forth a new level of philosophical intervention. It is not to classical speculative philosophy, however, which psychology must turn. The search for eternal truths of knowledge and reason, from the standpoint of the transcendental subject, is yielding to the scientific analysis of cognitive processes and living human relationships. It is not coincidental that psychology is recreating on a concrete level, the problems debated by the classical philosophers on an abstract level. The relation of totalities to parts, causality and motion, the nature of consciousness and the essence of human life have re-emerged as issues to be answered not by speculative philosophy in itself, but by concrete scientific knowledge *organized by the conscious application of philosophical principles*. The need for psychology to become conscious of its relation to philosophy is now widely recognized. That is, philosophy and science must find a new working relationship. Therefore, Marx's solution to the debates of classical philosophy should be of general interest to theoreticians of psychology.

Marx's Theses on Feuerbach are recognized as the key formulae in his effort to resolve the issues of speculative philosophy, and in particular, the notion of the transcendental subject. Marx critiqued Feuerbach's attempt to formulate a natural scientific concept of man because he saw Feuerbach's materialism as a crucial intermediate stage between speculative philosophy and science. This Feuerbachian 'man', the abstract human being, containing within itself the essence of humanization, has, as I have shown, remained with psychology to this day as its most basic precept.

Leontiev (1978, chapter 3) pointed to Marx's first Thesis on Feuerbach as the key to overcoming modern naturalistic transcendentalism. For Marx, human processes must be understood not as metaphysical internal qualities existing essentially outside of social reality, but as human activity itself. The human being exists only in an active relationship with the world of objects, not as a passive spectator. The principle of objective activity as the basis of human psychological processes, therefore, overcomes the opposition between the passive subject contemplating, or influenced by, the world of objects, on the one hand, and the internally motivated subject acting upon a passive world of objects, on the other. All psychological processes are seen as moments, or components, of the active subject-object relationship.

Leontiev, in his formulation of the theory of activity, attempted to provide a complete basis for understanding the relation of individual psychological processes to social reality. This formulation has been widely applied, particularly in the socialist countries, in the effort to develop a coherent and unified theory of human functioning on the basis of the human being's active social nature. This point of view has been applied in studies of cognition, motivation and personality, which stem increasingly from a social, interactive basis, replacing the old metaphysics of studying components in some imagined isolation from each other or from social reality (Kossakowski, 1980).

In the last decade, as this point of view developed, two basic problems have emerged. The assertion of activity as a philosophical principle does not in itself guide the organization of data into a scientific theory. The issue of the structure and systemic nature of activity emerged as investigation became competent at ever more complex interactions. First there is the question of the source of the structure, whether it is intrinsic or extrinsic. Theoreticians such as Rubinstein postulated the development of internal structuring mechanisms, while Leontiev came to insist that the fundamental structuring relations must be extrinsic. The actual relationship of external to internal factors is not solved concretely.

Even more serious logical questions are raised. Since human beings interact essentially with each other and not with objects, it is impossible to conceptualize the activity of any one individual in isolation from that of others. Complex, interactive forms of analysis are called for. But then it becomes increasingly untenable to speak of activity in terms of the individual subject. But if the subject is not to be the unit of analysis, then what is? What is the basis for the overall coherence of the theory? Most importantly, the theory of activity cannot be based upon the individual subject and at the same time explain the existence of this subject. In sum, while the theory of activity may be the basis for overcoming transcendental naturalism, it itself is not sufficient to do so. What is called for is a theory that explains the coherence and complexity of activity, its systemic, structural or logical basis. It is with these questions that Leontiev was grappling in his final works.

Systems theory

The most influential model for analyzing complex organized processes has been that of the various forms of systems theory, and this approach has been productively applied to the analysis of activity (Lomov, 1975). Ludwig von Bertalanffy, in formulating the principles of the systems approach, attempted to transform psychology along the lines of the revolution in the physical sciences. For von Bertalanffy (1978), interdependence, multidimensional correlation and causation, and the study of organizational properties have emerged as issues in the social sciences in response to the complex development of social life and the great technological transformations of this century. He envisioned a "general systems theory" in which questions of society, technology, biology and psychology could be understood in their complex interactions and basic unity of organizational principles. The systems approach, he hoped, would extend the study of interactions, relationships and principles, until the entire human domain was covered, and the human totality thereby grasped.

Although this goal has proven to be elusive, the systems approach, in its variety of forms, has been productive in organizing data and modeling processes in a far more complex way than previously possible. In its rejection of elementalism and simple determinist models, and in shifting the focus of investigation to organization and relationships, it has provided a way to conceptualize the interaction of people with technology and with a complex world in which information and communication seem to have taken on a life of their own, replacing direct human relationships, or at least constituting the definitive quality of relationships. The advances in cybernetics and information theory have provided useful models for describing human processes in a new complexity. Yet it is precisely here that the first problem arises. The fact that human activity and relationships take on certain properties and qualities at particular times should not lead to the conclusion that these properties are constitutive of the relationships themselves and therefore sufficient as models for their explication. It is a long logical leap, for instance, from the observation that communication has become a central feature in human relationships, to the conclusion that human relationships *are* communication, and that this is therefore a suitable *model* for explaining all human phenomena.

In considering the difficulties encountered in the application of the systems approach, it is important to distinguish between those that are transient, and those based on inherent limitations. As noted, the systems approach holds the promise of unlimited extension, therefore it is easy to identify as temporary difficulties what are actually fundamental problems. These latter are, in my opinion, as follows: 1) the issue of boundaries, that is, the objective definition of the system as a whole or totality, subsystems, and elementary units; 2) the laws of organization in their specificity and generalizability; 3) the source of motion and development.

Boundaries are understood by von Bertalanffy as essentially arbitrary. They may be conceptual, natural or social, and may be applied by the investigator in any way for the purposes of analysis. This arbitrariness, however, spreads to the entire theory, since there is then no explanation for the objective existence or coherence of its own subject matter. Relationships, the fundamental category, whether seen as communication or interaction, must be implicitly defined as relationships in their property of taking place at a boundary. Otherwise this process could not be seen as a relationship. But the boundary, we have seen, is arbitrary. Then, systems theory often claims that the entity or form in the relationship has come into existence *on the basis of* the relationship. In the study of the human individual this produces the tautologous theory that communication taking place between individuals produces the psychological functioning of these individuals. Since communication already implies a psychologically functioning individual, the latter is posited both *a priori* and *a posteriori*.

Equally important, wholes, such as a society or the human totality, or psychological functioning as a whole, are posited as simple aggregates of parts, while parts are posited as defined by intersections of processes characterizing the whole. Since there is no theory of the whole itself or its relation to the parts, explanations become deeply anarchic. There is no explanation for why individuals should not change altogether when moving from one informational or relational system to another, or why human processes or the personality have any particular coherence. This problem is usually avoided by recourse to a naturalistic functionalism of either the individual human organism, groups, or society considered as a whole.

Lacking a theory of the boundaries of its objects of investigation, the systems approach tends to generalize what it sees as natural laws of functioning from one system to another. Most importantly, it does not recognize the transition from natural laws to human laws, and it therefore attempts to reduce the explanation of human functioning to a preconceived natural level of analysis. That is, it understands laws to be generalizable to any object, and the particular operations of any system are seen as the working out of these laws. In the area of human affairs, we find that far from enabling us to grasp human processes in their coherence and specificity, systems theory dissolves them entirely!

Motion and development are particular problems, since the systems approach conceptualizes relations to be separate from motion. Apparently explanatory principles such as entropy, homeostasis, and regulation, are consequently imported from biology and cybernetics, in order to account for both coherence and motion. The result, far from a theory of a unified integrated human system, is a thoroughly fragmented anarchic aggregate, held together and motivated by hypothetical general functional postulates such as the goals and needs of society, the group, or the individual. Human events, in their historical motion, are reduced to a "state of nature", and we have not budged an inch, for all the modern terminology, from the thought of Bentham and Mill.

In sum, the seductive promise of the systems approach to provide a coherent account for human functioning cannot be fulfilled. While it has rejected simple elementalism and determinism, it holds fast to positivism, functionalism and naturalism. In its application to psychology, it has replaced the nineteenth-century naturalism, upon which much of psychology continues to be based, with a more modern version. However, in its recognition of complex processes, and the systemic nature of human interactions, it has made an important step toward the more developed form, which is dialectical logic.

Dialectics

Hegel's philosophy of dialectics addressed just such methodological problems as those discussed above, but it remained for Marx to apply this method to a concrete analysis. In his final work, Leontiev (1978, chapter 5) grappled with the logical dilemmas posed by the analysis of activity, of the formation of the subject, and the grasping of the human totality. He found in Sève's application of Marxist dialectics a crucial contribution to their resolution. Leontiev (1978, p. 110) credits Sève with the insight that "the true way to investigate personality lies in the study of those transformations of the subject which are the result of the self-movement of his activity in the system of social relations". Let us consider the way in which dialectical logic addresses this question, and succeeds when systems theory fails.

According to Sève, while Marx's first thesis on Feuerbach is indispensable for the overcoming of speculative transcendentalism, it is the sixth thesis that provides the key to dialectical methodology. "No genuinely relational theory of personality, no effective surpassing the impasses of psychological substantialism and naturalism, and therefore no really scientific theory of personality are possible so long as one does not take Marx's crucial discovery absolutely seriously: in reality the human essence is the ensemble of social relations within which men not only produce their means of subsistence, but are themselves produced" (Sève, 1978, p. 141). Marx, according to Sève, has not simply asserted mankind's sociability, but has placed the locus of causality, the basis of human phenomena, on the terrain of social relations. Leontiev (1978, p. 140) put it this way: "for Marx, man as generic being (Gattungswesen), is not the biological species *homo sapiens*, but human society". Feuerbach's naturalism, which sees the source of human phenomena as an innate essence within each individual was rejected in favor of the theory of social relations as the explanatory basis of human phenomena. The key idea here is that social relations are not interpersonal relationships which the individual, pre-existing, enters into, nor are they general relations of society which, through cultural and economic mechanisms come to influence the lives of individuals: they are the underlying relations of a social order. According to Sève, these relations have no existence apart from the concrete lives of individuals, while individuals have no existence apart from these relations. The life of individuals taken as a whole is therefore the living concrete logic of social relations. The task of dialectical thought is to trace this logic.

Dialectics, from the very start, has an epistemological uniqueness, since as a form of thought, it has a theory of its own origins. According to Marx, dialectical thought has been made possible by the objective historical coming into being of the human totality through the universalization of labor and exchange. The starting point for dialectics, therefore, is a theory of totality as an objective reality, not simply as a sum of parts or a conceptual device. The whole is not an aggregate but, rather, has the status of totality on the basis of the fundamental relationships which have produced it. The processes underlying the totality's coming into being are also the basis for the formation of its parts, and therefore, as Marx attempted to show, parts must be analyzed in their contemporaneous relationship with the whole, rather than from the point of view of their individual genesis.

Dialectical analysis traces relationships from the totality, through mediations, to the level of concrete phenomena. Individual phenomena are characterized by both general relations of the totality and particular relations of their own specificity. For Sève, this understanding of the existence of the general in the particular is crucial to dialectical thought.[1] The key to understanding how this could be, is that the fundamental categories of dialectics are *motion* and *contradiction*. Motion is seen to pre-exist and need not be explained through an outside *elan vitale*. The source of motion is inherent in the contradictoriness of the organization of matter, while matter has no existence outside of motion. If we imagine a totality as a temporal logic of motion, not as a spatial architecture or systemic nexus, it becomes possible to see how general relationships can exist in particular phenomena.

Dialectics contrasts sharply with systems theory on numerous points. Form, for dialectics, is a moment of motion produced by its contradictions, whereas systems theory continues the metaphysical opposition of matter to motion. The latter sees boundaries as the form by which motion comes to define itself but not as inherent in the motion itself. Both motion and matter, for systems theory, remain ultimately abstract and metaphysical, each posited to define the other. Human individuality, that is, the human form, for dialectics, is not simply an aggregate of processes, nor is it a natural phenomenon: it is produced as a coherent form by the contradictory relationships within the totality. These relationships exist in the form of *necessary matrices of activity* within which all human phenomena take place. These matrices have both a general and a specific logic, producing individuality as such and its various forms (see Dolling, 1978).

The separation of the inner world from the outer, the creation of the subject, is seen in this way to be based upon the contradictions that underlie a social formation. The apparent "opposition between individual and society," according to Sève (1978, p. 38), which has been the starting point for all psychological theory, "is itself a secondary form of society's opposition within itself". The inner world does not enter into the world of external social relations: it is its concrete human product. Therefore, in analyzing human activity, dialectics does not begin with activity of the subject or of the individual, but with human activity as activity of the human essence, which, in its concrete logic, produces individuality and the subject.

The individual is linked with the processes of society, not externally, but internally. Dialectics, therefore, discards any notion of a pre-existing individuality and attempts to trace the relationships of society to their concrete logic in individual life. Marx clarified his ideas on the methodology of tracing social relationships in his introduc-

---

[1] This idea runs throughout Sève's work but is developed most explicitly in chapter III, part 2, "Psychology of the personality and the psychosocial sciences".

tion to the *Grundrisse*. He rejected functionalism that sees societies as aggregates of individuals and groups, motivated, united and differentiated on the basis of goals, interests and functions. He termed this level 'the false concrete', and demonstrated that an analysis that begins on this level leads necessarily to anarchy rather than coherence. Far from being a precursor to systems theory, as von Bertalanffy and others have suggested, Marxist dialectics has fundamentally criticized it.

Dialectical analysis, according to Marx, must begin with the most general abstract determinations within a totality, and trace them to the concrete level, since it is these determinations which have produced both the totality and the concrete forms. These abstractions are not conceptual constructs, but are objectively existing relationships. According to Marx, "the simplest abstraction which modern political economy sets up as its starting point and which expresses a relation dating back to antiquity and prevalent under all forms of society appears truly realized in this abstraction only as a category of the most modern society . . . [E]ven the most abstract categories, in spite of their applicability to all epochs – just because of their abstract character – are by the very definiteness of the abstraction a product of historical conditions as well, and are fully applicable only to and under these conditions".[2]

Marx was referring here to the category of general labor which was then the basis of political economy, and he showed that general labor had only recently come into existence. The same argument applies to the category of the general human individual which, as Marx showed, has come into existence on the basis of general labor. The modern individual, seeming to have a general individuality apart from particular social relations, is in actuality a product of the highest development and generalization of these relations. The apparent immediate correspondence between the biological *homo sapiens* and the psychological individual is thus a product of a total circuit of social relations. Sève points to Marx's analysis of the relation between the labourer and product, and between labour and wages to demonstrate the way in which the basic relations in the modern era proceed through a total social circuit.

In sum, just as Marx rejected the category of general labour as the starting point for economics, dialectics in psychology would reject the general individual as a starting point and begin with the analysis of the production of individuality. For Marx, underlying *relationships between things*, as in circulation and exchange, is to be found the *relations of the production of things*. The dialectical method in psychology, similarly, would leave the level of interaction, communication and the innately self-interested individual, and begin with the level of production. While the study of human phenomena has benefited greatly from the various forms of systems theory, structuralism and semiotics, the overall coherence of the theory requires analysis at another level.

In its analysis of the essence and appearances of human psychological phenomena dialectics offers a coherent theory of the 'human factor', that is, what it is that is distinctively human. Dialectics, unlike systems theory, does not impose pre-conceived laws of functioning on a sphere of analysis, but rather, attempts to grasp the object in its own motion. Dialectics provides psychology for the first time with the possibility for explaining human phenomena entirely in human terms in its analysis of the human essence, its motion, and concrete appearances.

[2] See K. Marx, Grundrisse, chapter 1, sect. 3, "The Method of Political Economy".

The Copernican revolution in psychology

According to Leontiev, the analysis of activity leads necessarily to the "rejection of the traditional| ... egocentric, 'Ptolemaic' understanding of man in favor of the 'Copernican', which considers the human 'I' as incorporated into a general system of interconnections of people in society" (Leontiev, 1978, p. 139). I have shown how a dialectical understanding of these interconnections provides a coherent theory that accounts for motion, development, boundaries, the human totality and individuality without recourse to naturalism and functionalism. What are the implications for psychological theory of this 'Copernican' revolution?

Firstly, the starting point for theory is the creation, not of characteristics of this or that individual, but of individuality as such. That is, the way the inner comes to be distinct from the outer on the basis of the logic of activity. This requires that psychology abandon spatial and substantial concepts in favor of temporal ones. For Sève (1978, pp. 272–273), "personality is not an architecture; it is a system of temporally organized processes." The science of personality must be a topology "of the relations and processes in which a concrete personality is produced".

A temporal topology makes it possible to conceptualize how general relations exist in particular phenomena. Both the generality and specificity of psychological phenomena can be explained in a uniform theory. Psychology in this way need not be based upon a model of generally equivalent individuals within which individual differences are produced by chance experiences or predispositions. The coherence and commonality of cognitive processes and personality organization, as well as cultural, group and individual differences are explained on the bases of the logic of activity.

The analysis of the great range of human phenomena on the basis of concrete logic eliminates all normativeness from psychological theory. That is, the assumption that the *homo sapiens* organism *naturally* and *normally* produces a coherent, socially adjusted, psychologically functioning individual. I would argue, in fact, that it is precisely the surpassing of this organismic level of functioning that is the basis and prerequisite for distinctly human phenomena. The analysis of personality in terms of norms, deviations and pathology would be replaced by a comprehensive theory of all human phenomena, their contradictions and forms of appearance. The very great range of human experience, consciousness and personality, the moment to moment changes in functioning within any one individual, transformations in religious rituals, carnivals and other profound collective experiences, all would become comprehensible when a static normative structure is discarded in favor of a temporal topology.

The conception of the personality as a structure of components such as motivation, emotion, cognition, would be rejected along with the Ptolemaic conception of the whole. The coherence of the functioning of the individual and the various aspects of this functioning come into being together. The deep interconnections between the various facets of psychological functioning would no longer be seen as some remarkable interdependence of separate systems, but quite on the contrary, as a developing diversity and complexity of functioning which begins with biological evolution and proceeds with human history. All questions pertaining to the relationship between various aspects of functioning, therefore, are ultimately historical questions. The emotional, cognitive and motivational potentials of humans may have only begun to appear.

The topology of individuality is at the same time the topology of consciousness. All questions of epistemology, the relation of consciousness to being, become concrete, scientific, rather than abstract, philosophical, questions, since being is now understood only in determinate forms, not abstractly. Consciousness, like being, only exists in concrete historical logic. Forms of organization of consciousness and the historical progress of these forms need not be attributed to innate structures, but may be understood in relation to real historical development.

Dialectics is above all a theory of motion, having surpassed the metaphysical barriers between form and motion, structure and development. Questions of motivation, the sources of motion in human affairs, are basic to this new conception. Since form is produced in the topology of its motion, the production of individuality and the basic laws of its motion are one and the same, both for individuals in general and for any one individual. Put another way, individuals are not affected by social contradictions, they *are* these contradictions in concrete form.[3] The positing of inner drives and outer goals, in whatever forms and combinations, is superseded by a theory that is based upon the contradictions of motion and development. Furthermore, the changing importance of individual motivational structures in relation to the collective, can itself be analyzed as an historical question. The relation of the individual to the motion of history would become more comprehensible, and the influence of factors such as ideology in this regard would be seen as secondary to more basic processes uniting and differentiating the individual with the collectivity.

Psyche and soma

The relation of the psychological to biological levels is particularly troublesome and controversial and a clarification is a prerequisite to the above reviewed reformulations. Leontiev, in his final work, drew upon Sève's interpretation of Marx's Sixth Thesis in attempting to clarify this issue. For Leontiev (1978, p. 8), when the personality is seen as a "*quality* that a natural individual commands in a system of social relations," then "anthropological properties of the individual appear not as determining personality or as entering into its structure, but as genetically assigned conditions of formation of personality, and, in addition, as that which determines not its psychological traits, but only the form and means of their expression". Since the human essence is seen to be in the "ensemble of social relations," not in the *homo sapiens* body, the *basis* of psychological processes is in the relations, while the body is the *support* for their transformation into forms. The relation of psyche to soma is of two realities of an entirely different order. Far from seeing the human body as antagonistic to human development, a theory some still subscribe to, this view sees the *homo sapiens* organism as a product of evolution with the unique capacity of bringing human phenomena to life.

This view calls for an understanding of human psychology as itself not a static composite of traits and abilities, but as a process of development, emergence and consolidation. Human psychology has not appeared at once, but has emerged gradually and is still in a process of consolidation. It is this, *distinctly human* psychology that is

[3] Sève's analysis of 'abstract activity' a neglected aspect of his contribution, is crucial here.

18

distinct from biological processes. Not all aspects of human functioning, therefore, are directly part of human psychology, and it is the task of psychological theory to sort this out.

The relation of economics to geography sheds light on this question. Recently, the United States witnessed a series of volcanic eruptions that have been perhaps the greatest natural cataclysm in U.S. history. Yet the effect on the overall functioning of the U.S. economy is precisely zero. Under other circumstances, at another time or place, this cataclysm could have obliterated a civilization, forced a mass migration, or fundamentally altered an economic structure. While the volcano had local effects on the economy of the region, no economist would seriously conclude that volcanos are capable of having a determining effect on the U.S. economy. The laws of economic functioning have become *essentially independent* from local geographic events, and therefore can in no sense be understood as composites of these events. While factors such as soil conditions and climate have local short term influences, they no longer have determining influences on economic dynamics as such. Through technology and the multinational nature of economics, these dynamics have become freed from particular geographical determinants, while relying on geography for their support.

According to Sève (1978, p. 221), "while it is true that it was from natural conditions that the development of mankind *started*, the whole of human history precisely consists in the transformation of those natural facts into historical facts . . . It is no longer geographic 'facts' which are the basis of developed history, since they themselves have increasingly become *historical results:* it is history which is its own basis and the real basis of these geographical 'facts'. This inversion of the natural and the social . . . is the secret of the whole process of humanization".

This illustration from geography is not a mere analogy to the relation of psychology to biology: there is a deep correspondence in the process of the freeing of human activity from its natural presuppositions. As Marx showed in this *Grundrisse* it is the freeing of economics from geography, in the system of universal exchange, which at the same time produces individuality in its modern form – the universal individual freed from natural ties. This modern individuality therefore represents a new stage of the relationship between psychological and biological organization in which the logic of human psychological organization has assumed a full coherence, because human social organization has for the first time achieved a full social logic. With this completeness, human psychological processes become functionally independent from biological organization, and they come to have a coherent, self-enclosed logic. This is why Descartes discovered the non-substantial *ego* when he did: in earlier times it did not exist.

In sum, the basis and logic of human psychological functioning, as *human* functioning, does not correspond to the *homo sapiens* body, but to what Marx termed mankind's *inorganic body*, the ensemble of relations considered as a material substrate (Sève, 1978, p. 224). This inorganic body has, with the advent of capitalism, assumed a new coherence, and therefore, so too has human psychism. The logic of human psychism is the logic of this inorganic body and the logic of its appearance in individual forms is the logic of the individual's activity in relation to the inorganic body. The Cartesian search for the relation between the human *essence* and *substance*, must, therefore, proceed through the dialectical logic of the relation between the essence and its forms of appearance.

Perhaps the crucial point is that human psychology must be understood not as "whatever it is that humans do," but as the contradictory motion of human development in its individual forms, as manifestations of human development and emergence from earlier forms. Similarities observed between human functioning and that of our animal forbears, and the continued influence of biological determinants on individual behavior, may be interpreted, not as limiting conditions of an innate animal nature, but as indications of how far we have yet to go to realize the potentials of the human species. The often posed question of why mankind makes use of but a fraction of its cerebral capacity is then easily answered: we have realized only a fraction of our social potential.

Psychology might well look upon the *homo sapiens* organism as a natural resource, whose mysteries and potentials have only begun to be tapped. The key to the development of this resource lies in the social possibilities for real human progress.

References

BERTALANFFY, L.: General Systems Theory. New York: George Braziller, 1978
DOLLING, I.: Zur Dialektik von Individuum und Gesellschaft. Deutsche Zeitschrift für Philosophie 8, 1978
KOSSAKOWSKI, A.: Theoretische Voraussetzungen und Konsequenzen einer tätigkeitszentrierten Analyse und Interpretation psychischer Erscheinungen. Deutsche Zeitschrift für Philosophie 4, 1980
LEONTIEV, A. N.: Activity, Consciousness and Personality. Prentice-Hall, 1978
LOMOV, B. F.: Systemic Approach to Psychology. Voprosy Psychologii 2, 1975 (eng. trans. U.S. Gov't doc's JPRS 65806)
SÈVE, L.: Man in Marxist Theory and the Psychology of Personality. Sussex: Harvester Press, 1978, p. 141

Structure and Function of Personality

KAZIMIERZ OBUCHOWSKI

The thesis of my paper is based on the methodological approach to personality established in the Poznan Branch of the Psychology Department of Polish Academy of Sciences.

The following general assumptions were the starting piont for this programmes:

1. A resarcher deals with two ontologically different forms of reality: *the picture* and *the model* (Obuchowski, 1970, 1982, in press). A picture is a description of concrete facts and processes. A model is a conception of the origin; the existence, and changes of a picture. A picture may indicate possibilities of relationships between various research results. A model shows causal relationships not only between various results of research but also between various results of deductive thinking.

2. In our understanding of the psychology of personality, a picture is a reality described either by means of situationally defined notions such as "lazy", "prosocial", "effective", etc. or by means of notions defined through a definite research method, for instance "highly intelligent (having an IQ over 130), "extraversive" (having a high score on the appropriate scale of the MPI), etc.

The first kind of notions are called *"situational"* notions, while the second are called *"indicative"* notions (Obuchowski, 1981 a).

A more detailed analysis has allowed an assumption that situational notions provide a shortened description of an individual's conduct, but they do not describe indirectly any of his psychological properties. Those psychological properties which, we suppose determine the individual's conduct, constitute a picture of personality, or more simply-*personality*. Personality we describe by means of indicative notions.

Therefore we should clearly distinguish between the picture of conduct, and the picture of personality, between conduct and personality.

We should differentiate also between *conduct* and *activity*. Conduct is a sequence of activities characterized by a common direction and by a form particular to a given person – a sequence covering, in some cases, many years of human life. Conduct is a procedure in the framework of which an individual shapes reality in his or her particular way.

It is activity when someone is hammering a nail. We may describe and explain it by conception of general psychology. When this nail is hammered into the door because we don't want to let somebody we don't like come in – this is conduct. It should be explained in terms of the theory of personality.

3. A model is a theory of personality, serving to establish casual relationships between the personality of a given individual and his or her conduct. Detection of such relationships we called explanation. Theoretical notions are the basic elements of a

theory of personality. *Theoretical* notions are related to mechanisms or systems of mechanisms, by the functioning of which a conduct of an individual is explained. Theoretical notions belong to the third class of notions (besides situational and indicative notions) specific to the psychology of personality.

Being a product of abstract thinking, a model is not directly related to reality, and as such can be subject to unrestricted operations, as for instance approaching it at different levels of generality, adding it to or identifying it with other models (according to the analogy principle), or educing definite pictures from it. The possibility to educe definite pictures and their consonance with intersubjective reality is a criterion of the model's quality.

Besides consonance with reality, a model has to have a heuristic value, i.e. it should be possible to derive either other models or pictures of the future (prognosis of personality) from the original one. In this sense, a model ist "unabolishable". It can only be rejected and replaced by another model, i.e. by one which would be either better verified or more useful (or meeting both criteria).

Let us conclude:

Three separate categories have been distinguished in the framework of psychology of personality, i.e. *personality, conduct*, and *theory of personality*. Psychology of personality aims at establishing casual relationships between personality and conduct.

4. Assumptions that follow concern practical recommendations resulting form the above considerations. It seems that the most important directions in the present situation of psychology of personality should be:

a) research into developing the description of personality with new elements. This needs a lot of exploration. For many years, personality has been described by means of a few, always the same, categories. Often they are, in fact, situational notions and for that reason refer to conduct and not to personality. Moreover many existing categories are simply useless.

b) exploratory work on the most important directions of human conduct, made by means of other methods than those used in typical personalyty research. This seems to be reason enough for cooperation with sociology and theory of culture.

c) construction of open models of personality. Very few (except, perhaps, psychoanalytical) conceptions of psychological mechanisms, explaining relationships between personality and conduct, are at our disposal at present. We also lack large, complex theoretical systems, which have, at the same time, operational advantages.

d) Pictures and models of personality should be useful in depicting and explaining the changes of personality in all phases of human life (Obuchowski, 1981, in press).

5. Those were the most general postulates directed towards psychology of personality.

For the purposes of the concrete research programme, serving here as an illustration of the problem, the following sequence of steps has been carried out.

The programme deals with the basic dimension of every mode of conduct, i.e. with its level. In our culture, this dimension is determined first of all by its functioning in the occupational sphere. Assuming that cases of various disfunctions resulting in a low professional effectiveness will be found at one of the extremes, cases of persons showing a particularly high professional effectiveness will be found at the other one. But the situation is more complicated than it seems to be, because the professional effectiveness of an individual could be determined by the organization of his or her work, the level of technology, and other factors which might be treated as marginal ones, from the point of view of personality research. Thus, in our programme such occupations have been chosen in which success depends primarily on the individual. They were called "complex" professions. Such kinds of professions meet three basic criteria:

a) Their realization requires creative inventiveness,

b) personal fate of an individual depends on the efficiency of realization of occupational functions,

c) there are no clear-cut standards for the performance of professional activities.

Examples of such occupations are high-level managers, scientists and artists.

High-level managers have been chosen as subjects for the main part of the research. A more detailed analysis showed that their outstanding functioning has been frequently due to favourable external conditions and to the application of proper management techniques. Personality traits seemed to play rather a background role. However, properties of personality proved to be a decisive factor in a longterm effectiveness, lasting for many years.

The research group has been divided into three subgroups, established according to the level of a long-term effectiveness: "low effective", "medium effective", and "highly effective" subjects. The level of effectiveness has been judged by subjects' superiors and colleagues (Obuchowski, 1981 b).

Next, a large amount of explorative research has been carried out. Free interviews, psychometric and projective methods, as well as some original methods based on our theoretical assumptions (e.g., the Map of Tasks Organisation) were used.

6. At the same time, an attempt at constructing a theoretical model of personality has been made. Two separate systems of personality have been distinguished in the framework of this model: the *Programming System* and the *Basic System* (Obuchowski, 1980, 1981 b, in press).

The Programming System involves the organisation of information fulfilling three basic functions:

a) The function of *Knowledge*. Information gained from the external worls and from the individual's own reflexive thinking are the basis for interpretation of reality. Knowledge can be described by means of various codes and involves various systems of meanings, dependent on its origins and purpose.

b) the function of *Individual Tasks*. The organization of tasks is an "axis" of individual conduct. It also has a decisive influence on properties of a long-term motivation and on the degree of utilization of the acquired knowledge.

c) the function of *Emotional Attitudes*. Emotional attitudes have a decisive influence on preferences for individual tasks and on evaluation of the outcome of realization of tasks.

The Basic System involves properties often referred to as formal properties of personality. In many cases they are direct manifestations of the state of cerebral tissues and of the brain organization of the state of cerebral tissues and of the brain organization. They are not learnt, and they change either in the course of maturing and ageing or in consequence of various diseases.

It has been assumed that properties of human personality are subject to constant changes of at least four kinds (Obuchowski, 1981 a, 1980, 1976, in press).

The basic one, common to all human beings, is the mechanism of *continuous changes* resulting from maturity and aging. From this point of view, the efficiency of highly effective managers from our research group should be expected to decrease with age. Thus, the fact that they still show high effectiveness seems to be a paradox, especially when we remember that in the case of successes at managerial level, the degree of difficulty of tasks usually increases.

The second category of changes is related to mechanisms connected with various illnesses; to a certain degree, everybody suffers from something. This category has been called *decompensative changes*. A lot of our subjects reported suffering from various somatic diseases and psychological inner incompatibilities, making their work harder. Thus also from this point of view a decrease in effectiveness should be expected instead of an increase.

The third category of changes has been called *compensative changes*. There is not much to say about the mechanisms of compensation of diseases (apart from the over-simple Adlerian concepts), and ageing influences. The impact professional experience could be constructive in many cases, but it could be destructive as well. Many subjects introduced either a strict health care discipline or some new forms of recreation into their everyday life, but such steps might be considered as disturbing subjects in their work, rather than increasing their effectiveness in the professional sphere.

In order to explain a lasting, long-term effectiveness, we had to try to find a fourth kind of mechanisms of personality changes. These are – *task-oriented changes.*

It has been assumend that the specific property of the Programming System is its ability to "tune up", to accommodate to tasks faced by an individual. When tasks are directed towards adaptation to external demand only, an impoverishment of the organisation of the Programming System should be expected. When tasks are related to past experiences and their consequences only, pathological changes in the Programming System, and consequently – changes in the Basic System should be expected.

The only changes that could be considered as developmental ones (which are the most desirable) are changes consisting in accommodation of the Programming System to the realisation of a *long-term task*, integrating all other tasks into a whole. Such tasks, have been definied as *principal tasks*, giving a basis for an individual's sense of life, and at the same time, surpassing limits of an individual life.

A conception of long-term tasks and additional criteria of personality development as one of the forms of task – oriented changes of personality, have been elaborated.

The conclusion drawn from the above model is that different levels of long-term effectiveness correspond to different organizations of personality, especially in the framework of the Programming System.

Research carried out independently of the theoretical level, has confirmed its assumptions and added much important data.

The result of this research permits the conclusion that the *fundamental function of personality is maintaining a high level of effectiveness, which is tantamount to the development of personality*.

The development of personality is related to such properties as knowledge, tasks, and attitudes, understood as a personality's system, programming the conduct of an individual. They form various structures of personality, in the framework of which, the organization of an individual's tasks seems to play a decisive role.

Properties of the Basic System, although being the main field of interest of psychology, do not have a decisive influence on personality functions. Their role could be either a facilitating or a strenghtening one.

Concluding, I would like to remind the reader that in our approach three categories have been distinguished: conduct, personality (both being descriptive ones), and theory of personality. Psychology of personality aims at explaining the causal relationships between conduct and personality. Research on the basic dimension of conduct – long-term effectiveness has shown that it was tantamount to developmental changes of personality and that different levels of effectiveness corresponded with different organisations of personality. Only one type of its organisation warrants the development of personality. These assumptions have been verified indirectly by means of research on groups of scientists.

References

OBUCHOWSKI, K.: Cognitive Codes and Structure of Emotional Processes. Warszawa: PWN, 1970 (in Polish)

OBUCHOWSKI, K.: The Individual's Autonomy and Personality. Dialectics and Humanism 1, 1976

OBUCHOWSKI, K.: Einige Probleme der entwicklungsfähigen Persönlichkeit. In: A. Kossakowski (Ed.), Psychologie im Sozialismus. Berlin: Deutscher Verlag der Wissenschaften, 1980

OBUCHOWSKI, K.: Individual and Personality. Some Theoretical Aspects of Developmental Personality. Warszawa; PWN, 1981 a (in Polish)

OBUCHOWSKI, K.: Personality and Effectivity. In: K. Obuchowski (Ed.), Personality and Effectivity. Wroclaw: Ossolineum, 1981 b

OBUCHOWSKI, K.: Orientierung und Emotion. Berlin: VEB Deutscher Verlag der Wissenschaften, 1982 and Köln: Pahl-Rugenstein Verlag, 1982

OBUCHOWSKI, K.: Some theoretical aspects of Developmental Personality. In: E. Zolik and L. Grzesiuk (Eds.), Psychology in Poland. (In Press)

OBUCHOWSKI, K., and L. GRZESIUK (Eds.): Psychology in Poland. (In Press)

Cognitive Theory of Personality Assessment

Hans Thomae

The chances for prediction of behavior offered by cognitive theories of personality were demonstrated by very different approaches. Cognitive structures such as those defined by personality through perception approaches facilitated prediction of different aspects of cognitive behavior, of coping with conflict, of self concept formation, and interpersonal behavior. The analysis of cognitive systems within the dimension concrete-abstract (Harvey, Hunt & Schroeder, 1960) pointed to close relationships between formal cognitive structures and stages of personality development. Personal construct theory (G. Kelly, 1955) especially in its operationalization by Bieri identifies evolution of personality and formation of personal constructs the analysis of which is instrumental in predicting interpersonal behavior.

Even more successful were approaches such as defined by generalized expectancy (J. Rotter). The construct of expectancy goes back to Tolman's pioneer work on cognitive theory of learning and motivation. Therefore it can be regarded as a link between learning theory and personality theory. The development of research on generalized expectancy of internals vs. external control showed, however, that any kind of operationalization of cognitive constructs exposes to the risks and dilemmas of trait contered personality theories. Just to mention one example: The ambiguity of recent findings on the adjustment of externals vs. internals (Phares, 1978) can be solved by additional constructs like that of the *defensive external* only partially. This points to the interaction of situation and person in the elicitation of reactions and questions the usefulness of constructs derived from process oriented theories like cognitive theories which are transferred into trait-oriented theories by their transformation into tests- and questionaires.

This paper raises the general question how much cognitive theories loose of their relevance as process oriented theories as soon as they become represented in testlike measurement instruments. If this is true we are faced with the problem of alternate methodological approaches. An *alternative* is seen in the *semi-structured interview* and its standardized evaluation by judges. This methods enables us to come as closely as possible to the decisive variable in any kind of cognitive theory, namely the process of cognitive appraisal of the present situation by different 'belief-value matrices' (Tolman, 1951).

The place of cognitive theories in personality theory

According to traditional trait-centered personality theories behavior is the outcome of the elicitation of more or less specific mechanisms which are labeled by some trait name or factor symbol. This interpretation is supported by Raymond B. Cattell's emphasis on the determining function of personality factors (Cattell, 1966). By additive cumulation of situational, trait, and state variables Cattell's specification-equation tries to predict behavior of specific persons in specific situations. Cognitive theories on the other hand point to close relationships between situation as perceived and behavior. They focus on the assessment of the formal and content aspects of these situation perceptions and on the formation of person as well situation specific predictions derived from these qualities. These perceived qualities of the cognitive representation of the situation are the outcome of cognitive appraisals which can be influenced by the nature of the personal constructs as developed by the individual, by generalized expectancies, and preference for certain attributions of success and failure. With increased measurement of cognitive structures by instruments designed under the control of traditional test theory the real process of cognitive appraisal of situation and its cognitive representation very often becomes neglected and non-situation-specific predictions are preferred which hide the variability of behavior as existing in reality.

In agreement with models of 'cognitive appraisal' of situations like formulated by Magda B. Arnold and R. S. Lazarus this paper will focus on the concrete cognitive appraisals and reappraisals. The semistructured interview on specific aspects of life history and present situation enables us to study these concrete appraisals and re-appraisals.

The conclusions to be drawn from anextended version of these cognitive appraisal models for the prediction of behavior and personality assessment will be discussed from the findings of several studies conducted at our Bonn Psychology Department.

Real and perceived life space in adolescents of different SES

Using a Dailey round type of interview Lehr and Bonn (1974) tested the hypothesis of a more restricted life space of lower middle class adolescents. This hypotheses had been confirmed by McKinley (1964) and Uhr et al. (1969). According to the analysis of longitudinal data on achievement orientated activity during 8 years of observa-tion Uhr and I (1969) found that the life space of lower class children and adolescents provided only a limited degree of interindividual variability in development: These Ss received either consistently low or slowly rising scores in the measured variables. On the other hand, middle class children and adolescents showed a great variety of developmental patterns: consistent medium and high scores, falling, rising, falling and again rising or rising and falling scores as well as repeatedly changing scores. We concluded that this higher variation in the developmental patterns in middle class children reflected a life space more open to change in different directions.

Lehr and Bonn (1974) however, found very clear differences between the 'openess' of the real life space and its cognitive representation. While the objective environ-ment of middle class children and adolescents in terms of private space in family home, access to higher education, opportunities to travel and to meet more people from different social strata was more open this was not true for perceived life space. The young people in this class perceived themselves more restricted and controlled by prescriptions and rules than lower class adolescents. Therefore the cognitive appraisal of the life space by middle class adolescents was more negative.

The differences between the findings of Uhr et al. (1969) and Lehr and Bonn (1974) are to explained partially by cohort-as well as age-related differences. In any case it can be concluded that the study of the objective environment is insufficient for the prediction of behavior as the cognitive representation can differ from its objective quality. This cognitive representation as to be assessed by semi-structured interview is the decisive variable in selecting responses to any situation.

Cognitive representation of parental behavior and achievement in school

Another study correlated perceived parental behavior as measured by a questionnaire (PME) with achievement in and adjustment to school (Kerpa, 1979). Girls who perceived the parental attitudes of their mothers as tolerant had higher grades in subjects like German, Mathematics and Natural History and higher adjustment scores than those who perceived their mothers as less tolerant. On the other hand the adjustment and achievement scores of boys who perceived their mothers as less tolerant and nurturant were higher than those of boys who perceived their mothers as tolerant and nurturant. From semi-structured interviews Kerpa (1979) could demonstrate the greater power of this instrument: we can mention here only those findings which are related to the hypothesis of adverse effects of *working mothers* on the adjustment of their children. She studied the objective and perceived home environment and leisure time of children of *working* and *non-working* mothers. Contrary to many beliefs there was no difference in perceived stress due extra jobs in the household or similar commitments for children of working mothers in the two groups. There also was no difference in perceived intensity of contacts in the family. Children of non-working mothers more often appraised the closeness of their family contacts in a negative way. Regarding leisure time children of working mothers perceived not more restriction than those of non working mothers. From these evaluations of the cognitive representation of their present life situation it can be expected that no behavioral differences between children of these groups of mothers will turn out. This expectation was confirmed by Kerpa as well as by many other studies. The very frequent warnings against adverse effects of work of mothers can be regarded from these findings as misleading constructions of children's cognitive representation of their family situation. The failure to find any reliable behavioral differences between children of working and non-working mothers points to the impact of cognitive representation.

Cognitive representation of academic training

Another recent study from Bonn (Hirsch 1979) tested the contribution of semi-structured interview for the predication of academic success in medical students: one group failed in the first examination (Physicum), the other one was successful. The cognitive appraisal of the situation at the beginning of the first year of training did not differ in a positive or negative direction. Both groups experienced the training as important to the same degree. However there were clear differences regarding perceived control of the situation: Successful ones perceived the situation as more changeable by themselves and they reported of more congruence between their expectations regarding training and the real situation at university. Sizeable differences were found regarding perceived difficulties and challenges in training. While both groups emphasized great difficulties the less successful ones did so to a significantly greater degree. While perceived insecurity in training was greater in the failure-group, perceptions of positive stimulation by the training was greater in the success group. The differences in reported perceptions were supplemented by those related to reactions. Successful students reported of more achievement related behavior and less evasive behavior than the failure group who had a tendency to leave things to chance. From these findings we may conclude that the semi-structured interview on cognitive representations of important aspects of the life situation can be regarded as an important tool for prediction and modification of study behavior.

Future time perspective and behavior

Lewin pointed to future time perspective (FTP) as an important area of cognitive structures. The formation of the mature personality from childhood to adulthood according to him is a function of the differentiation of FTP.

There are findings on relationships between restricted FTP and juvenile delinquency as well as different forms of psychopathology. In different samples from the normal population we studied the behavioral correlates of the cognitive structure of FTP. Uhr in 1967 analysed semi-structured interviews of men and women (19–20 yrs) who had been followed through their 6–14 years in the Western German Study on Postwar children regarding extension and differentiation of FTP and attitude toward the present. She differentiated between a more 'problemcentered' and a 'naive' attitude toward the present. Extended FTP was significantly correlated with greater degree of problem-centeredness'. The same was true for the correlation between differentiation of FTP and problem-centeredness.

While this finding may have relevance only as a confirmation of a global dimension such as differentiation it deserves more attention by the antecedents of the various FTP and present time attitudinal patterns. During their school-time those assessed as 'problem-centered' showed very often inconsistent and asynchrone scores for achievement oriented activity. On the other hand there was no relationship between any longitudinal pattern in the development of achievement oriented activity and any aspects of FTP. We should like to conclude that at least in adolescence and young adulthood there exists no consistent relationship between FTP and achievement related behavior.

Another aspect of FTP was studied by Mudrich by interviewing mothers facing the empty nest reaction (the youngest child leaving the home). This situation was coped with in a more successful way by those women who had a more positive attitude toward future, more realistic expectancies regarding later adulthood, believed to be competent to meet the situation, and who were active in the adjustment to the situation. The data from a semi-structured interview point to relationships between different cognitive representations of present and future, perception of own competence, to master the situation, and the reactions as elicited by these cognitions. Therefore they stress the predictive power of the study of cognitive structures by semi-structured interviews. At the same time the findings point to possible ways of intervention.

Dreher (1969) analysed interviewdata with workers from steelindustry (50–55 years of age) and retired persons (70–75 years) of the same companies regarding adjustment to retirement. Contrary to many expectations in literature and practice of preretirement training no significant relationship between degree of anticipation of retirement and adjustment to retirement was observed. On the other hand there was a significant correlation between a more positive appraisal of FTP as defined by retirement and adjustment to retirement. This finding coming from semi-structured interviews is important especially in connection with medical contributions to preretirement training related to increased possibility of disease and impairment in old age.

We could report more findings from BLSA related to the contribution of semi-structured interview to the assessment of cognitive structures and their behavioral implications. To mention just one example: Olbrich demonstrated from our data by the use of pathanalysis that the medical diagnosis 'sclerosis' or 'heart insufficiency' was less related to active coping with disease than the perception of health by the subject himself as assessed in an interview.

For our discussion on methodological aspects of cognitive structures and their impact on behavior we should like to stress that we don't believe that semi-structured interviews are the only instrument to be recommended. In a study on the impact of cognitive structures such as the generalized expectancy of unchangeability of stress and deprivation in old age (Thomae, 1981) we used a scale for measuring this variable (Expectancy of unchangeability = EU-scale), including items like 'a person of my age should not expect that hard times will change for the better'. The sample consisting of aged persons with chronical disease, physical dispairment and/or low income was also interviewed with special emphasis on the way how they reacted to their life situation. From the many findings we want to mention just one: Subjects scoring high in the EU-scale more often reported of reactions to their problems like revision of own expectancies, depression, and active resistance against medical advice or diet prescription than those scoring low in this scale. The close relationship between the cognitive structure 'expected unchangeability of stress and deprivation' (EU), and the preference for maladjusted reactions to the own life situation points to the relevance of cognitive theories for psychological assessment as well as for the intervention against chronical disease or increasing impairment due to passive or problem behavior.

Discussion

From the last study reported here it becomes evident that we do not want to stress a methodological 'monism' which excludes any other approach aside from the semi-structured interview. However it will be the only choice for the analysis of concrete and specific situations and the reactions to these situations. As far as trait-like cognitive structures such as 'generalized expectancies' are concerned scales and questionnaires may be used as their methodological basis is trait-oriented, too.

The validity of our EU-scale, however, was tested again by the use of the semi-structured interview. About 30% of the sample of chronically ill persons of our EU-study (Thomae, 1981) belonged to the panel of the Bonn Longitudinal Study of Aging (Thomae, 1976). These subjects had been interviewed and tested for 12 years before the EU-scale was administred for the first time. From the interviews we rated (among hundreds of other variables) the degree of perceived definitiveness of the own life situation. Subjects who scored high in the EU-scale in 1977 had consistently higher scores in the scale rating 'perceived definitiveness' during the years 1965–1977. But they differed in other aspects, too, they had a some-what lower SES, lower IQ, poorer objective health, poore perceived health; were always more concerned about the restrictiveness of their life space, and were less interested on social participation and intellectual stimulation.

From these data we could conclude the continuity of two life styles one of which is more restricted by physical and economic deprivations and low degree of counter reactions where as the other one is more open for change, activity and involvement. However this continuity was only true for the extreme groups. Those scoring medium in the EU scale had very complex patterns of consistency and change in their adjustments.

Summarizing we might state that the semistructured interviewed analysed by rigorous rating procedures offers the chance for the assessment of specific as well as generalized cognitive structures. As these structures are the main determinants of behavior the prediction of personality development will make progress only if the method of the semistructured interview and its analysis by rating procedures becomes increasingly sophisticated.

References

ARNOLD, M. B.: Emotion and personality. New York: Columbia Univ. Press, 1960
CATTELL, R. B. (Ed.): Handbook of Multivariate Experimental Psychology. Chicago: Rand Mc Nally, 1966
DREHER, G.: Die Anpassung an die Pensionierung als psychologisches Problem. Phil. Diss. Bonn 1969
HARVEY, O. J., D. E. HUNT and H. M. SCHROEDER: Conceptual Systems and personality organisation. New York–London: Wiley, 1960
HIRSCH, M. A.: Die Auseinandersetzung mit Schul- und Studienanforderungen. Phil. Diss. Bonn 1979
KELLY, G. A.: Psychology of personal constructs. New York: Norton, 1955
KERPA, U.: Mutterrolle und mütterliche Berufstätigkeit im Erleben des Kindes. Phil. Diss. Bonn 1979
LEHR, U.: Frau im Beruf. Frankfurt: Athenäum, 1969
LEHR, U.: Persönlichkeitsentwicklung im höheren Lebensalter. In: H. Löwe, U. Lehr and J. E. Birren (Eds.), Psychologische Probleme des Erwachsenenalters. Berlin: VEB Deutscher Verlag der Wissenschaften, 1982
LEHR, U., and R. BONN: Ecology of adolescents as assessed by the daily round method in an affluent society. In: H. Thomae & T. Endo (Ed.) The adolescent and his environment. Basel–New York 1974, 67–79
MCKINLEY, D. G.: Social class and family life, New York 1964
MUDRICH, B.: Der Wegzug des letzten Kindes aus dem Elternhaus im Erleben der Mutter. Unveröffentl. Diplomarbeit Bonn 1978
OLBRICH, E., and H. THOMAE: International Journal of Behavioral Development 1, 1978

PHARES, E. J.: Locus of control. In: H. London & J. E. Exner jr. (Ed.), Dimensions of personality. New York: Wiley, 1978, 163–304.

ROTTER, J. B., J. B. CHANCE and E. J. PHARES: Applications of a social learning theory of personality. New York: Holt Rinehart Inc., 1972.

THOMAE, H.: Das Individuum und seine Welt. Eine Persönlichkeitstheorie. Göttingen: Verlag für Psychologie, 1968.

THOMAE, H. (Ed.): Patterns of Aging. Basel–New York 1976

THOMAE, H.: Expected unchangeability of Life stress in old age. A contribution to a cognitive theory of aging. Human Development 1980

TOLMAN, E. C.: A psychological model. In: T. Parsons & E. Shils (Ed.s) Toward a general theory, of action. Cambridge, Mass. Harward Univ. Press, 1951

UHR, U.: Untersuchungen zur Entwicklung in der Adoleszenz und im jungen Erwachsenenalter. Unveröffentl. Forschungsbericht Bonn 1967

UHR, R., H. THOMAE and J. BECKER: Verlaufsformen der seelischen Entwicklung in der Jugendzeit. Zeitschrift Entwicklungs- und Pädagogische Psychologie 1, 1969

Structural Analysis of Interpersonal Abilities

HARRY SCHRÖDER

1. Proposition and starting-point

The development of an efficient psychological personality diagnostic that meets the needs of social practice is connected with premises that are first of all to be provided by personality-psychological research. The level of formation of personality-psychological theories is reflected, mostly with a certain time lag, by our diagnostic methods and eventually also by our findings and diagnoses. It is a well-known fact that it is easier to formulate general requirements for a theory than to put such premises into practice – and if possible up to the construction of methods of inquiry and the empirical control of a field of subjects. The present paper should be taken as an attempt to utilise, from the structure-analytical aspect, principles of a personality psychology indebted to the concept of action in psychology (cf. Leontjew) for analysing abilities in a limited field of demands. Therefore, we want to give a short report on our research. Their aim was to find out structures of psychic functional potentials necessary for successfully meeting interpersonal demands of man. A comprehensive survey of this topic is provided by the book by M. Vorwerg and H. Schröder (ed.): "Persönlichkeitspsychologische Grundlagen interpersonalen Verhaltens", Leipzig 1980.

If starting from the central concept of action, from the conception of the individual as an open system in correlation between individual and environment, the aim of research cannot, on the one hand, be a system of situation-invariant universal dispositions of behaviour. On the other hand, it is not unstable regulating quantities for behaviour that are concerned, but psychic functional potentials in the meaning of a potential by means of which the personality meets repeated actual efficiency demands. The basis for analysis must therefore be the objective structure of demands and levels of action of the correlation "personality – environment". Starting from these, structural statements on the specific quality of psychic components of the independent regulation of action would be aimed at. This is an expression of the fundamental position of the personality theory based on Marxism-Lenism and thus also of personality psychology, in the concept of which the "personality" is a rating conception. According to this interpretation it is not sufficient to state a system of formal descriptive quantities. Moreover, starting from an estimation of the results of action, the "social quality" of man and its premises of action in the meaning of social efficiency are to be determined. As a general rating criterion to be verified in empirical work, the "level of active conscious configurative and functional competence (Schmidt, 1977) in face of social efficiency demands can be taken. Since these are concrete for every individual, we bring that in each case into relation with the predominant sphere of activity of the personality.

We restrict ourselves here to interpersonal performance situations as they are given for teachers, managers and psychotherapists. Thus, in the case of a teacher the question could be: what social behaviour, which interpersonal action potentials are necessary in a given social formation for attaining defined educational objektives of this society? In this case the structure of abilities referred to action would be identical with aspects of the psychological profile of this profession or with the part to be played in society. We will come back to this point later.

2. Methodical concept of analysing variables

By means of which methodical conception can the matter in question be mastered? To begin with, I will confine myself to the methodics of the analysis of variables applied here. According to the question asked, the first task was to deduce hypothetical ability components for interpersonal performance situations. For this purpose two fields of event had to be put into systematic relation: a) characteristics of the objective structure of action had to be referred to b) regulating functional units of the individual. On the basis of this relation functionally significant qualities had to be deduced. This required, of course, the development of concepts for a) and b). This was the concern of part of the work. The single elements of the analysis of action, which will not be explained in detail here, are based on the following general definition of what is understood here by *interpersonal performance situation:* demanding

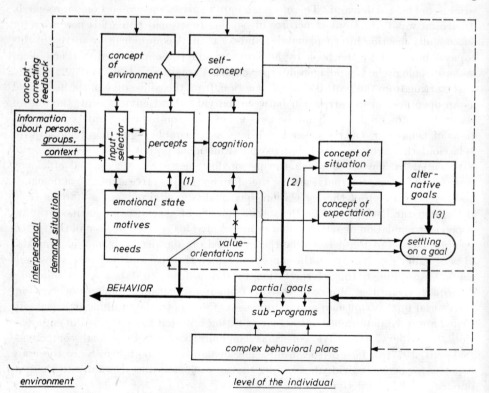

Fig. 1: A general diagram of the action process (Schröder, 1980).

situations in which persons are in direct communication, with influence being exercised on changes in behaviour-complying with standards of the other person through acts of behaviour. In this connection the shaping or modification of psychic regulation peculiarities of the interaction partners is aimed at. The elaborate action elements can roughly be grouped into: 1. situation analysis, 2. definition of problems and determination of the objective, 3. choice of means, 4. objectivedirected stimulation and 5. process and result supervision. The parts of the action structure were then referred to function units of the action regulation. For this purpose a specifically designed scheme of the general action process with a comparatively great number of dispositional regulation sequences was used.

Fig. 1 gives an impression of the components of the scheme without the framework of relations being explained (environment and self-concepts, cognition, situation concept and expectation concept, alternative objectives, complex patterns of behaviour with sub-programmes, motives, valueorientations etc.). In the analysis of variables, for example, the question was, which progressional qualities of the behaviour regulation according to the action scheme are significant for the first action sequence (situation analysis with its many partial demands). This aims in this case mainly at individual peculiarities of cognitive concepts, first of all at the structures of characteristics and at the rating structures. In the stage of demand "definition of problems and determination of the objective" of the action demand, decentering and interpersonal problem solving presumably unite to form a complex determining the performance. This was worked through step by step for all elements of action and all stages of regulation and resulted in a set of hypothetical partial abilities. The determination of variables in this phase served as an intermediate step for preparing empirical real analyses. On the other hand, it was not a final step of a work programme to be followed only by the construction of the procedure and the diagnostic application. Therefore we refrain here from presenting in substance the non-reduced field of variables ranging from cognitive characteristics via motivational peculiarities to qualities of the instrumental behaviour. Further on the spheres of variables were exactly defined, suitable measuring points were fixed, variables operationalised and rendered measurable by means of scales. In what follows we will confine ourselves to the presentation of some selected results of empirical analyses by means of the whole set of variables (complex analysis).

3. Empirical results of "Complex Efficiency Analyses"

The hitherto existing set of hypothetical ability components for interpersonally successful behaviour (competent behaviour) was very extensive and it was necessary to reduce it. According to what criterion should this be done? Answering this question is connected with the principal problem of rating individual peculiarities of behaviour regulation – in our case with the question as to the criterion of interpersonal competence (as to the concept of competence see M. Vorwerg and Schröder 1980). According to our normative conception of the concept of personality we primarily rate on the basis of normative demands of the specific sphere of life and activity of the personality. From this the class of construct-external criteria of success in action is constituted. After defining relevant psychic regulation peculiarities, it could be extended by the class of construct-internal criteria. On the stage of analysis just described and for the example of the activity of a teacher we establish and use the following characteristics as selecting criteria: dimensions of readiness of the pupil to identify with the teacher (socially-personally, politically-ideologically, with reference to performance), synthesized external and estimated judgement on variables of the success in action of teachers, belonging to criteria groups "psychic sane" and "patients of psychotherapy" respectively.

In empirical research only an extensive set of person variables was to be related to some criteria of objectives, with a comparable valuation of influences to be theoretically interpreted being aimed at. The data are based on a systematic random test of teachers of the Secondary Polytechnical School of the German Democratic Republic ($n = 100$), its about 2500 pupils and on a random test of psychotherapy patients ($n = 86$). As mathematico-statistical methods of analysis were used: special transformation within the framework of factor analysis, canonical correlation analysis and discrimination analysis. Repeatedly proved *findings verify thereby the following fact*: there is a limited number of variables that can be taken as performance-determining functional potentials for interpersonal-competent behaviour in the field of activity dealt with here. These are, according to the empirically ascertained valuation, primarily as follows: complexity of information digestion in socio-personal problem situations, communication confidence in front of the group, self-image "self-control", communication readiness, communication confidence as leader in dyadic situations, decentering, cognitive complexity in personrating and some characteristics of behaviour such as emotional warmth and understanding.

4. "Complex Structural Analysis"

Of course, no statements as to relations between structural components are connected with the results mentioned here so far. All parameters were dealt with equally as "person variables", regardless of their hypothetical significance in the process of behaviour regulation. Therefore the following step interdependence relations between them are of interest. We grouped our field of variables as follows:

1. cognitive variables of the self- and social understanding of environment,
2. general requirement-related behaviour,
3. traits of instrumental behaviour,
4. success criteria of the dominant field of action.

The purpose was to probe "chains of influence" between the variables of these groups. Thereby the dominating, significant direction of relation had to be found and the specific weight of influence determined. For this purpose multiple linear regression analyses were calculated, where the variables of one stage were valid as predictor variables for each seperate variable of the following sequence. In this way a relatively tight net of variable relations was made.

Fig. 2 is an example of a path diagram for the criterion variable "identification readiness I".

The explained paths and influence weights show important aspects as to the contents. Some of them will be illustrated in more detail. One can see that the assurance of communication of a leader or instructor standing before a certain group within

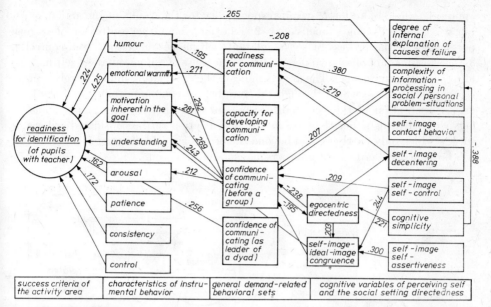

Fig. 2: Path diagram of effect variables in the field of "Interpersonal Abilities" (Schröder, 1980).

this field of requirements is of great importance. Important traits of behaviour are linked with it, which, in turn, themselves are direct premises of educational success. This concerns above all the aspects of motivation and activation of pupils; not so much the emotional relations. The path diagram also shows important degrees of influence for this aspect of assurance of communication. It depends on decentered orientation and on the reflexion about the self-control and is, in addition, in a defined relationship to the complexity of informational processing and self-acceptance. According to this a teacher will only communicate quite confidently in his classroom and show himself as an effective identification object, if he has a positive attitude to himself, and assesses himself as very self-controlled and besides is able to analyse social-personal problem situations distinctively. Besides, he must be able in the sense of changes of perspective to take the subjective position of his pupils. In this complex of relations two basic points are obvious that were also present in the previous analysis of variables: the cognitive analysis of the environmental conditions by the individual that corresponds to the objective situation in connection with the self-related certainty to be able to control oneself appropriately. This relation embodies the bearings of cognitive external control (in the sense of environment control by the individual) and of self-control as a presupposition of a successively regulating changes of environment. As will be seen, some more blended structural parameters may be worked out. The indicated aspecting of the degree of influence could be supported by similarly made regression-analyses that related to other successful criteria. A general view is given in Fig. 3.

The variables of the first stage reflect in one part the field of orientated external control and thus important formal characteristics of the social reality concept of the personality. A second group of variables represents special aspects of self-consciousness. To this belong 1. the reflexion about individual possibilities of action in the appropriate field of action (e.g. self-responsibility for the results of the action, capability related self-image-dimensions), 2. reflexion about the control of one's own personality in the process of self-regulation (self-image dimension, "self-control"), 3. the assessment of ones' own personality in the sense of self-acceptance (self-image – ideal image – congruence). The arrows indicate the dominating influence-relations on the variable groups, which through the variables of communicability and the integrated orientation of the personality represent operative features of instrumental behaviour. In this paper they are in sketched relation to the considered criteria of success which only partly extend beyond the pedagogic field of action. In Fig. 3 they will be shown as "criteria of interpersonal success of action".

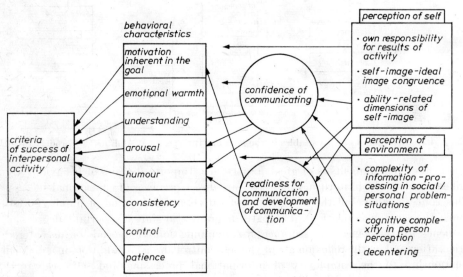

Fig. 3: Salient influence relations in the field of variables of "Interpersonal Abilities" (Schröder, 1980).

5. Conclusions for a general model of interpersonal abilities

The hitherto indicated grouping of variables seems to be of importance not only for people who are involved in pedagogical work but also for those that have a much greater field of action. This led us, as a generalisation of our hitherto gained knowledge, to model conceptions about the general structure of interpersonal competence (Fig. 4).

It becomes concrete always in relation to the type of requirement of the appropriate field of action. So, for example, in an assumed equal general structure, special cognitive concepts will make the oriented ability of action and action-relevant operative behaviour characteristics will make the regulating competence of action. This also concerns the other components in making them concrete with regard to contents. In the current situation of action the interaction between the situational requirements and the potential performance ability yield the appropriate situational competence. In every person it undergoes intraindividual fluctuations depending on the specific features of the task given and the variable additional conditions (for example indisposition of the individual).

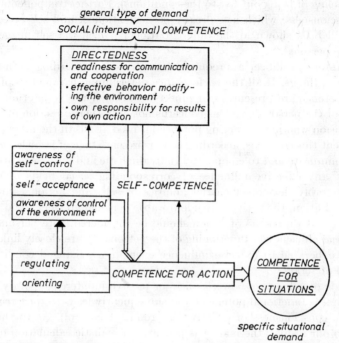

Fig. 4: A general ability structure of social (interpersonal) competence (Schröder, 1980).

The general construction of interpersonal competence can be divided into the competence of action and self-competence. The former comprises two aspects. The orientated competence of action concerns psychic predispositions for a subject adequate cognitive control of the environmental conditions. It involves the differentiated representation of the determining components of the environment, the realistic explanations and forecasts of events of the subject-field. Regulating competence of action comprises the operative ways of behaviour, with which a changed influence on the conditions of requirements is carried out. They are those features of behaviour, tactics and strategies that represent the requirement related forms of the reactive or active action and make up the individual degree of stimulating control of the environment. About the reflexivity of the subject there are close relations between the competence of action and the self-competence. The latter comprises above all the relatively consistent reflexion about the regulating and controlling efficiency of behaviour in the appropriate field of action – the external control consciousness (in the sense of reflected active control of the environment by the individual). It represents a cognitive scheme about one's own possibilities of behaviour and determines the situational complex in the process of the regulation of behaviour, the expected success of one's own behaviour and also the decision for a behaviour. This field of self-image integrates the reflexive concept about the effectivity of one's own possibilities of action, in the sense of a complex performance concept. Disorders of the external control consciousness are an incriminating disturbance of the environment relationship and are even in clinical aspects an important psychopathological phenomenon (as with depressive patients or overstrained people, that do not feel themselves to be active but who develop a feeling of being outcast to the conditions). Further components are the self-control-consciousness, which has already been mentioned, and self-acceptance that has above all been shown in the differentiation between the self-image and ideal-image of the personality.

To be enabled to fulfil certain requirements and to act according to this ability are quite different things. If all the performance determining parameters of action and of self-competence are present, their object-determined use is determined by basic orientation of the personality. This concerns not only their direction of activity but also the decision whether the acting potential is used at all. In the interpersonal field of requirement this concerns, according to our present stage of knowledge, the readiness to communicate and to co-operate. Individualistic and autistic attitudes cannot bring about any effective influence of corresponding social fields of action even though favourably developed partial abilities of self- and action competence are present. In addition, the active attitude towards personal efficiency and self-responsibility for one's own results of action should be considered. Interpersonal effectiveness and social efficiency of functioning of the personality are closely linked with the conviction to be able to exercise influence even under changed conditions in the specific field of action.

An attitude of subjective powerlessness or passive indifference paralyses the normally favourable functional potencies and subsequently leads to their regression (for example the consciousness of effective environment control). As to this question, according to our results, the matter is primarily a realistic calculation of one's own possibilities of action. Under the given objective conditions one must decide if an active behaviour modifying the circumstances is indicated in the particular situation or, if, now and then reactive ways of behaviour for attaining the aims of action are necessary.

The indicated structural analyses of interpersonal abilities present a special concept of ability analysis and, together with this, the results gained and theoretical generalisation to be discussed. The attempt to use active psychological researches for studying special aspects of the personality structure in the presented variation seems to us to be useful and worthwhile developing, as, already after the first phase of complex studies, empirically proved psychological parameters have been elaborated which are shown in their structural entanglement and could be grouped into a general hypothetic model. The achieved results could serve as a basis for a personal psychologically proved psycho-diagnostics and modification of behaviour.

References

SCHMIDT, H.-D.: Normativer Aspekt und Persönlichkeitsbegriff. Probleme und Ergebnisse der Psychologie 48, 1979
VORWERG, M., and H. SCHRÖDER (Eds.): Persönlichkeitspsychologische Grundlagen interpersonalen Verhaltens. Leipzig 1980

The Analysis of Personality Variables of Pathogenetic Relevance in the Mentally Sick Person

Harald Petermann

First investigations served to examine the psychopathological relevancy of the initial concept. Proceeding from personality psychological model conceptions we tried to examine dispositional variables of action control on the basis of the disfunction in samples of psychiatric patients. Persons with directedness and self- or environmental control turned out to be of special import- ance for further clinical-psychological studies. Seen in its entirety, the method of involving abilities related to communication and cooperation in clinical-psychological analyses and develop- ing the diagnostic features for such studies proved fruitful. Therefore it is necessary to concentrate the selection of variables within different fields of action control more on central groups and to involve variables of other sequences of the field of action. For future studies we also contemplate extending the reference of requirements to everyday situations and involving other groups of psychiatric patients who are relevant to health policy (alcoholics, psychopaths).

1. Introduction

The interrelationship between personality psychology and psychopathology in the widest sense of the word is, at present, insufficient. We regard the conceptional notion of psychopathology as one of the reasons for this. According to Weise (1979) this notion, among other things, conditions which branches of science are used in solv- ing current research tasks and conditions the competence of the representatives of various scientific branches. The most widespread notion of psychopathology which is also predominant in this country is the traditional medical-scientific concept (Schneider, 1955). It interprets psychopathological phenomena as symptoms of organismic pathobiological processes. Thus, psychopathological symptoms seem to be phenomena following internal somatic rules. Within this theoretical framework personality psychological research approaches are irrelevant. However, within the last few decades psychological and sociogenetic models for explaining mental disease have gained influence. A result of this was that psychiatric research increasingly con- sidered social and personal variables. The concept of regarding psychopathological phenomena as disorders of the interaction between person and environment on the basis of social learning processes (Weise, 1979) basically changes the importance of personality psychological issues. Personal and social conditions are regarded as relevant partial causes for the psychopathological syndrome and as essential starting points for therapy and rehabilitation of the mentally sick person. Of special interest in this respect are those intrapersonal conditions of maladjustment which affect the disordered interaction between individuals in a relatively consistent way, thus being related to the psychopathological situation. It is especially in this field of clinical psychological diagnosis where future research work still has to fill a gap. Most of the procedures used by the clinical psychologist in trying to diagnose personality basically only confirm the syndrome diagnosis. They allow only a few conclusions to be drawn with regard to areas of personality that may be studied psychotherapeutically. It is in this field that concepts of the personality psychology in solving psychopathological problems might fill a big gap.

2. Approach

The aim of the present investigation is to record fundamental personality psychological data about the behaviour regulation of mentally sick people. We are especially interested in the interindividual variability of person variables which include, in a relatively consistent form, the personality in the individual – environment interaction in the field of social behaviour. The theoretical starting point was a structure model of interpersonal abilities based on action psychology (Schröder and Vorwerg, 1978; Schröder, 1980). Related to this is a set of operationalised variables obtained by the method of analysing objective activity demands on the basis of a general action model of personality. These variables served as a basis for examinations of mentally sick people chosen at random. The value of this model approach in the field of psychopathology results from the content of modern concepts in psychopathology. They interpret phenomena and forms shown by human disorders, as a result of psychological, social, and somatic influences, thus avoiding a unilateral biological view of mental disease. Psychopathological phenomena are regarded as disturbances in the interaction between individual and environment. Thus, in psychopathological research to an ever growing degree arises the question of the psychic functional potential of the patient, which is used for coping with communicative requirements. What advantages, then, qualify the model approach of interpersonal abilities for use in clinical samples?

1. Regarding psychopathological symptoms as a result of a disordered person – environment relationship is incompatible with a rigid dispositional concept. Thus, it is essential to include relevant areas of activity of the mentally sick person. Our approach, which is adjusted to interactions with persons, with certain groups, and to demands made by social interactions meets this requirement. This range of demands is of clinical relevance because of the variety of communicative disturbances in mentally sick people.

2. Empirical analyses from the personal point of view should also include the person in his entirety in the psychopathological field. Our conceptional notions, starting from the process of action regulation, comprise variables of different levels, e.g. of the self-concept, of the concept of environment, of motivation and person perception. In this way, statements on combinations of characteristics become possible, which may include variables of different regulation levels.

3. Variable concept

The determination of variables was oriented along the general action model of personality mentioned above and the demand characteristics of interpersonal performance situations (Schröder, 1980). The set of variables represents essential stages of behaviour regulation.

In question were variables of person perception, decentering, variables of the self-image, of social abilities, of decision behaviour, social communicability, variables of inadequate expressive behaviour and fixed maladjustment.

The fields of inadequate expressive behaviour and fixed maladjustment were additionally incorporated into the set of variables for examining mentally sick people. They represent special variables of social incompetence.

The defined variable ranges were specified and made measurable by the method of fixing measuring points on scales. For this, comparatively extensive conceptional and methodological work was required, in the course of which operationalisation and the scale arrangement of abilities related to communication and cooperation represented a special imperfection.

4. Findings

The empirical findings are based on the examination of 86 mentally sick people (Möhring and Roeber, 1979). These were mainly patients suffering from neurosis. The teacher's profession is represented by 32 subjects, the other 54 patients being of different professions.

The first task was to find out about functional relations between personality variables and hypothetically determined objectives. By doing so we aimed at testing the psychopathological relevance of the variables of our initial concept.

The starting point in determining the criterion variables was theoretical positions of clinical psychology and our own considerations. Neuroticism, decentering, variables of the self-image and readiness for communication were the effect variables chosen. For the present purposes the discussion of findings is limited to the last of these effect variables. When determining the variable of readiness of communication as target factor, the following clinical-psychological facts had to be considered: In the majority of psychiatric patients, disturbances in communicative behaviour are an important psychopathological syndrome. In the field of psychiatry it is above all the patient's ability to communicate with his fellow men according to standards which is considered an expression of social competence.

A successful rehabilitation is often measured by the extent and the frequency of the patient's communicative relations. The variable of readiness of communication can be regarded as an essential personality-psychological precondition of this desired communicative behaviour. In the clinics it is of special interest how this variable is determined and what personal characteristics are related to it. If we knew all influencing factors for certain, we could influence the patient therapeutically in a more controlled way.

To be able to determine the relative importance of the variables within the statement of variables we chose as a statistical procedure the multiple linear regression analysis. After gradual reduction of the regression statement the reliable influencing factors were left whose standardized partial regression coefficients determine the relative importance of the influencing factors in comparison with the target factor. The findings have been compiled in Tab. 1.

Tab. 1: *Findings of the regression analysis of the "Readiness of communication"*

Variables crossed out in the regression statement in sequence of reduction	Standardized partial regression coefficients
1. Interpersonal ability of irritation	Readiness of communication =
2. Cognitive simplicity (K)	+.20 configuration of communication
3. complete self-image	+.15 behaviour of contact
4. Rigidity	−.41 social-communicative rigidity
5. Decentration	−.19 lack of interpersonal initiative
6. Communicability of feelings	−.18 behaviour of assertion
7. Self-control	−.18 empathy and prediction of behaviour
8. Individual perception and evaluation	

The configuration of communication and the self-image dimension of the behaviour of contact turned out to be reliable influencing factors. This result proves the close relationship between the abilities of interaction and the readiness of communication. This is a fact which was pointed out several times by Argyle in particular (1974).

Only very slightly less important is the influence of the self-image dimension of 'behaviour of contact'.

The variables of social-communicative rigidity, lack of interpersonal initiative and the self-image dimensions of behaviour of assertion and empathy and prediction of behaviour turn out to be reliable negative influencing factors which significantly correlate with the target factor and other influencing factors. The determination of social-communicative rigidity and lack of interpersonal initiative as being negative influencing factors is entirely in accordance with the hypothesis. Only the importance of social-communicative rigidity, which is much higher than of any other influencing factors, is surprising.

This result illustrates again the pathogenetic relevancy of variables of fixed false attitudes.

On the other hand, the interpretation of the self-image dimension of behaviour of assertion as well as of empathy and prediction of behaviour as negative influencing factors for the readiness of communication seems to be difficult. A pronounced readiness of communication combined with the empathic personality's fear of possibly disturbing another person or of being inopportune can be thought of as incompatible. Therefore the above mentioned therapeutical starting points for increasing the readiness of communication mainly consists in the formation of social-communicative flexibility and interpersonal initiative by developing abilities of interaction that improve the self-image of one's own behaviour of contact (see Vorwerg, 1971, Schmidt and Alberg, 1980).

In a second stage of analysis we tried to reduce the number of single variables to basic factors. While doing so we aimed at making the mutual relations of the variables easier to survey. Furthermore it was interesting how the abilities related to communication and cooperation, which are still often neglected in clinical psychological research, would prevail in connection with the variables of other fields of action control and selfimage. We used the factor analysis as a multivariant method of analysis.

Four factors proved to be worth interpreting. A survey of the findings is given in Tab. 2.

Tab. 2.: *Structure of factors of the set of variables in psychiatric patients after orthogonal rotation (extract)*

Variables	Factors					
	I	II	III	IV	V	h^2
Neuroticism	−0.01	−0.75	−0.09	−0.22	0.00	0.63
Cognitive Complexity (constructs)	0.36	0.18	−0.21	0.09	−0.25	0.28
Cognitive Complexity (objects)	0.09	0.10	−0.21	−0.23	−0.22	0.17
Communicability of feelings	−0.15	0.04	−0.11	0.22	0.47	0.30
Behaviour of assertion	0.05	0.47	−0.33	−0.07	0.28	0.42
Total self-image	0.16	0.33	0.15	0.07	0.86	0.92
Communication assurance 1	0.32	0.18	−0.06	0.52	0.16	0.44
Communication assurance 3	−0.08	0.13	−0.06	0.69	0.22	0.56
Communication assurance 4	0.10	0.24	−0.08	0.59	0.03	0.43
readiness of communication	0.53	−0.05	0.66	0.13	−0.03	0.75
Configuration of communication	0.57	−0.01	0.24	0.26	−0.16	0.48
Reliability	0.65	0.19	−0.06	0.16	0.08	0.50
Pro-social behaviour	0.65	0.06	0.06	0.06	0.01	0.44
Inhibition	−0.53	−0.08	−0.23	−0.62	0.13	0.76
Unguidedness	−0.14	−0.61	0.13	−0.22	−0.08	0.47
Offensive behaviour for solving problems	0.48	0.12	0.17	0.60	−0.02	0.64
Introversion 1	−0.28	0.04	−0.73	−0.18	0.02	0.66
Introversion 2	−0.18	−0.22	−0.56	−0.45	−0.04	0.61
Social-communicative rigidity	−0.54	−0.24	−0.62	−0,09	0.00	0.76
Intoleration of ambiguity	−0.11	−0.76	−0.13	−0.13	−0.04	0.60
Abnormal ambition for conformity	−0.27	−0.57	−0.16	−0.38	−0.00	0.59
Orientation toward failure	−0.33	−0.59	−0.33	−0.16	−0.02	0.60
Intoleration of frustration	0.12	−0.66	0.04	−0.05	−0.02	0.45
Absolute variance	3.88	4.20	3.43	3.60	1.66	
Share of total variance	10.50%	11.36%	9.28%	9.72%	4.49%	
Share of explained variance	23.15%	25.05%	20.47%	21.43%	9.90%	

Beside neuroticism (factor 2) and extro/introversion (factor 3) the factors of general communicability/inability (factor 1) and communicability related to performance (factor 4) were extracted. Thus we have groups for description that describe a large part of the variables involved without much redundancy. When related to the general structure of interpersonal competence (Schröder, 1980) there are striking similarities in essential aspects, with the results of studies of normal persons. It is therefore not difficult to assign extro/introversion and general communicability/ inability to dimensions of directedness. It refers to aspects of basic motivation for social integration, according to Vorwerg (1980). The components summed up in the factor of communicability related to performance are cognitive schemes about one's own varieties of behaviour and are therefore variables of the awareness of alien control of a specific aspect of self-competence. Awareness of self-control is represented by substantial loadings in neuroticism factor.

These first factor-analytic studies with variables of the concept of social competence within the scope of clinical studies have not yet been repeated with other clinical samples. But we consider the results to be encouraging for further studies.

References

ALBERG, T., and J. SCHMIDT: Trainingsbedingte Modifikation der psychischen Verhaltensregulation. In: M. Vorwerg and H. Schröder (Eds.), Persönlichkeitspsychologische Grundlagen interpersonalen Verhaltens. Manuskriptdruck. Leipzig 1980

ARGYLE, M.: Soziale Interaktion. Köln 1974

MÖHRING, W., and A. ROEBER: Untersuchungen interpersonaler Bedingungen sozial ineffektiven Verhaltens. Diplomarbeit Leipzig 1979

SCHNEIDER, K.: Klinische Psychopathologie. Stuttgart 1955

SCHRÖDER, H., and M. VORWERG: Soziale Kompetenz als Zielgröße für Persönlichkeitsstruktur und Verhaltensmodifikation. In: M. Vorwerg (Ed.), Zur psychologischen Persönlichkeitsforschung 1, Berlin 1978

SCHRÖDER, H.: Struktur interpersonaler Fähigkeiten. In: M. Vorwerg and H. Schröder (Eds.), Persönlichkeitspsychologische Grundlagen interpersonalen Verhaltens. Manuskriptdruck. Leipzig 1980

VORWERG, M.: Persönlichkeitsforschung des sozialistischen Leiters durch Verhaltenstraining. In: Probleme der Entwicklung sozialistischer Persönlichkeiten. Berlin 1971

VORWERG, M.: Grundlagen einer persönlichkeitspsychologischen Theorie des sozialen Verhaltens. In: M. Vorwerg and H. Schröder (Eds.), Persönlichkeitspsychologische Grundlagen interpersonalen Verhaltens. Manuskriptdruck. Leipzig 1980

WEISE, K.: Psychopathologie – Symptomatik und Interaktion. In: J. Helm, H.-D. Rösler and H. Szewczyk (Eds.), Klinische Psychologie. Theoretische und ideologische Probleme. Berlin 1979

Development of an Individual: Conceptualization of the Problem

W. J. Paluchowski

The tradition from works by Stern and Allport (Allport, 1937) conceives of personality as a "being" stabilizing individual behavior. More precisely, the assumption of personality makes it possible to account for both trans-situationally repetitive behavior of an individual and his uniqueness. But do individuals really behave similarly in different situations? Early studies by Hartshorn and May in 1928 (cf. Mischel, 1968) showed that this might not be so, at least for some situations and for certain types of behavior. It is also obvious that behavioral variability, described on one level of generalization, disappears when the analysis is performed on a higher level of abstraction (cf. Magnusson, 1976, or the concept of reliability as understood by test theory as presented by Lord and Novick, 1968).

And finally how can one reasonably argue for personality changes if personality, as such, is defined as a property which protects an individual from behavioral variability? The problem is by no means solved by weakening the initial assumption on stability when adding to it the adjective "relative". Should we not talk, rather, about changes in person rather than in personality?

1. Social interactions as a field of behavior

Irrespective of the assumptions concerning the ontic character of personality (cf. Sanocki, 1978), it is assumed here that personality is not manifested – and thus cannot be measured – directly. Personality exists through an individual's behavior, i.e., through all those acts which fulfill the following conditions:

1. they are realized in a social environment,
2. they do not bear a singular character,
3. they take place in a time.

The assumption that human behavioral acts are social in character frequently leads either to specifically understood sociologism which takes into account a macro-social perspective in explanation (which should be respected when historical origins of human beings – humanity – are dealt with, but which should or can be disregarded when the object under discussion is an individual being) or to reduction of the essence of human beings (humanity) to singular interactions. It should be emphasized, however, that human essence is not identical with individual personality. One should agree with Sanocki (op. cit.) that any individual is a concretization of the human essence proper for a given social group but that is not tantamount either to it or to the essence of humanity as a species.

Properties of an individual's behavior cannot be entirely (or even generally) accounted for by features of social macrostructures. What is important for psychological explanation is individual behavior as revealed in interactions with other individuals (some more specific cases are disregarded here). Therefore we shall specify the first condition mentioned above and focus our attention only on those human actions which are realized in social interactions. We shall thus conceive of situations as made up of those contents and structural properties of individual interactions, which define the external conditions of human actions. Characteristic individual behavior in those conditions is subject to personological explanation.

2. Structure and direction of behavior

So far, we have not made any distinction between two aspects of human action: its direction and style. Let us now try to distinguish between the "what" and "how" of human behavior, focusing more attention on the former. Behavioral style means here much the same as "structure of behavior" (Tomaszewski, 1963) and encompasses behavioral features which are similar in form. By changes in individuals we mean both changes in structure and direction of behavior. It should be assumed, of course, that the individual is capable of choosing both the goals and the means of his actions, at least with reference to behavioral aspects.[1] However, only directional changes in behavior are considered as significant when defining change.

Knowledge of the direction of behavior is a prerequisite of valid observations and conclusions drawn from psychological research. Only by knowing the direction of action are we in a position to analyse its effectiveness. We must distinguish here between results and goals of action on the one hand and values on the other. Result is defined here as a certain state of the individual's environment or of the relationship between the individual and his environment. Goal is a state of the individual's introspective consciousness, while value is a criterion according to which the individual evaluates those alternatives which lie at his disposal[2]. Similar meanings should be ascribed to such terms as hierarchy of values, task structure or expected result of action (Reykowski, 1975; Tomaszewski, 1963; Obuchowski, 1974).

The following assumption will thus underlie the theoretical framework presented here in which individual changes can be studied:

1. An individual's field of behavior consists of his social interactions.

2. These interactions are potentially multidimensional.

3. The "multi-alternativeness" of interactions is cognitively and primarily behaviorally accessible to the individual.

4. Content and structure of human interactions are reflections of their actions.

5. The objects of study are changes in content and structure of human interactions and actions.

[1] Personological explanation is possible only when the behavior accounted for is realized in conditions which offer different goals (means). By no means does this imply that the individual must be aware of the alternative solutions, it is sufficient – as in personality tests – that behavioral variance in different individuals is stated.

[2] The criterion is used by the researcher as an explanation of individual behavior and not a generalized description of his behavior.

48

3. Conceptualization of the problem – the empirical relational system

Conceptualization of the problem was inspired by Lazarsfeld's model of latent structures (1959). The model assumes that the n-dimensional space of manifested behaviors can be reduced to $n-k$ dimensional latent space accountable for by theoretical constructs. Relationships between a latent trait and its manifestation is probabilistic in character: the person defined by a respective value of the latent trait may be ascribed (with different probability) different trait manifestations (the so-called *latent probability*); and vice-versa – observation of the person's concrete behavior allows us to ascribe to him (with different probabilities) certain values of the latent trait (the so-called *recruitment probability*). In other words, a person may be fully defined only with the full distribution of probabilities with which his manifest behaviors are realized (latent probability) and a respective value of the latent trait.[3] Gulliksen's physicalistic assumption on the one-univocal relation between trait value (true result) and manifest behavior (observed result) has been refuted by Lazarsfeld, Lord and Novick (op.cit.). Outside test theory, however, the so-called propensity distribution introduced by the latter is still understood as an assumption that a trait value determines individual behavior with the precision allowed for by the measuring instrument and the researcher's extent of knowledge on the full range of significant variables. This assumption is false, since we would have to assume that the individual can be described by one result only, equal to the extreme of the function determined on the basis of observable behavior. With such an assumption the observed interindividual variance of behavior in the same situation would have to be accounted for by interindividual differences in trait value (function extreme). This does not, however, allow us to account for the fact that an individual is capable – not only in his imagination but in real actions – of different behaviors in the same social situations. In other words, it is often disregarded that any situation is multidimensional not only for a set of individuals but also, and mainly, for a particular individual (cf footnote 1). According to the suggestion by Lord and Novick, it should be assumed that the observed behavior of an individual is not a representation of the "pointlike" trait (defined as an interval only due to the stochastic character of procedures of its empirical identification) but that a given individual should be characterized by the whole trait dimension along with a description of probability of realization. In other words, it is assumed that different values of the same trait coexist in the same individual. What differentiates one individual from another is not differences in trait intensity but different probability distribution described in terms of these values.

The full manifest space consists of n behavioral dimensions and m situational dimensions. Latent space is its empirical generalization. For clarity of argumentation let us assume that latent space pertains to behavior only.

Let us assume that we are dealing not with one but with k traits which make up the latent space of manifest behavior. An individual is then identified by pointing to the k-dimensional space and to the function defining probability of realization of the dimensions. Number and type of dimensions are not identical for every individual, each individual is described by a subset P of a set N, on which a probability function

[3] Let us mention here that "trait" is understood according to Guilford rather than Allport (Buss and Poley, 1976).

is determined.[4] If we now assume that our interest lies only in those values of the function which are higher or equal to a certain value *psi*, we can say that an individual can be identified by a certain *l*-dimensional sub-space; cf. footnote 4.

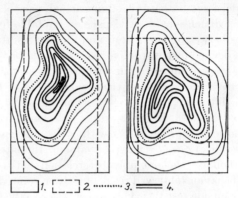

1. ☐ 2. ⌈⌉ 3. ⋯⋯ 4. ══

Fig. 1: Latent space and subspace for an individual P_i and an individual P_j.
1. *k*-dimensional space
2. *l*-dimensional space
3. psi values
4. probability function

The model of relational system accepted here is not identical with Lazarsfeld's model. Despite its undoubted heuristic value it assumes that parameters which describe an individual (latent position and distribution of latent probabilities) do not change in time. Wiggins (1973) has presented a modification of Lazarsfeld's model and assumed that both parameters may change in time. Of the nine models for studying individual changes which he described, those assuming systematic changes of latent positions are feasible.

One of the probable reasons why Lazarsfeld's model has not been applied in psychology, particularly in the psychology of personality, is its low explanatory value. The manifest space reduced into the latent space is an empirical generalization only – it makes possible a description of the structure of reality but nothing more. This weakness is characteristic of all factorial theories of personality: the procedure of data aggregation cannot lead to explanation. Additionally, explanations of purely personological or situational character have already been refuted in psychology (or are more and more frequently being abandonded). What is being explained now is behavior, understood as a result of interactions of an individual with his social environment (Endler and Magnusson, 1976; Magnusson and Endler, 1977). It is thus necessary to give up the assumption that latent space may be described in terms of behavior only and include the situational elements as well. As a reduction of manifest situations (interactions) is analoguous to that of behavior, we shall not describe the procedure again.

[4] We should emphasize, however, that it does not mean that assemblages of individuals may be identified by the k-dimensional latent space. The space together with the probability function determined on it, can characterize one individual only. When identifying a particular individual (i.e., defining the set $P = \sum_{i=1}^{1} n_i$ we reduce set $N = \sum_{j=1}^{k} n_j$ of all those elements (traits) for which the probability function equals zero).

50

4. Suggested conceptualization of individual changes

Let us assume that manifest space is described on n behavioral dimensions and m dimensions pertaining to conditions of behavior realization (situations). By reducing the full space to the latent space, we obtain a latent sub-space, restricted by values of probability with which the behaviors are realized in given situations, higher or equal to psi values. This sub-space of latent space is then explained psychologically with theoretical constructs including relationships between subjective and objective determinants of behaviors[5] in a particular individual.

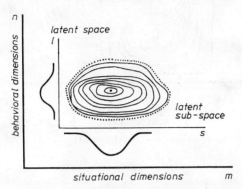

Fig. 2: Mutual relation between manifest and latent space and latent subspace for an individual P_k.

The latent sub-space, defined above, enables a full identification of a particular individual. In other words, an individual is characterized both by the probability distribution represented by empirical generalizations of his behavior (traits) and by the probability distribution represented by empirical generalizations of behavior realization. Having reduced this hyper-plane into a plane we can present it in graphic form.

Using the philosophical suggestions of Nowak (Nowak, 1977; Magala, 1977; Łastowski, 1977) we shall accept two kinds of changes in an individual-continuations and transformations (Fig. 3). The criterion for this differentiation is the conditional probability of a given change, or to put it more figuratively – whether the movement takes place inside or beyond the latent sub-space.[6] In more precise terms, continuation will take place if the extreme of the probability function determined on full latent space in time t_{n+1} is included in values higher or equal to the psi value of the probability function determined on latent space in time t_n. In other cases we shall speak of a significant change in an individual, i.e., transformation.

In the framework of the suggested approach an individual may be identified on two complementary aspects:

1. static, when interest is focused on organization of the $1 + s$ dimensional latent

---

[5] These relationships are psychological mechanisms.

[6] We mean here latent space, as not every change in probabilities determined on manifestations is real change (Wiggins, op. cit.; Coleman, 1968). The simplest criterion of finding out whether we are dealing with change or unreliability of our procedure of data collection, is described by Coleman (op. cit.).

space, as when either no significant change in the space take place or one temporal moment only is considered;

2. dynamic, when psychological diagnosis pertains to rules of change in the organization of the 1 + s latent space, i.e., rules of transformations.[7]

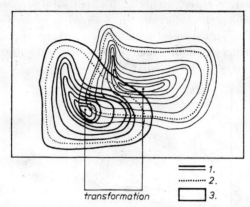

transformation

1.
2.
3.

Fig. 3: Illustration of significant change (i.e. development).
1. probability function
2. psi values
3. latent space

References

ALLPORT, G. W.: Personality. New York: Holt, 1937
BUSS, A. R., and W. POLEY: Individual differences. Traits and factors, New York–Toronto–London–Sidney: Gardner Press 1976
COLEMAN, J. S.: Introduction to mathematical sociology. Glencoe: Free Press of Glencoe 1964
ENDLER, N. S., and D. MAGNUSSON (Eds.): Interactional psychology and personality. New York: Wiley 1976
LAZARSFELD, P. E.: Latent structure analysis. In: S. Koch (Ed.), Psychology: A study of a science, Vol. 3, New York: Mc Graw-Hill, 1959
ŁASTOWSKI, K.: O możliwości adaptacyjnej interpretacji zasad dialektyki (On the possibility of adaptational interpretation of principles of dialectics), Poznańskie Studia z Filizofii Nauk, zeszyt 2, Założenia dialektyki (Poznań studies in the philosophy of science, vol. 2, Fundamentals of dialectics). Poznań: PWN 1977
MAGALA, S.: Zjawisko komplementarności w kategorialnej interpretacji dialektyki (Complementarity in the categorial interpretation of dialectics), Poznańskie Studia z Filozofii Nauk, zeszyt 2, Założenia dialektyki (Poznań studies in the philosophy of science, vol. 2, Fundamentals of dialectics) Poznań: PWN 1977.
MAGNUSSON, D.: The person and the situation in interactional models of behavior. Scand. J. Psychol. 17, 1976.
MAGNUSSON, D., and ENDLER, N. S. (Eds.): Personality at the crossroads: Current issues in interactional psychology. Hillsdale: Lawrence-Erlbaum Associates 1977. Mischel, W.: Personality and assesment. New York: Wiley 1968
NOWAK, L.: Koncepcja historii w kategorialnej interpretacji dialektyki (Concept of history in categorial interpretation of dialektics) Poznańskie Studia z Filozofii Nauk, zeszyt 2, Założenia dialektyki (Poznań studies in the philosophy of science, vol. 2, Fundamentals of dialectics). Poznań: PWN 1977

[7] To be more precise, changes in density of probabilities in the latent sub-space.

OBUCHOWSKI, K.: Osobowość a społeczna efektywność działania (Personality and social effectiveness of action). Bydgoszcz: TNOiK 1974

REYKOWSKI, J.: Zadania pozaosobiste jako regulator czynności (Nonpersonal taks as a regulator of actions). In: I. Kucz and J. Reykowski (Eds.), Studia nad teorią czynności ludzkich (Studies on the theory of human action). Warszawa, PWN 1975, 103–144

SANOCKI, W.: Koncepcja normy w psychologii klinicznej: Studium metodologiczne (Concept of normality in clinical psychology: methodological study), Zeszyty Naukowe Uniwersytetu Gdańskiego, Rozprawy i monografie, nr 1, Gdańsk 1978

SÈVE, L.: Marksizm a teoria osobowości (Marxism and personality theory) Warszawa, KIW 1975

TOMASZEWSKI, T.: Wstęp do psychologii (Introduction to psychology), Warszawa: PWN 1963

WIGGINS, L. M.: Panel analysis. Latent probability models for attitude and behavior processes. Amsterdam: Elsevier, 1973

An Action-Oriented Model of Personality Development in Ontogenesis

ADOLF KOSSAKOWSKI

In spite of intensive scientific investigations of problems of psychic development in ontogenesis (at least since the beginning of our century) many questions can not even now be solved. This can be seen in divergent theoretical positions especially concerning the developing psychic structure of personality, the course and the determinants of psychic development.

One could characterize these divergences in a rather generalized way as follows:
– Concerning the developing psychic structure, contradictions exist between an isolating consideration of psychic components of personality on the one hand and an interpretation of the structure of psychic components as an integrative unit on the other. Moreover, the psychic structure of personality described by some authors seems to be neither theoretically nor empirically based.
– Concerning the course of psychic development, the contradictions appear in interpreting the course of development as a continuous process by some authors and as a discontinuous one by others. Continuity and discontinuity are considered either only concerning different psychic qualities or concerning the whole psychic structure of personality.
– The strongest contradictions are expressed regarding the interpretation of the basic determinants of psychic development in ontogenesis. Up to now, there exist one-sided biologically oriented viewpoints, extremly socially oriented viewpoints as well as finalistic viewpoints (see Kossakowski, 1966; Chapter 1, Möncks and Kuvers, 1976).

The main reason of the divergences mentioned is – in my opinion – the *individual-centered consideration* of personality and its psychic development. This theoretical position is connected with an one-sided interpretation of the function and the structure of psychic processes and qualities.

For better understanding, I would like to explain it in a rather simplified way. Personality is often regarded as a relatively isolated individual confronted with the environment. Environment is viewed either only as a field of realization of psychic processes developing relatively autonomously (maturation theory) or as strict force opposed to the individual, who underlies, to a great extent, the influence of the environment (milieu theory). Also the finalistic, so – called emancipation theory (see Lange-feld, cit. in Möncks and Kuvers, 1976) assumes lastly a contradiction between the individual and the environment declaring that general aims (independently of real social aims and material environmental conditions) determine psychic development of personality. In these theories the psychic processes and qualities are viewed either as individual components existing independently of the environment which internally determine the organism behavior, or as "final products" of the psychic reflection activity whose function is exhausted in the perception and processing of information and which has no direct reference to the orientation and regulation of the individual's interaction with his environment.

This reductionism in interpreting the structure and function of psychic components makes it impossible to give a scientifically founded classification of them and to describe the actual interrelations between the classified psychic components within the structure of personality (see Kossakowski, 1980, Chapter 1).

A scientifically based interpretation requires, in my opinion, a consistently action-oriented analysis of psychic components of personality and their ontogenesis.

It is possible to explain this assortion in a short form:

1. The starting point of our theory of personality development in ontogenesis is the assumtion that an individual and his (or her) environment has to be considered as a closely connected unit of interaction that the psychic development of personality takes place only within the interaction between individual and environment and that the main function of the developing psychic components consists in orienting and regulating this interaction on the basis of perception and processing of environmental information (see Rubinstein, 1962, p. 240).

2. In this process of interaction the individual plays an active role. This is possible by appropriation, processing and creative alteration (by the individual) of social conditions (i.e., social aims of activity, norms of behavior etc.).

The developing personality is never only a passive object of environmental influences, but increasingly a subject of its activity forming its own life relations and changing the environmental conditions according to its intentions (see Kossakowski, 1980, Chapter 2).

3. The physic regulation of interaction between an individual and the environment is considered as a more and more consciously regulated process within which the different psychic components – such as cognitive, emotional and volitive processes and contents – are closely interconnected.

This integrative interconnection of psychic components of activity regulation holds for the functional units, e.g. the orientation, the motivation, the implementation and the control of action, as well as for the habitual psychic qualities, e.g. the qualities of knowledge, the attitudes, the abilities etc. Therefore, psychic development of personality has to be considered as mutual development of the whole structure of psychic components of activity regulation. Models of development overstressing the isolated development of different psychic components and underestimating the integrative connections between all psychic components are one-sided and inadequate.[1]

4. Because the main function of psychic contents, processes and qualities consist in regulating the activity of the individual, it seems to be suitable to classify them primarily on the basis of functional units of action regulation and to analyse the psychic structure of personality and its development on the basis of such functional units. The psychic properties should be interpreted primarily as habitual qualities of the functional units.

In such a way, it would be possible to overcome the relatively abstract and static

---

[1] This refers to the one-sided cognitive theories of psychic development as well as to one-sided motivational oriented theories of the ontogenesis of personality.

structures of the psychic components of personality predominating up to now and to analyse the development of the more dynamic functional units of action regulation (Kossakowski, 1980, Chapter 2).

Thus one could assume as main classes of psychic components of action regulation, functional units of different complexity and psychic properties mentioning again the close interconnection between cognitive, emotional and motivational components on all levels of functional units and in all properties of action regulation.

Such kind of classification is, in my opinion, also suitable for investigations of the psychic development of personality in ontogenesis.

5. The concrete course of development of the personality as a whole and of the individual characteristics of the psychic regulation components are considered as being determined by the quality of the activity of the developing personality. By changing the quality of activity the psychic regulation components change as well. This opinion is particularly stressed by Leontjew who described the close relations between the so – called dominant activity and the age – specific qualities (see Leontjew, 1964.)

6. The development of specific qualities of activity is, for its part, determined by the external (material and social) and internal conditions of this activity. The internal conditions of activity consist in the biological and psychical preconditions developed up to the time the activity begins, especially the ability of the acting subject to change the environmental conditions according to the intentions of the personality. So we are confronted with a very complex structure of determinants which makes it impossible to interpret the determinants of psychic development in ontogenesis one-sided.

7. The progress of psychic development is defined as progress of development of action regulating psychic components which enable the individual to act in an increasingly independent, conscious and creative way.

As valuation criteria of estimation the level of psychic development could be used
– the degree of self-regulation including the degree of reflexibility,
– the level of hierarchical structure of integration and differentiation of psychic regulation components,
– the degree of stability and at the same time, of flexibility of the psychic regulation components concerning the objective behavioral demands.

In the following part of my contribution I will try to explain the above mentioned general statements of an action-oriented model of personality development in ontogenesis concerning the periodisation of psychic ontogenesis.

1. In order to define the specific psychic structure of personality at a certain age period, we concentrated on the psychic regulation components and on the valuation criteria of psychic development mentioned. We have tried to describe the level of independent orientation of action, e.g., the ability to define concrete aims of action independently, to work out effective programms of action to more or less comprehensive classes of tasks; that means independently to find strategies of implementing of action referring to the special demands and conditions of special tasks.

The level of psychic development is also defined by the level of self-concepts (as the level of self-reflection and self-evaluation according to the difficulties of the tasks), the abilities of an individual to reflect upon the motives and consequences of their activities as well as by their possibilities to transfer the acquired strategies of action in a special field of other fields of action. Thus, the level of psychic development is also defined by the degree of generalization and flexibility.

2. Analysing the determinants of age-specific psychic regulationqualities, we always consider the already mentioned complex structure of these determinants. I should like to explain it (by using Fig. 1).

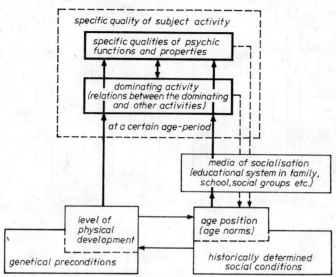

Fig. 1: Conditions for the development of specific psychic qualities at a certain age-period.

a) as the main and immediate precondition (to a certain extent we could say: as the cause) of development of age-specific psychic regulation qualities could be regarded a certain quality of activity or a certain quality of interaction between individual and environment (the so-called dominating type of activity in a certain age-period-Leontjew).

This position was pointed out in a very clear manner in Elkonin's model of periodisation of the psychic development in ontogenesis. He explained the primary development of the requirement sphere of personality in one age period as determined by an objectoriented activity and the primary development of the motivational sphere of action regulation in the next period as determined by a more socially oriented, communicative activity (see Elkonin, 1972).

b) The dominating activity for its part is determined by manifold conditions.
– To a certain extent the physical preconditions, e.g., the neurophysical mechanisms of information acquisition and processing as well as the emotional reactions typical of a certain age period play a role.

But one should not overestimate the role of physical components for development of a certain dominating type of activity and the corresponding psychic qualities.

In our own investigations regarding conditions of changing of psychic qualities in puberty, we couldn't find any immediate relations between physical and psychical development. We want to prove it only by the results of two tests.

In the first example the level of physical development using the Schwidetzky-scale and the level of interest characteristic for teenagers by 11 years old girls were correlated (see Fig. 2). As you see, a significant relation could not be found. We also correlated the level of physical development and the level of attitudes concerning a heterosexual partner by 14 years old girls (see Fig. 3). The expected relations also in this case couldn't be proved. Thus in both cases the expected relations between a certain physical and psychical level characteristic to the appropriate age group couldn't be proved.

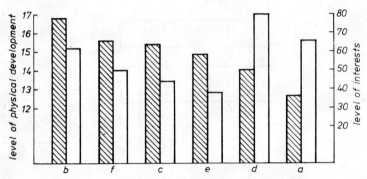

Fig. 2: Correlations between the level of general interests and the level of physical development by the 11 years old girls.

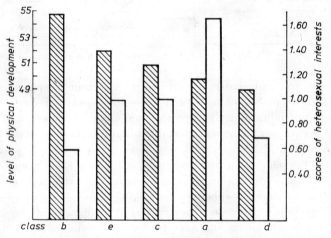

Fig. 3: Correlation between the heterosexual interests and the level of physical development by 14 years old girls.

On the other hand, great group-specific differences between various school-classes on the same educational level could be demonstrated.
– Also for the development of a dominating type of activity in a certain age period, the social conditions are to be considered as the main determinants.

They include the material conditions produced by society, social relations as well social ideas and norms of behavior, reflecting those relations.
– The age-specific norms of behavior that means both official and inofficial social demands and expectations concerned a special kind of behavior of numbers of a certain age group are of particular importance.

They lead to a special position of a certain age group in society and determine in this way specific educational measures as well as special influences of other socialization media, encouraging the developing individuals to an age-related behavior. Through active interaction with his social conditions of life and especially with the age-norms and their educational consequences, the individual acquires this external "behavioral patterns". Step by step they become internal "behavioral patterns".

c) The age norms and the appropriate social position for its part are determined above all by specific social conditions existing in a certain society, in certain nations, social classes or groups. Therefore they are different in different societies, classes etc. (This is, by the way, the main reason for different kinds of psychic development by children of the same age, living under different social conditions).

Of course, the age-related behavioral norms and the appropriate age positions are also determined by the level of physical and psychic development attained up to a certain age. These preconditions impose certain limits which are narrower the younger the children are.

(This example shows, by the way, that interdependences between external and internal conditions and between biological and social determinants of psychic development of personality exist in different aspects.)

Furthermore, the developing individual brings his influence to bear on the external behavioral patterns, on the educational measures etc., changing them according to his own intentions and expectations. In this way he plays an active role in originating the dominating type of individuals' activity. Therefore we can state dialectical interrelations between internal and external conditions, between social influences and the personal activity of the developing individual on his own psychic development, between processes of interiorisation an exteriorisation during the psychic ontogenesis of personality.

This very complex structure of conditions of psychic development of personality explained here is a cause of the difficulties which appear in discribing age-specific psychic qualities as attitudes, kinds of achievmental behavior etc.

The manifold possibilities of variation of the developmental conditions described lead to significant group specific and individual characteristic differences in development of psychic components of behavior regulation by children of the same age.

This could be shown very clearly in investigations of the socalled cultural-anthropologic school of psychology as well as in recent cross-cultural-studies.

In our own investigations we were able to show that with pupils of the same age,

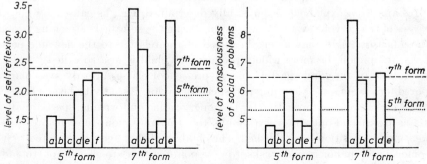

Fig. 4: Group specific differences of psychic qualities.

attending the same school very different group specific psychic qualities exist between single school classes even concerning such properties as self-reflexion, consciousness of social problems etc., which are generally assumed as characteristic to a certain age group (see Fig. 4). The individual differences were, of course, even greater than the group-specific differences.

3. A similar complexity holds also for those conditions determining more or less fast *changes* or even "jumps in psychic development" of action regulating components in ontogenesis. Also in this case we assume changes of the dominating activity as the main conditions of changes of psychic components. There changes in dominating activity for their part are also determined in a manifold way.

a) They may be based at first in action-internal contradictions as it is assumed, e.g., in Elkonins theory of periodisation. For example, it may be possible that special psychic qualities developing in a special kind of activity (which dominates in a certain age period) help the individual to a higher kind of activity. In that case the individual will spontaniously try to realize a new quality of activity. The new expectations of the developing personality originated by the conditions, existing in a certain age period, may lead to new kinds of interaction between the individual and his environment which have to be seen as typical of a higher developmental stage. Thus the future-oriented activity of the developing subject of activity plays an important role in the transition from one kind of activity to an other.

b) The main condition (or also the actual cause) of changes in the dominating activity and the appropriate changes in the psychic qualities during the transition from one developmental stage to the next higher one is, however, a *socially caused change* of the social age-position and the corresponding agenorms.

When entering a new age-group the developing individuals are often very rapidly confronted with new expectations and demands, they must learn to adjust to those new expectations or try to resist them. In either case, however, – and that often in a relatively short time – their position in life, their life relations and especially their dominating activity undergoes a change. This really seems to be the main precondition for more or less rapid changes of intellectual performances as well as of social attitudes etc.

As an instructive example we may regard the transitional period at the age of between 5 and 7 years. During that time, as several authors maintain, a transition can be observed from a predominantly total to a more analytical kind of environmental perception, from more egocentric attitudes to predominantly object oriented attitudes, from more fantastic to more realistic relations to the environment. These changes are often explained as physically determined, e.g., as caused by maturing processes of the nervous system which occur during the so-called "streching period".

These factors might play a certain role. But the relation to the new age position can, in my opinion, be more widely proved. The child is in a so called "mediation group". It is in the kindergarten and in pre-school classes already systematically prepared for an organized learning and social behavior. Its activity begins to assume a serious character. In preparation for learning, reading and writing, special analytical exercises are carried out. In everyday life, too, the continuous reference to the subsequent pupil's position is established. The children of that age are expected to have, at home as well, minor regular tasks, to give polite answers to grown-ups, to address them by their proper name etc.

The new position and the new demands connected to it lead, as we see it, to a shift in psychic development causing a discontinuous course of development. This applies to all ageperiods, where by transitions to new social positions or systems of demands, such as the transition to new educational stage within school, from school to vocational training, from vocational training to professional life etc. play an important role.

This especially holds for higher developed social systems in which the official educational systems plays an important role from the early child-hood up to about 20 years. Parents, teachers and also the developing individuals are oriented on expectations and demands connected with certain educational stages. Furthermore some social conditioned events in the course of life of the developing individuals as, e.g., the juridical independence, the beginning of professional work, etc. are important points for changing the social position.

Thus, we could show in own investigations that changes in age norms and corresponding age positions correspond to relevant stages within the educational system in our country (see Fig. 5).

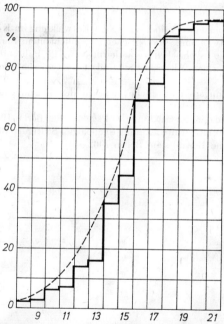

Fig. 5: Cumulative increase (expressed in percents) in behavior patterns expected or approved by adults in individual age groups (relating to the total number of items).

This figure demonstrates the changes of the profile of expectations and demands regarding certain intellectual performances, social attitudes, political standpoints and the like in certain age groups obtained by means of a standardized questionnaire which was answered by more than 2,200 teachers and parents (see Kossakowski, 1969).

It can be shown, that "jump-like" changes occur between the 13th and 14th, between the 15th and 16th as well as between the 17th and 18th year of age. They correspond to remarcable changes in our educational system from the 8th to the 9th, from the 10th to the 11th form etc.

Therefore it is possible, to distinguish the different stages of psychical development in ontogenesis according the main stages in our educational system.

By reason of the close interaction between external and internal determinands of the psychic development and as a result of the integrative structure of the psychic regulation systems mentioned the whole structure of psychic components of personality usually changes during transition from one age period to an other one. Therefore the psychic development of personality seems to be a discontinuous process comprehending the whole psychic structure of personality.

At the same time the complexity and the interindividual variability of the main developmental conditions leads to a great qualitative and temporal variability of individual courses of development. This makes it impossible to state general age periods exactly.

References

ELKONIN, D. B.: Zum Problem der Periodisierung der Entwicklung im Kindesalter. In: Psychologische Probleme der Entwicklung sozialistischer Persönlichkeiten. Berlin 1972
KOSSAKOWSKI, A.: Über die psychischen Veränderungen in der Pubertät. Berlin 1966
KOSSAKOWSKI, A.: Altersnormen, Altersposition und „alterstypische" Verhaltensweisen. Jugendforschung 10, 1969
KOSSAKOWSKI, A.: Handlungspsychologische Aspekte der Persönlichkeitsentwicklung. Berlin 1980
LEONTJEW, A. N.: Probleme der Entwicklung des Psychischen. Berlin 1964
MÖNCKS, F., and M. P. KUVERS: Entwicklungspsychologie. Stuttgart/Berlin/Köln/Mainz 1976
RUBINSTEIN, S. L.: Sein und Bewußtsein. Berlin 1962

A Constructivist Cognitive View of the Development of the Person

Irving E. Sigel and Allan Holmgren

This entire discussion is admittedly schematic and there are many details to be filled in, but the basic argument simplistically is that we come to know about outselves through a knowing process. All knowing has intrinsic to it, elements, attachments if you will, of emotion. Knowing is not independent of affect, and affect is not independent of knowing. There is an integration between how we feel about things and people. The process of coming to know is developmental and structural. It involves knowledge, and social, physical and logical thinking patterns as well as the knowledge about the self as integral. The emergence of the self is through a process of continuous engagement, but the awareness of those engagements is not total. The fragmentation is artifactual. The person evolves as an organic unit, shifting or moving through various contexts, each of which elicits differential demands. Specification of these propositions is possible so that empirical tests of some of them are also possible. From our perspective, the schematic provides the skeleton. That skeleton has form and structure. What it needs is meat.

Over the past decade there have been shifts in the degree to which psychologists come to terms with the concept and definition of personality (Pervin, 1978). For some the term personality is too vague, too undefined, to warrant a legitimate place in the construction of psychological theory. For others, the concept of personality is too complex and multifaceted to have any value. Part of the reason for eschewing a construct of personality is the complex problems in generating reliable and valid measures. The traditional measures used to assess personality, especially for adults, were based on the notion that a set of stable traits and behaviors could be identified as durable. But Mischel (1968) has warned us of the dilemma we face in dealing with the issue of durable traits as well as values, goals, skills and behaviors in terms of the variation across situations.

Let us move away from trait theory which implies a static fixed model of the person, to a dynamic-organismic model wherein the person is conceptualized as a developing organism, integrating and reintegrating new experiences as he or she engages in various environments. To be sure, a person can be characterized in trait terms, e.g., likeable, aggressive, honest, anxious, cheerful, etc. These trait names are labels which one attributes to classes of behaviors or expressed attitudes. They are often decontextualized abstractions. Of course, these traits can be useful in characterizing individuals, but, they should be qualified in terms of situational or contextual referents. Thus, Mr. A is a cheerful person at home, but taciturn and morose on his job. If, however, one is asked to characterize Mr. A relative to his personality characteristics at work and at home, the characterizations might not be correlated. Does this mean that Mr. A is inconsistent or unstable in his behavior? Not necessarily. What it means is that Mr. A's behavior is contingent on the demands of the context in which he finds himself. The contingency does not necessarily require Mr. A's physical presence in that context, but does include the cognitive representation and meanings he attributes to that situation and concomitantly the meaning he attributes to interpersonal relationships in that situation. There is a dynamic relationship between the person and the context.

Further, this relationship does not just involve that particular interaction, since that particular work-related setting is only a part of the larger whole of Mr. A's total life environment. To get a better understanding of Mr. A requires getting to know him and his views of himself and of others in authority-collegial relationships, etc., i.e., in a variety of contexts. In essence the traits Mr. A exhibits in a work setting are part of a network of characteristics that comprise the whole Mr. A. This authoritative trait is dependent on other traits and is organized hierarchically in a system of traits. The expression of this particular characteristic will be determined by contextual requirements along with perceived salience. In addition, changes are possible for Mr. A because developmental changes in his construction are occurring. This brings us to the point in this conceptualization wherein the developmental idea becomes relevant. Development is an ongoing life process which involves accumulations and transformations in the cognitive, socialemotionol and biological domains. Quality and quantity of developmental changes will vary with the domain involved, e.g., cognitive development changes may be more rapid at certain periods than biological changes, etc. But, to hold that development per se is only related to the very young or the adolescent is to deny the fact that the person as a living system in continuously striving to create and to maintain dynamic equilibrium. This is how we adapt to various contexts. This is the intrinsic dialectic – the striving to maintain the dynamic coordination of the system and the conflict generated by environmental forces.

It is in this context that we shall present our developing conceptualization of the developing person.[1] Before articulating our model, let us present the theoretical perspectives from which this model was constructed.

Psychologists operate from a model of behavior without articulating their constructions of these realities. Psychologists, as all other humans, have an implicit set of assumptions about the nature of human nature. This is no different than the layman. Each of us has a construct system which serves us just as a scientific theory serves the scientist. We test our ideas, usually informally, and may not even be aware of the fact we do this. This testing results in changes or maintenance of the idea depending on the degree to which it is consistent with our perspective (Kelly, 1955). The view we have of humans is not a simple question of bias or a simple question of point of view, but rather, it is a basic question of a model of the person and of social reality with which we work.

The fact that each of us has a world view of human nature should be looked at in terms of the historical, social context. In the United States the view of human behavior and the study of human development in the 1950's tended to be generally either a psychoanalytic or behavioristic model. With changing times and for reasons yet to be precisely identifid, there has been a trend toward looking at the individual as a cognizer with the capacity for self-regulation, choice making, and seeking alternative routes in his engagement with the environment. This orientation indicates a

---

[1] This is but the beginning of a theoretical integration. We are fully aware that some basic contradictions may exist in the underlying assumptions of these writers. However, there are levels of commonality which allow for rational integration.

reintegration of cognition as a mediating process. Before discussing cognition, let us define what we mean by the word "cognition". *Cognition refers to the knowing process. Cognition refers to the understanding process. Cognition refers to the individual's coming to know through coming to understand, and conversely, through understanding, coming to know.* The model that we shall present in the following discussion will derive from the very basic assertion that cognitive processing is a fundamental point of contact between the person and his/her environment. The novelty of this approach rests in its effort to bring together a number of theorists such as Piaget (1971), Polanyi (1958), Kelly (1955), Leont'ev (1969), and Beck (1976) in a developmental framework. It moves away from the constructs of stability and traits in the more traditional framework, because traits are heuristic labels used in the course of our conception of the individual. Also, the term personality may or may not be relevant. What is critical is that we are discussing the person as an organic, knowing, living, developing whole. Fragmenting the individual into various components is a tool for thinking and abstracting. It is a Western way of thinking. But our underlying assumption is that the person is an integrated, coherent system of a variety of subsets of many systems, all of which do function in systemic synchrony.

Our effort is not one of an eclecticism which is a mere amalgam, an addition of various perspectives. Rather, the perspective presented here will speak to particular components of these various theoretical models which do, in their relationship to the subsets of information or concepts, provide the beginning efforts at an integrated and coherent unity.

For Piaget, a concept of development is the essential point of departure (Piaget, 1971). Development, in Piaget's terms, can be viewed as a series of transformations over time wherein new cognitive structures evolve. The process of development is one of assimilation and accommodation as these structures emerge, with the basic equilibration principle serving to maintain the coherence of these structures as a system. Although Piaget tends to focus on the development of logical thought, it is reasonable to extend the structural point of view toward the study of the person more generally, including what we think of as the thoughts, the feelings, the attitudes, the conceptions themselves etc. Interestingly enough, a structural approach to personality is not new. Freud himself spoke of personality structure, offering three organizational units as core constructs and also provided a developmental framework (Freud, 1938). However, development for Freud is conceptualized in psychosexual terms, motivated by instinctual drives which are molded by social experience with minimal attention paid to the power of conscious cognitive control. It is more like what in Pepper's terms would be a mechanical metaphor, i.e., although dynamic in concept, it has the implication of a mechanical model of an organism being impressed, or imprinted, by the social experience (Pepper, 1942). On the other hand, Piaget's position is a cybernetic feedback model where the individual functions as a constructor of his reality, and in that construction the individual engages experience. The feedback expresses itself in continual integrations and reintegrations of experience. We shall have more to say about that issue later.

Polanyi's contribution to the thinking here resides in his very interesting and important concept of tacit knowing (Polanyi, 1958). He provides an example of what he means by analyzing an experiment in which someone is exposed to a shock whenever he happens to utter associations to certain shock words. Eventually the subject learned to prevent the shock by avoiding the utterance of such associations. But, as Polanyi says, on questioning it appeared that the subject did not know he was doing this. Here the subject got to know a practical operation but could not tell how it worked. What Polanyi is saying is that certain skills are acquired and that we do not know quite how we got them. We do know the subject did know that he was attending to an electric shock, but he didn't know that somehow there was a tacitness in his not responding to get additional shocks. Tacit knowing is exemplified in our learning how to hit a tennis ball. We learn each element, but all elements are integrated and there is tacit knowledge of the integration of these elements. However, this knowledge can be articulated. As we shall see later, this becomes an important dimension in the model I am proposing.

George Kelly's contribution is in his model of the person as the scientist. Kelly's perspective stems from his basic assumption that the person functions as a quasi-scientist and in so doing utilizes an as-if scientific method; namely, one of consistent hypothesis testing to deal with the environment and to make the appropriate actions. This then suggests an anticipatory sense, an if-then attitude. The product of these actions is a system of constructs by which one defines the environment and builds subsequent hypotheses for verification or rejection.

Two other perspectives contribute to our conceptualization: the work of Vygotsky (1978) and Leont'ev (1969). Vygotsky's emphasis on the role of the social context and language as influencing the development of cognition and Leont'ev's view on actions will round out our initial effort at constructing a model of the developing person. Each of these writers provides not just a contemporaneous perspective, but places the development of the individual in the socio-historical context, in contrast to just relegating development to the individual's particular life space epoch. This construction of action is placed in the context of work. Leont'ev's concept of work holds that " . . .work is crystallized or assumes final form in its product. Whatever manifests itself as activity on the part of the subject takes the form of a potential quality in the product – that of existence or objectivity . . ." (Leont'ev, 1969, p. 425). In a sense, this perspective can be broadened to include the idea that ". . . the full force of its significance [activity] emerges when we analyze the process from a different standpoint, when we consider it not in terms of the objectification of human abilities but in terms of the way these abilities are learned and adopted" (Leont'ev, 1969, p. 425).

For Leont'ev (1969), "For the individual to discover the human aspect of the objects in his surrounding world, he has to relate to them through some activity which is adequate to those objects" (p. 425). Objects, however, are not to be viewed solely as physical, but can also be "objective conceptual phenomena" created by humankind, e.g., language, concepts, etc. The child must come to know these social products if he is to function actively and adequately in the society. This becomes possible by virtue of the child's interchange with adults. "The child is not simply thrown in the human world; he is introduced and guided in this world by people in his environment" (Leont'ev, 1969, p. 426).

The significance of Leont'ev's perspective is his concept of activity which is more complex than described here. It provides a way of relating the development of the person to the world of objects in the broadest sense, not merely as abstractions, but as concrete manifestations of the history of the society.

Vygotsky's perspective provides some of the bases for Leont'ev's thinking.

Vygotsky's special interest is in children's cognitive development, with particular reference in this case to *meaning*. Vigotsky contributes to the developmental perspective by indicating how activity relates to cognitive growth. While space does not permit a detailed discussion, let this quotation from Vygotsky (1978) speak for itself:

While action begins as the numerator of the $\frac{action}{meaning}$ structure, now the structure is inverted and meaning becomes the numerator. Action retreats to second place and becomes the pivot- meaning is again detached from action by means of a different action. This is another example of the way in which human behavior comes to depend upon operations based on meanings where the motive that initiates the behavior is sharply separated from fulfillment. The separation of meaning from objects and action has different consequences, however. Just as operating with the meaning of *things* leads to abstract thought, we find the development of will, the ability to make conscious choices, occurs when the child operates with the meaning of *actions*. In play, an action replaces another action just as an object replaces another object (p. 101).

For Vygotsky and Leont'ev, actions and meaning can be reconciled with the constructivist perspective, since it is through these actions that the individual comes to know and this knowing, we contend, comes through active participation with the object world.

For us, each of these theorists must be brought together in these various dimensions tied around the concepts of dialectics and cybernetics. The dialectic element is relevant since assertions often have their counterassertions which can be viewed as the principle of contradiction. Human organisms find the maintenance of contradictions very difficult unless they separate the two elements as though they are not on the same dimension and not related to each other. The resolution of contradictions is not only presumed to appear through a synthesis of the relevant elements of the polarities, but also can be said to be resolved through a feedback situation where the contradiction begins to influence the propositional statements and there is an active feedback model (cybernetics).

In our opening remarks we alluded to the idea that all theorists are constructors, building their own system of constructs by which they define their reality. We are no exceptions. We used these theories as a basis for our model, which reflects the direct and indirect influence of each of the theorists. Reading the work of these theorists reveals contradiction with each other as well as with us. We contend, however, that each of them simply is not complete enough to encompass what we believe are the necessary ingredients for model of the *persona*. However, they exhibit sufficient complementarianism to allow for some reconciliation without violating their individual integrity. Working with these theories we were able to generate a set of proposition which we propose as necessary, although not sufficient, to develop a model of the person, which on further elaboration provides the basis for empirical testing. These propositions are presented below.

Basic propositions

1. *The human organism has an innate capacity to respond to events affectively*. The developmental course of these affective responses will depend on cultural conventions as well as idosyncratic experience.

2. *All experience is filtered through a knowing system which we call cognition*. This experience is mentally represented and organized into schemata which are representations of events and experiences. These schemata evolve over time and are transformed into increasingly differentiated subsets operating within a generic overarching organization. They may be hierarchical in nature. For example, the child develops a schema of his mother through interactions which change with increasing age. Eventually this schema is embedded in a matrix, or nested in a nest of schemata about people in general.

3. *All knowledge which is assimilated is assimilated with some affective component*. Our basic assumption is that no knowledge is assimilated in a totally neutral way. Rather, knowledge is assimilated with minimal to maximal range of affect (Piaget, 1967). Looking out the window and seeing a tree is not a totally neutral thing. There is some interest, otherwise the attention will wander from that. Evidence of even young infants searching for novelty suggests that there must be some element of excitement or tension which provides the nexus or the coherence of the affect system and the cognition.

4. *The world of knowledge can be dealt with epistemologically as the world of the social, the physical and the logico-mathematical knowledge system*. This is consistent with Piaget's formulation (Piaget, 1971). Social knowledge is transmitted in a sociogenetic model and this primarily refers to knowledge that emanates from engagement with human beings (Waddington, 1960). Various systems are used to classify knowledge. Academia has its category system of sciences, humanities, and art, for example. However, social, physical, and logico-mathematical knowledge do encompass the major knowledge systems. Within the physical domain we subsume cognitions of the physical world (physics, chemistry, for example) and in the logico-mathematical category, we subsume the understanding of classes, relations and numbers. Social knowledge is both transmitted and constructed in the social context – in other words, from the world of people (Leont'ev, 1969, Piaget, 1971; Vygotsky, 1978; Waddington, 1960).

5. *Knowledges derived in each of these domains involves, as indicated above, an affective component, and this affective component will vary in its salience depending on the context*. Knowledge constructed in the social context will be construed with more affect since it evolves in the course of relationships with significant others, e.g., parents, siblings, peers, etc. The knowledge that is assimilated in this process is assimilated through the active construction on the part of the individual.

5.1. *This subproposition derives from the assumption that all objects and events are polydimensional and that which is selected from this array is selected by virtue of particular saliences at certain points in time* (Sigel, Jarman & Hanesian, 1967). These selective features are dependent upon the individual's maturity level and the individual's opportunities for experience. Therefore this brings in the issue of the historical social context because experiences will vary in significance with developmental level.

6. *Construction of knowledge is a basic generic, human activity.* The activity will vary in quantity and quality as the individual matures and confronts various aspects of the environment. The construction of knowledge involves assimilation-accommodation processes which are intimately involved and without which new knowledge will not be acquired. Generation of new knowledge comes about through experiencing discrepancies between previous constructions and new ones, or between ongoing constructions. The metaphor we are working from is that the child is the builder where the base is laid down for the ultimate schematic organization of construct system as a function of life experiences.

7. *There is an ongoing developmental set of transformations of these schemata over time and as a function of particular experiences.* The person represents an open system which continues to evolve and change until death. Life always provides opportunities for engagement, confrontation and subsequent resolution of discrepancies. How the individual copes with these discrepancies, these changing schema, depends on biological and psychological functions. The individual with an intact mentation, an intact neurophysiological system, is capable of continuously assimilating and reorganizing experience. The reorganization of these experiences will be dependent upon the degree to which the schemate that emerge are bounded. When schemata are tightly bounded and impermeable using the biological cell analogy, it is unlikely that the individual will be able to assimilate new information. In fact, it is probable that the information will not even be seen or identified as salient. Most individuals have constructions of other cultures, other races, other political systems, and these constructs define what is selected. And, of course, this becomes possible because every culture, social system and race is a poly-dimensional array, so that any of a number of selections of features of the environment consonant with one's own system are possible.

8. *The conflict between schemata or constructs produces disequilibration.* The assumption is that this generally is undesirable unless the boundary systems are so tight that the individual is not aware of the disequilibrium. Such conceptions are evident among individuals who tend to fragment their world views which in turn avoid inner conflict.

9. *Every action involves the two levels of knowledge which we shall refer to also as awareness and non-awareness, similar to Polanyi's tacit and explicit knowledge.* The non-awareness refers to the fact that we cannot articulate the totality of an experience and whatever is presented through some communication channel is only a limited aspect of thet experience. When one goes to hit a tennis ball, one can only present a limited statement of the components of the action. Yet, these actions are integrated into unity and as far as the observer is concerned, there is a type of synchrony among each of these components. In addition to the behavior elements that are in part observable, there is also an array of feelings, both bodily and mental, that accompany these acts. The observer can only make inferences – some through direct observation, but mostly interpretation of that observation – and some through his general knowledge of motor behavior. However, the quality of the nonknowledgeable is unknown and probably can only be articulated in a piecemeal fashion. Lest this sound mystical, it is not the case, but rather a function of our human limitations. We are addressing the question of how we deal with the multitude of stimuli that are available to us, externally and internally. And the coordination of all these,

especially into linear language, precludes our giving total statements in more than one dimension.

If we could speak simultaneously in two or three dimensions, we might be able to articulate our experience more intensively. Perhaps some day through advanced computer technology or work with robots, some light can be shed on this intriguing problem of simultaneity. However, cognitive controls of response and concomitant feelings are experienced by most of us. This lends credibility to the assertion that the linear response is perhaps the manifestation of a more complex substratum of a latent schema.

These nine propositions do not enhaust the list. Other propositions can be derived from the vast theoretical base with which we are working. For now, let us leave these and turn to a discussion between schemata and operations which in Piaget's sense asks the question – What kinds of mental operations are employed by the individual in order to deal with the knowledge that he/she has? From a Piagetian perspective, knowledge is assimilated. Schemata are constructed as are operations which, in fact, are interiorized actions. These operations are classification, seriation, comprehension of intersection of classes, etc. They are, in a way, the tools of thought Schemata which may be figurative in the from of images, or which may be eventually transformed into some other symbolic system, become, in effect, internal representations of one's reality. It is the intersect between the operation and the schemata that speak to the individual's ability to define, alter, and reorganize schemata relative to the demands of that situation. Then schemata and the operations evolve in a sequential and stage-like order. Nevertheless, the invariance and the quality of that, we argue, will depend on socio-historical functions. While for Piaget these are universals, there is still some question of what that really means. The appearance of a universal at any point in time is only one way of determining their presence. Universals may not be observable in the sense that capability of the organism is never tested or opportunities are not provided for development (skills, for example). In primitive societies children do not have the chance to engage in activities with objects of play. Are the skills for symbolic representation still present? It is like the old problem of the bough breaking in the forest. Does the breaking bough make a noise when no one is there to hear it? The problem is complex because the non-presence of something from a behavioral perspective is presumed to be non-existant. Appearance of a behavior, however, is a function of the methods used to elicit it in that particular context.

Therefore, the decision to build a model which deals only with behavioral manifestation or potentials of the living organism inferring certain potential characteristics does bring us back to the question of what the model is.

From our perspective, the capability of assimilating knowledge, acquiring new schemata and building and reorganizing these schemata which form the cognitive base for operations, are generic to the human condition.

In all this cognitive theorizing, where is the persona? Who is the person?

The Person in the cognitive system

We are faced with a rather interesting issue here. The propositions described above bring together primarily *affect* and *cognition* and deal with the relationship between

70

these *domains of knowledge*. Is there a more central core? Is there an underlying integrating "self" – the knower who is the organizer, the integrator of experience? Are we merely touching at superficial bits and pieces if we focus on the cognitive, for example, and missing the inner core? In effect, have we described the development of a persona?

Implicit in our entire discussion was the sense of some internal integrity of the organism. This integrity, this coherence, is not a fixed core, but a cognition where the person becomes both a self and an object to himself. The George Mead notion of the *"I"* and the *"me"* had considerable heuristic value for use in this context (Mead, 1934). The "I" is the core. It is the trunk which is no fixed, but growing; not growing in disarray, but growing both in height and width and internal complexity. The "me" is the social element which relates and varies with context. In the course of development, three things are happening: One, the child is experiencing; two, the child is assimilating and constructing these experiences into knowledge wholes; and three, the child is engaging in many situations at different times and at different levels which provide confirming or disconfirming experiences along with basic knowledge. The child at home is considered to be cute and bright, but when he/she goes to school he/she is no cuter than anybody else and perhaps less bright than some. The child may ask himself, "Am I bright" Am I not bright? Am I cute? Am I ugly?" There is an implication in such internal inquiry that the child is comparing himself to internalized standards. The standards, we argue, evolve through social interaction with significant others. Significant others are those individuals whom the child construes as important and whose opinions the child values. They can be parents, siblings, peers, radio and television figures and the like. Social experiences with significant others can be construed as positive or negative. These social comparison judgments can also exist at different levels of awareness. Irrespective of level of awareness, however, the social context is one in which contradictions and/or consensus occur. Children's comparisons of actions, of status, of ideas with significant other's are embedded in an ongoing social context which can be viewed as a social dialectical environment. The construction of the *persona* emerges as part of the cognizing of these social relationships in a social context. We shall not go into the cognitive complexities involved here. Suffice it to say, for our present purposes, social interactions generate opportunities for creating cognitive conflicts necessary for development of the concept of "I" and "me."

In addition to learning about *self*, the individual is also learning about social rules and conventions. Acquiring such knowledge requires a structuring before the child knows that there is: (a) a rule and (b) what the rule is. It is not discoverable through engagement or self-regulated actions. On the other hand, physical knowledge – knowledge that if things are dropped, they'll break, or knowledge of weight, distance, speed – all of such knowledge is potentially discoverable through one's own participation. The level of discovery, however, is going to vary with what resources the child has. Knowledge of the object world can come about through exploration and discovery. In principle, the knowledge of the social conventions in the social world can only come about through being told or through watching others; more of an observational learning. And this distinction is quite well expressed in the research findings. It is consistent with Vygotsky's and Leont'ev's notions of the significance of socio-cultural exchange with children.

Over the life-span the individual engages in activity in many contexts. He extracts knowledge from these, thereby developing schemata or constructs. Central to these constructions is the core construct system of the knower, the self. It involves a feed-back system where each action produces a reaction, each reaction produces actions, and so on ad infinitium. This rather simplistic summary is the skeleton of our system. In the remaining pages we will present the different contexts which illustrate the model we have proposed.

Examples of research and clinical application of the model

The first situation we wish to describe is the ontogenesis of the *persona* in the context of the family. During the past five years we have been studying the development of representation in young children. Our conceptualization of the model involves three segments: the parents constructions of children's growth; the parents' distancing strategies (i.e., those strategies which have an implicit and explicit demand for the child to transcend the present in time and space; essentially demand that the child engage in representation of the past and/or contemporaneous and/or the present, and/or the future); and the child's representational competence which in turn may influence the parents' behaviors or beliefs regarding cognitive development. The results of this study demonstrate that the parents' belief system (constructions) do in fact influence children's representational competence (McGillicuddy-DeLisi, in press, McGillicuddy-DeLisi, Sigel, & Johnson, 1979) .

In effect, the family study is an example of how the propositions discussed above can provide the empirical research. The parents' constructions of the children's cognitive development, the classification of teaching strategies, and the use of representational competence as a dependent variable are all classifications of the reality of the family. These constructions, on our part, stem from our integration of Kelly's ideas on personal constructs, Leont'ev's, Vygotsky's and Piaget's ideas of dialectics, cognitive conflict, and actions.

The practical significance of our conceptualization is reflected in part in a report by Bendixen and Holmgren (1979). While this report did not use the model expli-cated in their effort, authors' conceptualization does reflext the propositions of this paper. Specifically, one of the authors of the report lived in a therapeutic commune (a separate home in the community) with six adolescents who were diagnosed as being neurotic. The young people, while living in this commune, do engage in activi-. ties inside the house (working and cleaning), and outside the house (school or job). These actions serve as catalysts for emotional growth. The young people are engaged in a "real life context" level and have to deal with the contradictions they encounter in both the commune and in school or job settings. Coming to terms with these con-tradictions is considered as part of the therapeutic process. The results of this ex-perience have proven to be valuable for the young patients. After several months it enabled them to become increasingly independent and live on their own or non-therapeutic environments. By structuring the therapeutic environment to engage the young people in productive meaningful activity, they were able to enhance their emotional adjustement and also free themselves from some of their emotional pro-blems through cognitive restructuring of their lives (Bendixen & Holmgren, 1979).

References

BECK, A. T.: Cognitive therapy and emotional disorders. New York: International Universities Press, 1976

BENDIXEN, C., and A. HOLMGREN: Jugendliche mit psychischer Störung in einer Wohngemeinschaft. Paper published in Proceedings of Kongress Kritische Psychologie, Marburg, Germany, 1979

FREUD, S.: Three contributions to the theory of sex. [In : The basic writings of Sigmund Freud] (A. A. Brill, Ed. and trans.). New York: Random House, 1938

KELLY, G. A.: The psychology of personal constructs (2 vols.). New York: Norton, 1955

LEONT'EV, A. N.: On the biological and social aspects of human development: The training of auditory ability. In: M. Cole & I. Maltman (Eds.), A handbook of contemporary Soviet Psychology. New York: Basic Books, 1969

McGILLICUDDY-DeLISI, A. V.: The relation between family constellation and parental beliefs about child development. In: L. M. Laosa and I. E. Sigel (Eds.), Families as learning environments for children. New York: Plenum, in press

McGILLICUDDY-DeLISI, A. V., I. E. SIGEL and J. E. JOHNSON: The family as a system of mutual influences: Parental beliefs, distancing, behaviors, and children's representational thinking. In: M. Lewis and L. A. Rosenblum (Eds.), The child and its family: Genesis of behavior (Vol. 2). New York: Plenum, 1979

MEAD, G. H.: Mind, self and society: From the standpoint of a social behaviorist. Chicago, Ill.: University of Chicago Press, 1934

MISCHEL, W.: Personality and Assessment. New York: Wiley, 1968

PEPPER, S. C.: World hypotheses: A study of evidence. Berkeley, Calif.: University of California Press, 1942

PERVIN, L. A.: Current controversies and issue in personality. New York: Wiley, 1978

PIAGET, J.: Six psychological studies. New York: Random House, 1967

PIAGET, J.: Biology and knowledge. Chicago, Ill.: University of Chicago Press, 1971

POLANYI, M.: Personal knowledge. Chicago, Ill.: University of Chicago Press, 1958

SIGEL, I., P. JARMAN and H. HANESIAN: Styles of categorization and their intellectual and personality correlates in young children. Human Development, 1967, 10, 1–17

VYGOTSKY, L. S.: Mind in society: The development of higher psychological processes, Cambridge, Mass.: Harvard University Press, 1978

WADDINGTON, C. H.: The ethical animal. London, England: George Allen & Unwin Ltd., 1960

Social Norms and their Internal Representation as Determinants of Behaviour Regulation

Karlheinz Otto

1. The anthropological significance of social norms

The behaviour of human beings, which is primarily determined by social aspects, is multipotent in its essence. This already applies to its genetical bases, which have a relatively high plasticity. In comparison with human behaviour, the behaviour of animals is restricted within narrow limits, because it is predominantly controlled by inherited systems of instincts and drives.

It is man, therefore, who has numerous and manifold alternatives of behaviour within a wide range. But out of the 'universe' of possible behaviour only a finite number can be materialized by the individual. Consequently, the individual has to select. These multivariable alternatives of behaviour are, for the individual, the basis of his all-round development of personality, but on the other hand, they cause a considerable insecurity which is the greater, the less sufficiently an individual can recognize conditions and foresee consequences of his actions.

In order to get over these insecurities in behaviour or, at least, to reduce them, man is trying to find "guarantees of behaviour". The best guarantees for socially adequate behaviour and successful activities are, without doubt, found in the objective laws of nature, of society, and of thinking, which are defined and based on science and from which the right norms can be derived.

But not all of the laws are known by man and even if a law is known, the individual may only know it incompletely. Dependent on this fact for the purpose of social communication and cooperation, a certain number of general regulations of behaviour, such as "social habits" are essential, expressed in the socalled group norms, sex norms, age norms and similar norms.

Common to all norms is, seen formally, their stabilizing function. They represent general instances of orientation and result in the reduction (or channelling) of behaviour variants to those forms that – under certain conditions – are necessary or usual. It is there norms that make life clear and make stabile social relations possible.

Norms and systems of norms are, therefore, of vital importance for both the individual and the society. Naturally, it depends on the particular social conditions, which of the systems will be the one to refer to, will be the norm of behaviour. "The necessity and possibility that man learns to control himself and his environment to an ever larger extent, is due to social progress. The scientifically based application of norms for regulating social relations is an important means to successfully increase control . . . Thus on the international field it is of increasing importance to deal scientifically with the essence, the function, the characteristics, and the laws of norms. For real socialism, the scientific investigation of norms and their purposeful application is a decisive means to intensify progress" (Loeser, 1979).

Social norms have always to be related to their historical conditionality and to social development. They result from special social conditions, they help to reach the aims of a society, support its interests for a limited historical period, and they are changing with its further progress. Consequently, social norms are by no means general, human, rigid, and absolute categories of orientation of actions. They are created and altered by man, who, therefore, should not comply with them in a passive way but should face them with an active and creative attitude.

Accordingly, human behaviour is in principle related to norms (Schmidt, 1974; Lückert, 1966). In this respect this may justify the fact that the behaviour norm is regarded as a basic term (Brandstätter, 1977) in psychology.

2. Types of norms

Norms form a system, which has many branches and is most complex. According to various aspects they can be categorized as types of norms which are generally grouped in a dichotomal way:

1. As to the aspect of the regulation of relations between men as well as between man and object, we can distinguish between *social* (ethical) norms and *technical* norms.

2. In the aspect of education we can make a distinction between norms of *behaviour* and norms of *performance*.

Norms of behaviour – related, for example, to the development of habits, attitudes, social qualities, etc.

Norms of performance – related, for example, to the acquisition of knowledge, the development of skills and faculties, etc.

3. In the aspect of realization we can differentiate between *ideal* norms (referring to the future) and *real* norms (referring to the present).

4. In the aspect of legal obligation we differ *juridic* norms (legal norms) from *conventional* norms (customs and manners).

5. Concerning the aspect of the general public, norms can be divided into *official* and *inofficial* (so-called unwritten laws) norms.

6. As to the aspect of frequency we can distinguish between *individual* norms and *statistical* or *group* norms (including sex, age, occupational norms etc.).

Obviously, the types of norms above mentioned do not exist isolated from each other, on the contrary, they always appear in a complex as various aspects of this or that concrete norm. For example, one specified social norm (e.g. for the protection of people's property) can be a social, a real, a legal, and an official norm at the same time.

3. On the ontogenesis of acquiring social norms

According to action theory norms and systems of norms represent regulations of behaviour, impulses or barriers of behaviour. As a rule, they even contain complete programmes of behaviour. Norms, however, can only accomplish this task, if they have been internalized, if they have become internal, functional systems of behaviour orientation and action regulation.

Those norm systems which are necessary for the regulation of social life are ever increasing, specifying and differentiating in the course of social development. This phenomenon makes high demands on the individual, above all on those growing up, who have to be made familiar with the norms, and who must, after having discussed them, internalize them. Thus the individual cannot be expected to take into consideration all the most important social norms from the very beginning. What then is the right way of organizing this process of confrontation with norms in the course of man's psychological development?

Previous studies and experiences in education indicate that the acquisition of norms has the characteristic features of a process as well and takes a progressive course. This sounds trivial, but it is this fact that is often ignored in educational practice because of the false assumption that a child only needs to know the norms and he will observe them in his actions, i.e. he is willing and able to do so. In this very respect, children are often overtasked, misjudged, or treated in an unfair way.

From the ontogenetic point of view, two facts are of special importance:

1. As already mention ed, the numerous social norms cannot be internalized all at the same time. They must be internalized gradually, i.e. systematically, one based on the other. In which order should the new and higher norms be bred into children? In other words: which stages of development are the most adequate for the internalization of particular norms, such as "keeping one's clothes clean", "being honest", "helping each other", "acting with responsibility", etc.? To give the right answer to these questions is most difficult, among others this depends on a second problem:

2. Most social norms are of a highly complex nature. As a rule they have a most differentiated inner structure, the more even, the wider their range of validity is.

In most cases, therefore, the complete internalization of social norms takes an ontogenetically long period.

Internalization of norms is a most complicated process which is mainly realized by means of learning activities. In addition to special knowledge of things, knowledge of values and of techniques; Lompscher integrates, with reason, knowledge of norms as a separate category of knowledge. Until now, little has been known about the specific character of acquiring social norms. For this reason the special subject of our symposium is of great importance.

Obviously, the well-known general laws of learning are also valid for the internalization of behaviour norms. Further factors, however, are of great importance, first of all the conditions of motivation and attitudes.

For example, when special knowledge is acquired, the process is generally completed after reception, intellectual digestion and storing of knowledge. With the acquisition of norms, on the other hand, the agreed end will not be reached until the norms of behaviour, which are now part of the individual's knowledge, are integrated into the personality's systems of motivation and attitude and until adequate abilities of selfcontrol have been developed, which allow an independent regulation of behaviour.

An all-round and thorough internalization of norms is not possible before the individual has had the opportunity to tackle social norms in an active, creative and deliberate way.

References

BRANDSTÄTTER, J.: Normen. In: Th. Herrmann et al. (Eds.), Handbuch psychologischer Grundbegriffe. München 1977

LOESER, F.: Die wissenschaftliche Begründbarkeit von Normen. Deutsche Zeitschrift für Philosophie 27, 8, 1979

LÜCKERT, H. R.: Die Normation. In: H. Thomae (Ed.), Die Motivation menschlichen Handelns. Köln/Berlin 1966

SCHMIDT, H.-D.: Normativer Aspekt und Persönlichkeitsbegriff. Probleme und Ergebnisse der Psychologie 48, 1974

Social Regulation of Behaviour as a Function of Communication

E. V. Shorokhova

The theoretical basis of the study of the role of communication in the social regulation of behaviour was laid down in the works of the classics of Marxism-Leninism. K. Marx and F. Engels wrote that "the development of an individual is determined by the development of all the others with whom he is directly or indirectly associated, and that the different generations of individuals entering into relation with one another are connected with one another, that the physical existence of the later generations is determined by that of their predecessors, and that these later generations inherit the productive forces and forms of association accumulated by their predecessors, their own mutual relations being determined thereby. In short, it is clear that a development occurs and that the history of a single individual cannot possibly be separated from the history of preceding or contemporary individuals, but is determined by this history" (Karl Marx and Friedrich Engels, The German Ideology, Progr. Publ., Moscow, 1964, p. 482).

In the complex system of social behaviour, communication has many aspects, such as interaction between individuals, information exchanges, individual attitudes and individual influences, mutual emotional experiences and mutual understanding.

Communication as exchanges of information, interests, moods, feelings and attitudes equals, in its essence, social influence. It is, in fact, the individualised form of social relations, their personal psychological concretisation. The peculiarity of the personal forms of manifestation of social relations in communication is determined by the character, social experience and all the characteristics of communicating individuals – different individuals, performing social roles and coming into social relations (direct or indirect) with other individuals, demonstrate a different performance of social ,,instructions" and "demands", contained in different types and modes of activity and in different relations. This depends on their understanding of their social tasks, their place and role in the solution of these tasks, on their personal attitude and degree of interest; on the presence of the required personal qualities, such as knowledge, abilities and skills, necessary for the successful implementation of their tasks and establishing the necessary relations with other people with the aim of satisfying social and individual needs; on the activity of individuals, responsible for certain functions, on the energy and emotion they demonstrate; and on the concrete situation. The social function of communication is also to be found in the fact that it constitutes the necessary condition for the existence of the community as a number of individuals. The community is characterised by people's belonging to stable social groups, by internal spiritual solidarity of communicating people and by the stable spiritual relations manifested in mutual understanding.

Communication produces inter-personal forms of behaviour regulation. They manifest themselves in the processes of identification, assimilation and differentiation of individuals. Assimilation is the result of the solidarisation of the personality with the community he belongs to, while differentiation results from individual uniqueness and individual peculiarities, which indicate the personality's membership of many other social communities, as well as the variety of social relations and social roles of the personality.

The dialectics of differentiation and assimilation of the personality within the community characterizes all spheres and structures of human communication.

The social regulation of behaviour is performed with the implementation of all communicative aims: (1) the planning, organisation and control of joint human activity, (2) the influence on an individual or group of people with an aim of achieving certain actions or deeds, changing views and opinions, modifying life principles or forming the individuals' characteristics, (3) the assimilation of the experience of the previous generations, and (4) the satisfaction of the need for communication itself.

The social regulation of behaviour is to be found, in a varying degree, at all stages of communication, such as the establishment of the special, psychological and social contacts, and all other forms of interaction. From the point of view of the content, communication can be regarded as a communication process consisting in the mutual expression of the mental state and in information exchanges. From the point of view of the form, one can speak about the behavioural aspect of communication, materialised in the interaction of people and their behaviour towards one another.

Communication performs its social regulative function, primarily, in the form of speech. This manifests itself, to a varying degree, in various functions, i.e. informational, expressive and imperative. The direct, "influencing" regulative designation of the communication demonstrated by such forms of the imperative function of speech, as orders, requests, demands, prohibitions, proposals, suggestions, etc. They materialise the activating and interactive social influence.

The well-expressed regulative function is performed by the normative factors, operating in the communicative process itself, emerging spontaneously in the society or established consciously by certain individuals or institutions and extended to the choice of communication channels, the use of communication means, the inter-individual information exchanges, the decision-making in communicative situations and the choice of potential communicators. The ethnic, social, professional and cultural environments determine the contents and the form of the normative requirement to the character and means of communication. In the modern society, normative communication includes documented elements as an indispensible factor. A document, being a reliable long-term text, most often in written form, meeting the normative requirements and fixing the information about the essence of relations between individuals, is a means of productive social communication, i.e. leading to the materialisation of these relations.

The social regulative meaning of communication is most apparent when communication acquires the form of a specific type of activity sa propaganda, agitation, advertising, etc. The mass information media, used in these types of activity, are directed at organising and maintaining the social informational relations between individuals in a society and between different elements of the social structure. These functions have different social meanings in different social and economic formations.

In capitalist society, the main task of these forms of communication is the psychological conditioning of the public aimed at its adaptation to the dominating standards of the bourgeois way of life and thinking. In the socialist society, they provide an effective instrument of the mass information, propaganda and education of broad masses to achieve an allaided development of the personality, to expand the personality's outlook and the understanding of the modern world so as to intensify human activity for the progressive change of the society.

The social regulative effect of communication depends on its individualisation and understanding between the communicators. Understanding between communicators helps to solve many tasks of the social regulation of behaviour. It achieves coincidence, similarity or likeness in the world outlooks of different people in their value orientations, the understanding of the individual peculiarities of each other, the understanding, or even a guess, of behaviour motives and the possibility of a certain type of personal behaviour in a given situation, the acceptance of the roles performed towards one another, the mutual acceptance of self-evaluation and of the evaluations of personal abilities, etc.

We studied experimentally trusting and handicapped communication as forms of the social regulation of behaviour. The specific features of trusting and handicapped communication are determined by the aims and means of the communication, by the communicative situations, by the social (the distribution of social roles) and social psychological characteristics of the communicators (their system of values, attitudes, and orientations) and by their individual psychological traits (a personality type, etc.).

Research by E. V. Tsukanova revealed that handicapped business communication develops in situations of joint activities under the influence of the factors breaking into the following groups: the nature of inter-personal relations established between partners in joint activity; the personal psychological peculiarities of the partners; the nature of their involvement in the joint activity; and the peculiarities of the situation. In life situations of the joint activity, a handicapped business communication develops in the form of social psychological manifestations of a general and particular nature.

The general manifestations of such communication, developing both under the influence of inter-personal realtions and individual psychological peculiarities, result primarily in the changes of the functional, dynamic and qualitative characteristics of the communication.

The particular manifestations of a handicapped communication, emerging in life situations of the joint activity primarily under the influence of any one factor, acquire the form of phenomena, specific in their social and psychological nature: the manifestations of a handicapped communication, caused by inter-personal relations are registered in changed styles of business communication, pretending disagreement, intentional misinformation of the partner, the avoidance of business communication and the growth of the share of non-business communication in the general volume of communication. The manifestations of a handicapped communication, caused by individual psychological peculiarities, are registered in shifts in dialogue structures, irregularities in the use of contextually-conditioned ellipsis in business dialogues, in spontanious non-verbal means of communication, and in behaviour, inadequate to the communication situation and the nature of business activity.

The general and particular manifestations of a handicapped communication in life situations of the interaction in the joint activity perform the function of the secondary factors, causing the difficulty, which deteriorate the disharmony of business communication and reduce the effectiveness of the joint activity.

The difficulties discovered in communication have a particular importance for diagnosing the kind of difficulties and barriers in communications, expecially for the professions which largely depend on person-to-person relations and for activities performed under extreme conditions. The development of means of the optimisation of communication will therefore increase its social effect on human behaviour.

Activity Environment, Social Class and Voluntary Learning

AIRI HAUTAMÄKI

The mediating nature of family activities

The explanation of social class differences in the acquisition of voluntary learning (Husen, 1972; Clausen, 1966; Hess, 1970) demands studies into the ecological environment of the child (Bronfenbrenner, 1979a) and it is related to the problem of how the social is mediated to the individual through family socialization (Takala, 1979, Hautamäki, 1979a). In this study the focus is on social psychological mechanisms which are assumed to underly the transformation of certain social conditions into the activity and self-regulative capacities of the pupil in the family.

The mediating nature of the so-called environmental forces of the home which impinge on the developing child has been the object of research in the studies of learning environments (Bloom, 1964, Dave, 1963, Weiss, 1974, Marjoribanks, 1979). It has been found out that global social class indicators are poorer predictors of the personality development, especially cognitive performance, than the more sensitive parent interview measures of the learning environment. Using path analytic techniques Marjoribanks has distinguished the contextual and individual (indirect and direct respectively) effects of the socioeconomic status on the development of the child (Marjoribanks, 1977). The indirect effect of the socioeconomic status is mediated through different learning environments created by the families. In this study it is assumed that the effects of the living conditions associated with the parents' educational level and the mothers' language code are primarily indirect, i.e., mediated through the activities of the family (Hautamäki, 1979b).

Social psychological mechanisms of mediation

Although the research of learning environments has made use of environmental process variables, the problem of the conditions and nature of the transformation of the environmental forces (physical, social, or intellectual) into the abilities of the child has not yet been solved. Some attempts have been made, for instance, by Marjoribanks (1979, 130–150) to apply an interactionally oriented frame of reference.

The influence of the environmental forces has not, however, been related to the level of the self-regulated activity of the child.

L. S. Vygotsky analyzes the emergence of self-regulative capacities of the child in the ontogenesis, the prerequisite of which is the acquisition of historically developed sign systems under adult guidance (Vygotsky, 1974). As Wertsch (1979, 3–4) points out, Vygotsky is not primarily interested in the structural features of the sign systems acquired, but in the process of acquisition, i.e., in the emergence of self-regulation with the help of language and other signs. The origins of self-regulative capacities are to be found in adult-child interaction, where the adults provide the other-regulation (for the term Wertsch, 1979) necessary for the child to carry out the task to be learned. According to Vygotsky the child develops self-regulative capacities as he encounters communicative contexts involving other-regulation.

Thus learning under adult guidance creates the zone of proximal development, i.e., learning awakens a variety of internal developmental processes which start to operate when the child is interacting with the guiding adult (Vygotsky, 1978). Consequently the explanation of a psychological function has to be based on tracing this process of interiorization, the transition from interpersonal to intrapersonal psychological functioning.

If Vygotsky's ideas are generalized to the research of family socialization, it seems important to study such social interaction in which the adult is providing other-regulation in the zone of proximal development of the pupil, i.e., social interaction that facilitates the transition to self-regulated learning activity at the intrapsychological plane. In this study the forms of other-regulation provided by the parents are related to the level of the child's self-regulated activity according to Vygotsky's definition of the zone of proximal development as the distance between the child's other-regulated and independent problem solving (Vygotsky, 1978, 86) The other-regulation taken into account in the study is the parents' guidance[1], the parents' demands and model presented to the child. It is assumed that the development of voluntary learning is furthered, if the parents' guidance, demands and model in relevant aspects exceed the level of the child's self-regulated activity. These relationships might, with some reservations, be termed social interaction in the zone of proximal development. Consequently, the activity environment of the pupil is preliminarily defined as the environment which creates the zone of proximal development of voluntary learning activity and operationalized as the relationship between, on the one hand, the parents' guidance, demands and model and, on the other hand, the level of the self-regulated activity of the child (Hautamäki, 1979b).

According to the activity-centered approach outlined by A. N. Leontiev (Leontjew, 1971) it is important to specify the content of the activities. The activities mediate the relationship between the individual and environment and are defined by their objects. The definition of the psychological contents is related to the demands of the activity in question in regard to the child's self-regulative capacities (Kossakowski and Ettrich, 1973). Recently Urie Bronfenbrenner has also called attention to the investigation of molar activities according to their content (Bronfenbrenner, 1979a, 45), stressing that "molar activities as exhibited by the developing person serve as indicators of the degree and the nature of psychological growth; as exhibited by others present in the situation, they constitute the principle vehicle for the *direct* influence of the environment on the developing person".

In the learning environment research it has traditionally been assumed that there

[1] The parents' guidance of the child is similar to what Bronfenbrenner (1979b) terms a primary developmental context, i.e., a context in which the child can engage in ongoing patterns of progressively more complex activity jointly with or under the direct guidance of persons who possess knowledge and skill not yet acquired by the child.

are such general environmental forces which can be generalized across different areas of activity (Wolf, 1964). As the environmental forces have usually been identified and composed by using factor analysis, this assumption is legitimate. But the problem concerns the representativeness of the original items regarding the different areas of activity.

Consequently the learning environment has not been sufficiently specified according to the object and content of the child's activities.

In the present study an attempt is made to broaden the areas of activities usually mapped in the research of learning environments. Thus the activity structure in the family is specified according to the objects which seem to differ in their psychological contents. At the same time they represent dominant activities in the child's ontogenesis. The activity areas are learning, hobbies, social interaction and working activities.

Thus it is possible to specify both the modes of activity and the activity environment according to the activity areas (see Fig. 1) (Hautamäki, 1979b).

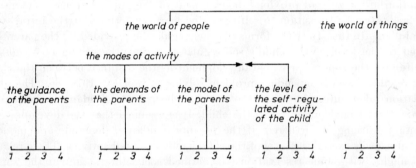

Fig. 1: The activity environment of the pupil in the family.
(1 learning activities; 2 hobby activities; 3 social activities; 4 working activities)

In the study two assumptions concerning the social psychological mechanisms of mediation are tested. Firstly, it is assumed that children characterized by differing living conditions will also differ according to their self-regulative capacities of learning and according to the extent to which the parents' guidance, demands and model exceed the level of the self-regulated activity of the child. Secondly, the degree to which the parents' modes of activity exceed the level of the self-regulated activity of the child in learning and hobbies draws a demarcation line between parents of different educational levels and language codes.

Voluntary learning

The learning activity differs from previous dominant activities in regard to its goal structure, time perspective and societal orientation. As Rosenfeld (1974) points out, the goal of voluntary learning is primarily outside the activity, not inherent in it. According to the Marxist image of man Rosenfeld stresses the growing orientation of the pupil's learning activity at other people and society in general. But the pupil is capable of grasping and conceptualizing the societal meaning and goals of learning

Tab. 1: *The modes of activity and their related characteristics used in the interview schedule*

1. The parents' guidance of the child	2. Parental demands	3. The model of the parents	4. The level of the self-regulated activity of the child	5. The world of things at home
1a The parents' guidance in learning – parental interest in school, support of the child's school work and knowledge of the child's educational progress – discussions held with the child concerning future education and occupational career – guidance to the use of books, periodicals and other literature *1b The parents' guidance in hobbies* – the introduction and encouragement of different hobbies by the parents – extent and content of indoor and outdoor activities with the child – extent and purpose of the use of T.V. *1c The parents' guidance in social activities* – knowledge of the child's friends *1d The parents' guidance in working activities* – discussions held with the child about the parents' work and the world of work – the child's visits to the working places of the parents – guidance to house-keeping activities	*2a Parental demands in learning activities* – parental expectations for the school work, the educational and occupational career of the child – stress on early independence in learning activities *2b Parental demands in hobbies* *2c Parental demands in working activities* – stress on early independence in house-keeping activities *2d Parental demands in social activities* – stress on early independence in social relations (sibling care, decisions concerning friends of different sexes, membership of political organizations)	*3a Parental model in learning* – the parents' model in occupational or other training, taking educational courses – the parents' reading habits *3b Parental model in hobbies* – the amount and nature of the parents' hobbies and the use of T.V. *3c The model in work* – the 'family tradition' in the level of qualification of work, i.e., the model of older siblings *3d Parental model in social activities* – the parents' formal (memberships in social and political organizations) and informal (neighbours), relatives, friends) extra-family interaction	*4a The level of learning activities* – use of library – use of books, periodicals, and other literature *4b The level of hobby activities* – the extent and nature of the child's hobbies, indoor an and outdoor activities, and extent and purpose of the use of T.V. *4c The level of the working activities* – the house-keeping activities at the responsibility of the child – the extent to which the child makes questions concerning the work of parents *4d The level of the social activities* – the extent and nature of the child's peer group associations	– the crowding ratio – the amount and nature of books, periodicals, other literature and news-papers – the amount and nature of children's books

only by acquiring an extended future-oriented time perspective. Consequently, a prerequisite for the development of voluntary learning is that the pupil learns to coordinate activities, set up and maintain subgoals of activities, and develop long-term motives which gradually permeate the entire activity sequences. Because of the demands of voluntary learning activity on the pupil's self-regulative capacities, the motives of learning represent primarily conscious and future-oriented motives (Hautamäki, 1979a).

Methods and measures

The sample consisted of 95 pupils aged 11–12 years and their parents from the town of Joensuu in Eastern Finland. The sample is representative of the town of Joensuu according to the parents' socioeconomic status and family constellation (Hautamäki, 1979a).

The parents were interviewed concerning the family activities with a half-structured questionnaire. The interview schedule was developed on the basis of Marjoribanks (1972, 1979), Takala (1977), and that theoretical assumption of the importance of contentspecific analysis. An attempt was made to measure both the intensity of the present activity environment and retrospectively gain a measure of the cumulative nature of the activity environment at home over time. 5- and 6-point rating scales were developed to score each item in the schedule. The score of each mode of activity was obtained by summing up the scores on the relevant environmental items. After one preliminary test of the schedule, the final questionnaire was adopted (see Tab. 1) (Hautamäki, 1979a).

The socioeconomic status of the families was defined in terms of five indicators:
– father's and mother's occupation (9-point scale),
– father's and mother's education (8-point scale),
– mother's language code (6-point scale).[2]

The children were investigated with tests aimed at measuring essential dimensions of self-regulative capacities in learning.

Learning motivation was assessed by Rosenfeld's phenomenological method (Rosenfeld, 1974) using Berg's classification scheme (Berg, 1971). Four indexes of learning motivation were developed: the time perspective, the societal extension, and the amount of motive grounds. A score for the hierarchization of motives was obtained by summing up the above-mentioned indexes (Hautamäki, 1979a).

Individual achievement motivation was assessed by Heckhausen's projective method (Heckhausen, 1963).

Personal time perspectives were also measured projectively according to Heckhausen (1963).

Cognitive development was assessed by the Finnish version (Hautamäki, J., 1980) of Shayer's science reasoning tasks (Shayer et al., 1976) based on Piaget.

---

[2] In the interview situation the mother's way of using language was observed and classified according to four dimensions (3-point scale), which were developed on the basis of Bernstein's language code concept (Bernstein, 1971). The line of demarcation was the extent to which the meanings in the mother's speech were context-free versus context-bound (Hautamäki, 1979a).

The verbal (V-factor), spatial (S-factor) and logical reasoning (R-factor) abilities were also measured.

School achievement was assessed by using the grade-point avarages.

Results

The reliability coefficients for each of the modes of activity scales were estimated by evaluating split-half reliability as an estimate of coefficient alpha (Nunnally, 1967). The coefficients presented in Tab. 2 were considered to be on an acceptable level.

Tab. 2.: *The reliability of the scales of the modes of activity*

Scale	Reliability coeffizient	Number of items
the guidance of the parents (A)	.63	19
the demands of the parents (B)	.73	7
the model of the parents (C)	.81	19
the level of self-regulated activity of the pupil (D)	.70	9
the world of people (A+B+C+D)	.91	54

The area-specific modes of activity were less reliable, the items of which were also fewer. The reliabilities ranged from .50 to .82. The modes of activity in learning and hobbies were more reliable than the modes of activity in social and working activities (Hautamäki, 1979a). The reliability of the language code was .87. This reliability coefficient was based on an inter-observer-consistency in the interview situation.

Hypothesis 1 was tested by path analysis. The direct effects of the variables were estimated as regression coefficients in standard form (Blalock, 1967, 675–676), and the indirect effects according to

$$(1) \quad \text{TIE} = r_{ij} - p_{ij} = \sum_k p_{ik} r_{kj}, \ k \neq j,$$

j = index of the explaining variable,
i = index of the explained variable,
k = index of all the variables that directly influence x_i,
TIE = Total Indirect Effect (Turner and Stevens, 1959).

The typical path model was as follows (Fig. 2).

Hypothesis 1 was confirmed. The path analysis suggests that the pupil's self-regulative capacities are related to the indirect or contextual effect of the socio-economic status (see Tab. 3). The direct effect of the socioeconomic status is small, but it effects markedly the modes of activity that parents are capable of providing for their children.

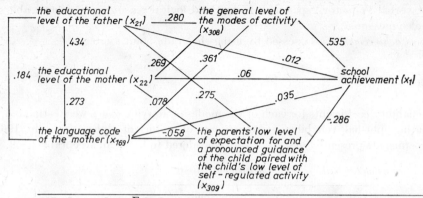

the educational level of the father (x_{21}) — .280 — the general level of the modes of activity (x_{308})

.434 .535

.269 .361 .012

.184 the educational level of the mother (x_{22}) .06 school achievement (x_1)

.273 .078 .275 .035

-.286

the language code of the mother (x_{169}) -.058 the parents' low level of expectation for and a pronounced guidance of the child paired with the child's low level of self-regulated activity (x_{309})

$$TIE = R_{IJ} - P_{IJ} = \sum_K P_{IK} R_{KJ} \; , \; K \neq J, \quad J = \text{index of the explaining variable, } I = \text{index of the explained variable, } K = \text{index of all the variables that directly influence } x_I,$$
$$TIE = \text{total indirect effect}$$

Fig. 2: A path model for relations between socioeconomic status, activity environment and school achievement.

Tab. 3: *Direct and indirect determination of the self-regulative capacities of the pupil by socioeconomic status indicators and modes of activity (indirect effects underlined)*

Explaining variables	Explained variables									
	School achievement		V		R		S		Expectancy of success	
	$P_{I,K}$	TIE	$P_{I,K}$	TIE	$P_{I,K}$	TIE	$P_{I,K}$	TIE	$P_{I,K}$	TIE
x_{308}	.535	–	.398	–	.149A	–	.300	–	.286	–
x_{309}	−.286	–	−.204	–	−.375	–	–	–	−.084A	–
x_{21}	.012A	.196	.096A	.120	.208A	.006	–	–	−.235A	.169
x_{22}	.060A	.225	−.045A	.223	−.001A	.169	−.087A	.147	.152A	.015
x_{169}	.035A	.275	.083A	.196	.268	.105	–	–	−.028A	.136
$100R^2$	42.20		25.60		31.60		7.20		11.7	

Explaining variables	Explained variables									
	Netto achievement motivation		Achievement motivation		Amount of motives of learning		Hierarchization of learning motivation		Time perspective of the past	
	$P_{I,K}$	TIE	$P_{I,K}$	TIE	$P_{I,K}$	TIE	$P_{I,K}$	TIE	$P_{I,K}$	TIE
x_{308}	–	–	.368	–	.388	–	.346	–	.275	–
x_{309}	−.206	–	.003A	–	−.191A	–	−.238	–	−.107A	–
x_{21}	–	–	−.296	.191	−.016A	.133	0.75A	.064	.122A	.099
x_{22}	.190A	−.037	.059A	.042	.027A	.146	−.021A	.134	−.016A	.183
x_{169}	–	–	−.035A	.141	−.011A	.191	−.090A	.173	.052A	.151
$100 R^2$	6.40		12.30		18.80		16.606		13.90	

Note: A indicates, that coefficients are not significant at the 0,05 level. $100R^2$ represents the percentage of total variance.

Thus the effect of socioeconomic status on the development of the pupil's self-regulative capacities is transmitted via the different modes of activity created and maintained in the parent-child interaction. Methodologically the socioeconomic status variables could be said to represent 'suppressor variables', whereas the modes of activity represent 'moderator variables' (Hautamäki, 1979b).

The trend in this study is the same as in the research of learning environments.

The model accounts for a large percentage of the variance in school achievement moderate percentages of the variances in reasoning and verbal abilities and small percentages of the variances in spatial ability and measures of motivation. The percentages of the variances of the personality traits accounted for by the model are somewhat lower than the results of the research into learning environments would suggest. But as Marjoribanks proposes, the correlations in some of the learning environment studies may be biased up wards (Marjoribanks, 1979, 45).

In order to study the social psychological mechanisms assumed to underly the mediating nature of the modes of activity, two fairly homogenous subgroups at the extremes of the three socioeconomic status indicators (the parents' educational level and mother's language code) were formed.

Group 1 consisted of 21 families. The parents represented occupationally unskilled manual workers and they usually had only elementary school education. Typically both parents worked regularly and had a regular income. The mother's language code was restricted. Most families in group 1 belonged to, what could be termed 'upper lower class'.

Group 2 consisted of 17 families. The parents represented typical middle class professions; they were semi-professional or professional white-collar workers. The upper (professional-managerial) class had, however, only a few representatives. The parents had usually a secondary school education (and in some cases also a high school education) and occupational training. The mother's language code approached the elaborated code.

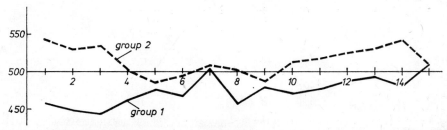

Fig. 3: Profiles of the self-regulative capacities of the pupil for each social group (in standard scores, $\bar{x} = 500$, $s = 100$).

1 school achievement	6 expectancy of success
2 verbal	7 expectancy of failure
3 reasoning	8 netto achievement motivation
4 visual	9 achievement motivation
5 level of thinking	10 time perspective of learning motivation

11 amount of motives of learning
12 hierarchization of learning motivation
13 time perspective of personality
14 time perspective of the past
15 time perspective of the future

The children of the two social groups differed significantly
– firstly, according to their logical reasoning abilities (at the 0.01 level)
– secondly, according to their school achievement and verbal ability which is an essential factor in enhancing school achievement (at the 0.05 level)

Thus the two social groups primarily differed according to the development of the cognitive self-regulative capacities of the pupil.

One social psychological mechanism assumed to explain the differences in the development of self-regulative capacities was the degree to which the parents' guidance, demands and model exceeded the level of the child's self-regulated activity. This was preliminarily termed family activities and -interaction in the zone of proximal development of the pupil. It was operationalized as the subtractive relation between the modes of activity and the level of the self-regulated activity of the child (both expressed in standard values).

The children of the two social groups differed significantly according to
– the degree to which the parents' guidance exceeds the level of the child's self-regulated activity (at the level of 0.01)
– the degree to which the parents' model exceeds the level of the child's self-regulated activity (at the level of 0.05).

The differences in the extent to which the parents' level of demands exceeds the level of the child's self-regulated activity, are, however, negligible (see Fig. 4).

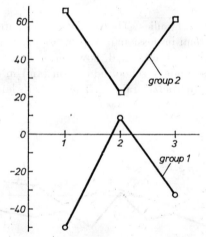

Fig. 4: Profiles of the extent to which the modes of activity of the parents exceed the level of self-regulated activity of the pupil for each social group.
1 (the guidance) – (the level of self-regulated activity)
2 (the demands) – (the level of self-regulated activity)
3 (the model)   – (the level of self-regulated activity)

The trend is the same, if an area-specific analysis of the relations between modes of activity and the level of the self-regulated activity of the child is made. The analysis is only preliminary, as the reliabilities of the area-specific modes of activity range from .50 to .82. Especially the degree to which parents' guidance and model exceed the level of the child's self-regulated activity in learning and hobbies draws a line of demarcation between parents of different levels of education and language codes (Hautamäki, 1979b). The results of the comparisons are presented in Fig. 5.

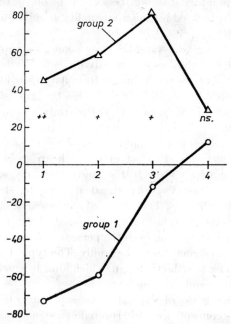

Fig. 5: Profiles of the extent to which the parents' area-specific modes of activity axceed the level of the self-regulated activity of the child for each social group (significant at the level of
$++ = p < 0.01, + p < 0.05$).
1 = (the guidance) − (the level of the self-regulated activity in learning)
2 = (the model)   − (the level of the self-regulated activity in learning)
3 = (the guidance) − (the level of the self-regulated activity in hobbies)
4 = (the model)   − (the level of the self-regulated activity in hobbies)

Discussion

The results cannot be generalized outside the town of Joensuu. Because of the size and nature of the sample (it does not, for instance, represent the whole spectrum of the social structure in Finland) the correlations might be biased downwards. The study confirms, however, some earlier investigations concerning the opportunities of various social classes to socialize their children according to the requirements of a formal learning situation. For instance, Hess and Shipman (1968) found a greater discrepancy between parental aspirations and expectations held for the child's educational career among lower social class mothers than among middle class mothers (see also Ogbu, 1974).

The more conflict-ridden attitude toward school and educational institutions among the lower social class parents is also manifested in this study: although the social class differences on the level of demands, i.e., on the level of parents' aspirations are slight, the lower class parents often seem to lack opportunities for guiding their child and for presenting a model in accordance with the level of aspirations. The differences are most conspicious in learning and hobbies, i.e., in the areas of activity approaching the demands of a formal learning situation at school and, at the same time, furthering the development of voluntary learning. This might be one of the social psychological mechanisms, through which educational inequality is reproduced from one generation to another.

In the study some of Vygotsky's and Leontiev's concepts were applied to the family socialization research, i.e., the less consciously guided activity and development of the pupil. However, Vygotsky and Leontiev formulate their ideas on a very general level. In one investigation it is difficult to bridge the gap between the theoretical concepts and their operationalizations. Thus the study was more a pilot study concerning the application of the cultural-historical tradition to persistent problems of family socialization research than an actual test of the ideas concerned.

The questions of method and object of research are essential in discussing the generalizibility of Vygotsky's ideas to the study of family socialization. With his experimental-genetic method Vygosky aimed at studying short-term, deliberately induced developmental changes. The object of the research of personality development in family interaction has, however, traditionally been conceptualized as long-term ontogenetic changes resulting from the persistent influence of fairly crystallized activity- and interaction structures in the family. The typical method has been interview research with an ex-post-facto design, which aims to grasp the more permanent structures of personality and environment.

This investigation made use of Vygotsky's concepts in its frame of reference. Consequently, Vygotsky's concepts were interpreted in a structural manner. In the study the adultchild interaction in the zone of proximal development of the pupil was not primarily defined as a changing characteristic of the interaction which takes different forms as the self-regulative capacities of the pupil emerge and the other-regulation gradually diminishes. Rather, it was defined as a fairly fixed relationship between the parents' modes of activity and the level of the self-regulated activity of the child. Thus the investigation focused on the conditions, not on the process of interiorization of the pupil's self-regulative capacities. The focus was on social psychological, not on psychological mechanisms underlying the process of interorization. However, in a correlational ex-post-facto research design a Vygotskian interpretation of the social psychological mechanisms of mediation might be tested only in longitudinal research.

Despite the problems concerning object and method in the application of Vygotsky's ideas to socialization research, some theoretical conclusions might be drawn. It seems that also in the research into family socialization it is important to catch the developmentally influential environment of the child. But according to Bronfenbrenner (1979b) "we still lack a scientific taxonomy for analyzing settings in terms of developmentally relevant parameters". In Vygotskian terms this implies an investigation of the parent-child interaction in the zone of proximal development of the child. Consequently, it seems important to relate the environmental influences to the child's developmental level as has been done in this study by relating the parents' modes of activity to the level of the child's self-regulated activity.

References

BERG, K.-H.: Über die Entwicklung der Lernmotivation bei Schülern der Unterstufe in einem Aufgabenlösen gestalteten Unterricht. Wissenschaftliche Zeitschrift der Humboldt-Universität zu Berlin, gesellschafts- und sprachwissenschaftliche Reihe XX, 441–461, 1971

BERNSTEIN, B.: Class, Codes and Control, Vol. 1, London: Routledge & Kegan Paul, 1971

BLALOCK, H. M.: Path Coefficients versus Regression Coeffizients. American Journal of Sociology 72, 675–676, 1967

BLOOM, B. S.: Stability and Change in Human Characteristics, New York: Wiley, 1964

BRONFENBRENNER, U.: The ecology of human development. Cambridge, Mass.: Harvard University Press, 1979 a

BRONFENBRENNER, U.: Contexts of child rearing. American Psychologist, Fall 1979 a (reprint)

CLAUSEN, J. A.: Family structure, socialization, and personality. In: L. W. Hoffmann and M. L. Hoffman (Eds.), Review of Child Development Research. Vol. 2. New York: Russell Sage Foundation, 1966

DAVE, R. H.: The identification and measurement of environmental process variables that are related to educationel achievment. Unpublished Ph. D. dissertation. University of Chicago, 1963

HAUTAMÄKI, A.: En psykologisk analys av relationen mellan individ och samhälle: Härledning och validering av en relationell modell för skolelevpersonlighetens verksamhetmiljö. Unpublished Lic. Ph. dissertation, University of Joensuu 1979 a (in Swedish)

HAUTAMÄKI, A.: The Mediation of Some Societal Influences to the Activity Environment of the Pupil. Paper presented at the XVII. International Seminar on "The Child and The Family in Changing Society", ISA, The Comittee on Family Research, Helsinki, Finnland, November 26–30, 1979 b

HAUTAMÄKI, J.: The Distribution of Piagetian Stages of Thinking in in a Sample of Finnish School Children. Paper to be presented at the 22 International Congress of Psychology, Leipzig, DDR, July 6–12. 1980

HECKHAUSEN, H.: Hoffnung und Furcht in der Leistungsmotivation. Meisenheim am Glan: Verlag Anton Hain, 1963

HESS, R. D.: Social Class and Ethnic Influences upon Socialization. In: P. H. Mussen (Ed.), Manual of Child Psychology, Vol. 2. New York: Wiley, 1970

HESS, R. D., and V. C. SHIMAN: Maternal attitudes toward the school a and the role of the pupil: some social class comparisons. In: A. H. Passow (Ed.), Developing programs for the educationally disadvantaged. New York: Teachers College, Columbia University; 1968

HUSEN, T.: Social Background and Educational Career. OECD: Centre for Educational Research and Innovation 1972

KOSSAKOWSKI, A., and K. U. ETTRICH: Psychologische Untersuchungen zur Entwicklung der eigenständigen Handlungsregulation. Berlin: VEB Deutscher Verlag der Wissenschaften, 1973

LEONTJEW, A. N.: Probleme der Entwicklung des Psychischen. Berlin: Volk und Wissen Volkseigener Verlag, 1971

MARJORIBANKS, K.: Environment, Social Class and Mental Abilities. Journal of Educational Psychology 63, 103–109, 1972

MARJORIBANKS, K.: Socioeconomic status and its relation to cognitive performance as mediated through the family environment. In: A. Oliverio (Ed.), Genetics, environment and intelligence. Elsevier: North-Holland Biomedical Press, 1977

MARJORIBANKS, K.: Families and their Learning Environments. London: Routledge & Kegan Paul, 1979

NUNNALLY, J. C.: Psychometric theory. New York: McGraw-Hill, 1967

OGBU, J. U.: The next generation. New York: Academic Press, 1974

ROSENFELD, G.: Theorie und Praxis der Lernmotivation. Berlin: VEB Deutscher Verlag der Wissenschaften, 1974

SHAYER, M., D. KUCHEMANN and H. WYLAM: The distribution of Piagetian stages of thinking in British middle and secondary school children. Br. J. educ. Psychol. 46, 164–173, 1976

TAKALA, M. et al.: Lasten sosiaaliset taidot ja niiden kehittymisedellytykset. Haastattelulomake liitteineen (The children's social competence and the conditions of its development. Interview schedule. In Finnish). University of Jyväskylä, 1977

TAKALA, M.: Perheen elämäntapa, vanhempien kasvatustietoisuus ja lasten sosiaalinen kehitys

(The way of life of the family, the child rearing consciousness of the parents, and the social development of the children. In Finnish). Reports from the Department of Psychology, University of Jyväskylä 219, 1979

TURNER, M. E., and C. D. STEVENS: The regression analysis of causal paths. Biometrics XV, 236–258, 1959

WEISS, J.: The identification and measurement of home environmental factors related to achievment motivation and self esteem. In: K. Marjoribanks (Ed.), Environments for Learning. Windsor: NFER Publishing Company Ltd., 1974

WERTSCH, J. V.: From social interaction to higher psychological processes. A clarification and application of Vygotsky's theory. Human Development 22, 1–22, 1979

WOLF, R.: The measurements of environments. In: A. Anastasi (Ed.), Testing problems in perspective. New Jersey: Educational Testing Service, 1964

WYGOTSKI, L. S.: Denken und Sprechen. Nördlingen: S. Fischer Verlag, 1974

VYGOTSKY, L. S.: Mind in Society. The development of higher psychological functions. Cambridge, Mass.: Harvard University Press, 1978

Self-Focused Attention and the Adherence to Personal Standards

Stefan E. Hormuth

"A theory of objective self-awareness" was introduced in 1972 by Shelley Duval and Robert A. Wicklund in their book of the same title. It is a psychological theory concerned with the effects of people's reflection on themselves. Several statements, based on a large amount of research generated by the theory, have since been added, refining the theory somewhat while leaving the basic formulation intact (Duval & Hensley, 1976, Frey, Wicklund & Scheier, 1978, Wicklund, 1975a, 1979, 1980).

The theory addresses the bidirectional nature of focus of attention. Consciousness can either be directed toward the environment, i. e. outward, or toward oneself, i.e. inward. In the early formulation of the theory, these states were called "objective self-awareness", where the self is the object of attention, and "subjective self-awareness", where the self is the subject of attention. Because these adjectives have created misunderstandings about the nature of the theory (Graumann, 1979), it is now usually referred to simply as "self-awareness theory". The term "self-focused attention" should be used to describe the fact that attention is paid to the self without necessarily implying the consequences proposed by the theory.

The core of the theory is concerned with assumptions about the conditions that bring about self-focused attention and the processes concomitant with self-focused attention. All stimuli that remind a person of himself or herself are assumed to turn attention from the environment and focus it on the self, even if only for a short period of time. Powerful stimuli of this kind are, for instance, one's photograph, one's own voice, one's mirror image, and the attention of others focused on oneself. Of those usually used in research, mirrors and audiences have been validated as a means of inducing self-focused attention (Carver & Scheier, 1978). When self-related stimuli are present, subjects are also more likely to make references to themselves (Davis & Brock, 1975). On the other hand, non-selfrelated, distracting stimuli can take attention away from the self.

What is meant by the statement that attention is focused on the self? The theory proposes that this attention is not focused indiscriminately on all aspects of the self, but only on those aspects that are specifically salient in the situation. Salience will most commonly be determined by the act performed while the person's attention is focused on the self. The person, however, is said to become not only aware of this behavior or cognition, but also of internal standards related to it. An internal standard can be a value, a norm, or an aspiration level one has in regard to a certain behavior or cognition. This is compared to the actual behavior. Thus, according to the theory, attention to a salient aspect of the actual state, the elicitation of a standard relevant to it, and the comparison of both are all postulated by the theory to be the consequence of self-focused attention.

It can probably be considered a truism that, even though not impossible, only rarely does our actual behavior exceed our ideal behavior. If it were the case, we would most likely set higher ideals. Therefore, in most cases when actual behavior and internal standard are compared, a negative discrepancy will result which, in the framework of the theory, is assumed to cause aversion and thus act as a motivational force. Two main strategies are used to discontinue this negative affect:

Avoidance. The confrontation with the self can be terminated either through the avoidance of self-focusing stimuli that turn attention from the self away to the environment. Avoidance is the simplest and probably preferred strategy in most cases (Wicklund, 1975b).

Discrepancy reduction. If it is not possible to avoid the state of self-focused attention, the individual will be motivated to reduce the discrepancy between internal standards and his or her actual state, feeling, or behavior. Since standards can usually be assumed to be more resistant to change than an actual behavior or cognition is, this discrepancy is more likely to be reduced by bringing the behavior in line with the related standard than through a change in the standard.

Summarized, self-awareness theory proposes that behavioral and cognitive changes following self-focused attention result from a comparison between a salient behavioral or cognitive aspect of the person and a relevant internal standard of correctness. Standards and their relation to actual behavior are therefore of primary importance to the theory.

Internal standards

A standard, according to Duval and Wicklund (1972, p. 3), "is defined as a mental representation of correct behavior, attitudes, and traits". The standard, as a representation of correctness, enables the individual to evaluate the behavior, attitude, trait or state that is salient while his attention is self-focused. Standards can relate to (a) what a correct person should be (in regard to traits and abilities), (b) what a correct person should attain (in regard to goals), (c) how a person should act under certain circumstances, and (d) the correctness of beliefs which can take the form of accepting other's beliefs as being correct.

Two further issues are important to understand the nature and function of standards. The first of these is whether the individual "attributes the standards of correctness to his own personal needs, desires, whims, and neuroses, or to the inherent qualities of the object constituting the standard of correctness" (Duval & Wicklund, 1972, p. 13). Duval and Wicklund presume that the person attributes correctness to the object that serves as standard, i.e. the individual does not consider correctness as the result of his own personal biases.

This presumption could easily lead one to the conclusion that, if the standard is the property of the object, everybody should hold the same standard in regard to the same object. This, of course, is not the case. Duval and Wicklund's own examples in their discussion of standards are those that allow large interindividual variations. They cite the example of a music teacher correcting her pupil's interpretation on the basis of correctness. The expected beauty, when the piece is interpreted according to the "correct" interpretation, is seen as a characteristic of the particular piece. Nevertheless, a large variety of possible interpretations can be given by various musicians.

The discussion of this point illustrates that even though correctness is by the individual considered to be a property of the evaluated object, standards can be inter-individually different. Some, of course, might be *generally* accepted and have frequently been referred to as *social* standards. Others might show inter-individual differences and are thus considered to be *personal* standards (see also Diener & Srull, 1979).

This leads to the second issue, namely the origin of standards. Duval and Wicklund state that standards can be the result of either one's own judgments or of social influences, i.e. they can be either internal standards, assumed to exist without social influence, or external standards, the acceptance of the attitudes, beliefs or traits of others as correct. What values does this distinction have for the theory and for the research in the context of the theory? As Carver (1974) notes, "the theory makes no distinction between personally held standards and those provided by an external agent but accepted by the subject as his own." The predictions of the theory do not concern themselves with the origin of the standard: the crucial element is that an "external" standard is accepted by the person as his or her own. From then on, the processes of comparison and discrepancy reduction can go on independent of the origin of the standard.

While the origin of standards is not an issue for the theory itself, their variation can be an important and interesting tool in the research demonstrating the theory's predictions. Using different operationalizations of standards, either by making use of a pre-existing standard or by creating a situational standard, self-awareness researchers have demonstrated a wide range of phenomena that are covered by the theory. Several demonstrations of the ways standards operate will now be presented.

Empirical evidence involving standards

Early studies within the domain of the theory of self-awareness usually made use of standards that could be assumed to be generally accepted. One of the first published studies (Wicklund & Duval, 1971, Exp. III) demonstrated performance facilitation as a result of self-focused attention. English speaking subjects were asked to copy as much German prose as possible during a given time period. During the first half of this time period, subjects in both experimental groups copied under identical conditions. During the second half, subjects in one experimental group faced a mirror as a means of inducing self-focused attention, whereas the other experimental group continued to work without being exposed to any new stimuli that would remind them of the self. It was hypothesized that self-aware subjects would perform at a higher rate, and this hypothesis was borne out by the data.

The standard that was acting in this situation was assumed to be the subject's own standard, and also was emphasized through the instructions. Wicklund and Duval assumed that a person's standard, namely the aspiration level in regard to the task to be performed, would exceed her performance. Therefore, self-aware subjects were expected to reduce the discrepancy between performance and aspiration level. At the same time, this standard that was assumed to be operating generally was additionally reinforced through the instructions that required the subject to copy as much prose as she could.

Different predictions can be made from the theory according to whether standards are assumed to operate generally, or are situationally created. This is illustrated in contrasting experiments by Scheier, Fenigstein, and Buss (1974) and Carver (1974). Both articles were concerned with self-awareness and physical aggression. Scheier et al. (1974) proposed that under certain circumstances self-awareness should decrease aggression. Specifically, they assumed that a generally accepted standard exists that prohibits aggression by men toward women. Their experiments demonstrated that this is indeed the case for subjects who experienced self-focused attention either as a result of being confronted with a mirror or being with an audience when there was frequent eye-contact. (The predicted effect was not obtained for an audience when eye-contact was infrequent).

Scheier et al. (1974) argued that the effect of decreased aggression might only be found under certain circumstances. In other situations, in which aggression might be justified, self-awareness would enhance aggression.

Such a finding was reported by Carver (1974). He created a situational standard by instructing subjects that aggression can facilitate learning in a presumed learning experiment. The procedure followed the Buss aggression paradigm (Buss, 1961), as did the earlier experiment by Scheier et al. (1974). Again, a mirror was used to induce self-awareness. The results clearly showed that self-aware subjects behaved according to the standard that was created in the experimental context. Subjects in the mirror group delivered significantly higher shock levels than those in the no-mirror group.

The results are thus in agreement with those hypothesized on the basis of self-awareness theory. But what exactly was the standard that was operating for subjects? A post-experimental questionnaire assessing the internal standard through the question, "How much do you personally oppose or agree with the use of punishment in learning situations?", showed no significant differences. Unfortunately, separate correlations for the two groups between attitude and aggressive behavior are not reported. More important, the overall correlation between attitude and behavior was very low ($r = -.04$). This suggests that this was not the operating standard, therefore it seems that a standard created by the experimenter was indeed operating. For lack of more evidence, however, it cannot be decided whether the standard was "aggression facilitates learning" or whether a standard similar to experimenter demand was operating, "follow the experimenter's instructions". Both should yield the same result.

In experiments such as this it is frequently difficult to precisely identify the standard upon which the self-aware individual is operating. Especially in cases in which the standard is not assumed to be pre-existing but created by the experimenter, the decision is difficult and the results are likely to be open to different *post hoc* identifications of the operating standard. Of course, even if the operating standard cannot be determined exactly, there still remains the obvious impact of the manipulation of self-focused attention on behavioral change.

Just as one can assume that "following the experimenter's instructions" can be an operating standard, group norms or the behavior or attitudes of others can also be accepted as standards of correctness. For instance, Wicklund and Duval (1971, Exp. I) demonstrated conformity with the attitudes of a positive reference group for self-aware subjects.

Several other experiments have shown that self-focused attention will bring individuals' behavior into line with generally accepted or situationally reinforced standards. Gibbons, Wicklund, Karylowski, Rosenfield, and Chase (1977), as well as Gotay (1978), researched the conditions under which people are more likely to behave altruistically and help as a function of self-focused attention. Along similar lines, Wegner and Schaefer (1978) showed that such helping behavior was stronger the more attention was focused on the helper and, therefore, the more self-focused attention was experienced by potential helpers. According to Duval, Duval, and Neely (1979), the effects of self-focused attention on helping behavior are mediated by an increase in felt responsibility for the needs of others. A feeling of responsibility for an outcome also increased equity behavior in research by Greenberg (1980) when attention was self-focused.

Honesty also is a moral standard brought out by self-focused attention. Diener and Wallbom (1976) had students take "intelligence"-tests, and those who were made self-aware cheated less on those tests when given the opportunity. Vallacher and Solodky (1979) pitted honesty and competence standards against each other through situational emphasis. For self-aware subjects, the emphasized standard prevailed. Two field studies by Beaman, Klentz, Diener, and Svanum (1979) took a developmental perspective. In their studies self-awareness did not influence behavior conforming to standards that were both situationally created as well as assumed to be generally prevalent in children of the age groups 1 to 4 and 5 to 8. However, the self-awareness effect was significant for children of the age groups 9 to 12 and 13 and above.

The studies described so far were concerned with standards that were assumed to to be similar for all subjects in the same study. They were assumed to be pre-existing and left intact in the laboratory, as in the studies by Scheier et al. (1974), or else they were created in the laboratory, as in Carver's (1974) experiment. Both of these approaches follow the strategy recommended by Duval and Wicklund (1972). To achieve clear predictions derived from the theory and successful applications, they recommend making use of standards that are either completely obvious and generally accepted or clearly and unambiguously created. The do not recommend the use of individual differences in standards, because subjects in an experiment may not be able to express all standards guiding their behavior (Duval & Wicklund, 1972, p. 220).

However, as was shown for the experiment by Carver (1974), an ambiguity in regard to the operating standards can still exist even if one follows Duval and Wicklund's recommendation. In Carver's (1974) experiment, it was said, the operating standard could either be "aggression is good for teaching" or "one should follow the experimenter's instructions." Also, if the operating standard works in the same direction for all subjects, e.g. strengthening of a response as in Wicklund and Duval (1971, Exp. III), the results are still open to alternative explanations. Drive theory (Spence, 1956) works as one such explanation, as will be elaborated below.

Some of these problems can be avoided if different standards on the same dimension are used. Carver (1975) used this approach when he pretested subjects several weeks prior to an experiment on their beliefs about the effectiveness of punishment and their willingness to use punishment in learning situations. Subjects expressing an attitude of opposition to the use of punishment (low punitive group) and subjects indicating belief in the use of punishment and a willingness to use it (high punitive group) participated in an experiment following the Buss aggression paradigm (Buss, 1961), the same paradigm as used by Carver (1974) and Scheier et al. (1974). For all subjects, the freedom to use their own attitudes as guidelines in determining shock level was made salient. It was predicted that subjects confronted with a mirror would administer shock level according to their previously measured attitudes, whereas smaller behavioral differences on the basis of the pretested attitudes were expected for subjects who were not confronted with a mirror. These predictions were clearly supported in two identical experiments. Additionally, it was shown that the correlations between attitude and behavior were high for the mirror subjects and low for the no-mirror subjects. The use of individual differences in standards here leaves less ambiguity as to which standard was operating in influencing behavior. The argument is additionally supported through the correlations.

There are other experiments with conceptually similar results that make use of standards that show individual differences. Gibbons (1978) used the different levels of people's guilt feelings in regard to sexuality in showing that self-aware subjects behave according to their individual standards when confronted with sexually explicit material. Rule, Nesdale, and Dyck (1975) and Scheier, Buss, and Buss (1978) studied the effects of self-focused attention on aggressive behavior on subjects with different levels of self-reported aggressiveness. The later study did not use a situational manipulation of self-focus, but rather a scale assessing self-consciousness as a personality disposition (Fenigstein, Scheier, & Buss, 1975). Pryor, Gibbons, Wicklund, Fazio, and Hood (1977) subjects' took a test of sociability. In two replications, there was a high correlation between self-reported sociability and behavioral measures of sociability, when the behavior was performed under conditions conductive to self-awarenesss. Correlations were low for subjects who were not self-aware.

The research on standards and self-focused attention can be summarized in the following way: From the very first published studies on self-awareness, researchers considered the issue of standards to be at the core of the theory. The standards used in research advanced from standards related to the performance on simple tasks to more abstract and even moral principles. They also changed from generally held or situationally created standards to personal standards with a range of individual differences, which make more unequivocal demonstrations of the predictions possible.

Generalized drive as an alternative explanation

While it can be accpeted as well-established that self-focused attention increases the consistency between standards and behavior, it can be asked whether the comparison between the standard and the actual behavior, as postulated by self-awareness theory, is the underlying mediating process. A frequently mentioned alternative explanation (e.g., by Liebling, Seiler, & Shaver, 1974) makes use of predications based on Hull's (1943) drive theory and its extension by Spence (1956). According to drive theory, the probability of the elicitation of a certain response is determined by its habit strength and the general drive level. Applied as an alternative explanation to some of the results of self-awareness research it would have to be assumed that self-focused attention creates arousal and thereby increases generalized drive level. It also must be assumed that a behavior that corresponds to a standard is high on a dominance hierarchy. Arousal, created through self-focus, would induce standard-conform behavior by increasing the probability of elicitation of such behavior. Liebling, Seiler, and Shaver (1974) pointed out that self-awareness researchers would have to contrast a *dominant* behavior with a *correct* behavior. If the drive theoretical alternative explanation were correct, the dominant behavior would prevail as a result of self-focused attention, whereas self-awareness theory would assume the correct behavior to be the result of self-focused attention. These different explanations of behavioral change through drive theory and self-awareness theory represent completely different concepts of human behavior.

Unfortunately, the experiment by Liebling, Seiler, and Shaver (1974) did not lend itself to a conclusive interpretation because of possible alternative explanations of its results within self-awareness theory (Wicklund, 1975b; Liebling, Seiler, & Shaver, 1975). But it did call attention to a number of problems in self-awareness research, and the original article and subsequent exchange proposed some requirements for the study of the notion of personal standards, as proposed by self-awareness theory, while controlling for an alternative explanation from drive theory.

Hormuth (1979) designed an experiment to contrast these two explanations directly while allowing a clear identification of the operating standard and the relevant response hierarchy. He selected a behavior that could be a representation of a personal standard and, at the same time, could be clearly established on a dominance hierarchy. The wish to be original was pretested as a personal standard, and the criterion behavior used was the originality of paired associations. For subjects high on the standard of originality, a correct response would be an original one, whereas a dominant response would be a nonoriginal, frequent one. Originality can be, already by definition, considered to be directly opposed to dominance.

Subjects who were not aware of the pretest's connection to the actual experiment were selected on the basis of high or low scores on the test for originality as a personal standard. They were randomly assigned to either one of three conditions: self-focus, arousal, or control, thus creating a 2×3 (standard by treatment) design. In the first part of the experiment, subjects were given a list of ten words paired with the most frequent associates of these words, selected on the basis of population norms on response frequency (Palermo & Jenkins, 1964). To further reinforce response dominance, subjects were asked to practice these dominant associations. The dominance of the responses was therefore high because it was clearly established based on the population norms as well as the practice trials.

At this point the experimental treatment was introduced. Subjects in the self-awareness condition were exposed to their mirror images, subjects in the arousal condition went through strenuous physical exercise, and subjects in the control condition spent a similar amount of time waiting. After this experimental treatment, subjects were asked to free-associate to the original stimulus words with *any* responses, whether they had been practiced before or not.

As the main dependent measure, responses were rated according to their originality based on the population norms. Additionally, subjects were asked for their own perception of the response originality and their awareness of their internal standard while responding. It was expected that subjects in the self-awareness condition would produce responses in correspondence to their strong or weak desire to be original, whereas subjects in the arousal condition were expected to produce generally less original, i.e. more dominant, responses, independent of their personal standards regarding originality.

Comparing the self-awareness condition to the control condition, the results clearly supported the hypothesis. When attention was self-focused, subjects' responses were clearly in accordance to their personal standards. Responses in the arousal condition were overall more dominant than in the self-awareness condition, as they were expected to be. But unexpectedly, they also corresponded to some degree with the subjects' internal standards. This had not been predicted by either one of the contrasting hypotheses.

The results could be interpreted on the presumption that the particular operationalization of arousal, namely strenuous physical exercise, raised not only drive level, as had been established in a previous study and through a manipulation check. It also provided self-related stimuli. This interpretation is supported through other findings within the self-awareness literature as well as additional data from the study. For instance, Fenigstein and Carver (1978) found that the perception of one's own heartbeat leads to increased self-attributions and increased activation of self-relevant information. Strenuous physical exercise makes one pay attention to symptoms like heartbeat. More specifically, Wegner and Guiliano (1980) have found that subjects who underwent strenuous physical exercise showed several of the signs as they are usually associated with self-awareness. In addition, questionnaire data of the present experiment showed that those behaviors that are indicative of self-awareness and are also compatible with arousal were found both in the self-awareness and in the arousal conditions, e.g. more accurate self-perception of actual responses and personal standards. These results, of course, also have implications for the manipulation of arousal, which seems to be difficult without also creating some self-focused attention.

Through this experiment, a drive interpretation of self-awareness effects could be ruled out. The data imply that through self-focused attention relevant standards will be activated and that a resulting discrepancy between behavior and standard will be reduced through behavioral change toward a correct response.

Implications for personality psychology and future research

An impressive body of evidence has accumulated over the almost ten years of research on self-awareness theory. The effects of self-focused attention as well as the limiting conditions have been demonstrated over a wide range. Some alternative explanations to the specific mediating effects as proposed by self-awareness theory could be ruled out (cf., Gibbons, Scheier, Carver, & Hormuth, 1979, Hormuth, 1979) and some new alternative models have been proposed (e.g., Carver, 1979, Hull & Levy, 1979).

Many of the standards studied are in themselves personality characteristics. Sex-guilt, aggressiveness, originality, honesty, morality, altruism, and others are all standards that are prevalent in individuals to different degrees. Although self-awareness theory does not concern itself with the content of such standards, but rather with the process acting on standards, the study of the distribution and individual prevalence of such standards will contribute to the understanding of individual differences.

A recurring problem of personality psychology is the frequently noted lack of consistency between self-reported personality characteristics and actual behavior (Mischel, 1968). Self-awareness theory offers a theoretical model that not only explains the reason for the lack of such consistency under many conditions, namely externally focused attention, it also offers ways of increasing such consistency. As such, it outlines some of the conditions under which people's behavior is more likely to be situationally influenced and the conditions under which people are more likely "to be themselves", to behave according to their own ideas, principles, values, or aspirations.

The disposition to focus attention on the self has also been studied as a personality characteristic. Fenigstein, Scheier, and Buss (1975) have developed a scale measuring attention to one's *private*, i.e. related to one's ideas and concepts, and *public*, i.e. related to the view of oneself as a social object, self. It has been demonstrated that the effects of private self-consciousness as a personality predisposition parallel the effects of situationally manipulated self-focused attention, as summarized by Buss (1980) and Scheier and Carver (1980a). Recent research has also pointed out that different manipulations of self-focus, namely private (e.g. a mirror) versus social (e.g. an audience) ones, parallel the different factors of private and public self-consciousness (Diener & Srull, 1979; Scheier & Carver, 1980b).

While the knowledge that self-focused attention affects standard-related behavior seems to be well established by now, a very important task remains for self-awareness researchers. The determinants of the salience of a given standard have to be identified: If more than one, or even contradicting standards are present in a situation, which is the one that will be operating? Wicklund (1980) and Wicklund and Frey (1980) have offered a theoretical resolution for such a conflict. Based on James (1910), *movement* ("features of self that are often in flux") and *uniqueness to self* are proposed to be the determining dimensions of salience. The suggestion that "the more unique or individual aspects of self come to light under self-awareness" (Wicklund, 1980, p. 205) both strengthens the link to personality psychology, as its very topic is the uniqueness of the person, and at the same time points out future areas of research.

Another issue may also be given more attention in the future. Research sofar has usually operated under the assumption that the self and its standards are stable components of the equation and that in most cases only the actual behavior will change to achieve consistency. Only for the rare case where behavior exceeds standards have basic assumptions about a change in the self been made, namely such that standards will be newly adjusted so as to prescribe a new goal. The conditions for change of standards and therefore in the self will be an important area of research for personality psychologists, both within and outside of the framework of self-awareness theory. One interesting idea can be taken from Hayden (1979), who did research suggesting that the self will remain stable unless a more meaningful notion of the self is found. Studying the issues of salience and change in the self by filling out, adding to, and possibly changing preliminary and still vague theoretical proposals will be some of the major issues for continuing research on the self.

References

BEAMAN, A. L., B. KLENTZ, E. DIENER and S. SVANUM: Self-awareness and transgression in children: Two field studies. Journal of Personality and Social Psychology 37, 1835–1846, 1979

BUSS, A. H.: The psychology of aggression. New York: Wiley, 1961

BUSS, A. H.: Self-consciousness and social anxiety. San Francisco: Freeman, 1980

CARVER, C. S.: Facilitation of physical aggression through objective self-awareness. Journal of Experimental Social Psychology 10, 365–370, 1974

CARVER, C. S.: Physical aggression as a function of objective self-awareness and attitudes toward punishment. Journal of Experimental Social Psychology 11, 510–519, 1975

CARVER, C. S.: A cybernetic model of self-attention processes. Journal of Personality and Social Psychology 37, 1251–1281, 1979

CARVER, C. S., and M. F. SCHEIER: Self-focusing effects of dispositional self-consciousness, mirror presence, and audience presence. Journal of Personality and Social Psychology 36, 324–332, 1978

DAVIS, D., and T. C. BROCK: Use of first person pronouns as a function of increased objective self-awareness and performance feedback. Journal of Experimental Social Psychology 11, 381–388, 1975

DIENER, E., and T. K. SRULL: Self-awareness, psychological perspective, and self-reinforcement in relation to personal and social standards. Journal of Personality and Social Psychology 37, 413–423, 1979

DIENER, E., and M. WALLBOM: Effects of self-awareness on antinormative behavior. Journal of Research in Personality 10, 107–111, 1976

DUVAL, S., and V. HENSLEY: Extensions of objective self-awareness theory. In: J. H. Harvey, W. J. Ickes and R. F. Kidd (Eds.), New directions in attribution research (Vol. 1). Hillsdale, N. J.: Erlbaum, 1976

DUVAL, S., and R. A. WICKLUND: A theory of objective self-awareness. New York: Academic Press, 1972

DUVAL, S., V. H. DUVAL and R. NEELY: Self-focus, felt responsibility, and helping behavior. Journal of Personality and Social Psychology 37, 1769–1778, 1979

FENIGSTEIN, A., and C. S. CARVER: Self-focusing effects of heartbeat feedback. Journal of Personality and Social Psychology 36, 1241–1250, 1978

FENIGSTEIN, A. M., F. SCHEIER and A. H. BUSS: Public and private self-consciousness: Assessment and theory. Journal of Consulting and Clinical Psychology 43, 522–527, 1975

FREY, D., R. A. WICKLUND and M. F. SCHEIER: Die Theorie der objektiven Selbstaufmerksamkeit. In: D. Frey (Ed.), Kognitive Theorien der Sozialpsychologie. Bern: Huber, 1978

GIBBONS, F. X.: Sexual standards and reactions to pornography: Enhancing behavioral consistency through self-focused attention. Journal of Personality and Social Psychology 36, 976–987, 1978

GIBBONS, F. X., M. F. SCHEIER, C. S. CARVER and S. E. HORMUTH: Self-focused attention and the placebo effect: Fooling some of the people some of the time. Journal of Experimental Social Psychology 15, 263–274, 1979

GIBBONS, F. X., R. A. WICKLUND, J. KARYLOWSKI, D. ROSENFIELD and T. C. CHASE: Altruistic response to self-focused attention. Unpublished manuscript. The University of Texas at Austin, 1977

GOTAY, C. C.: Helping behavior as a function of objective self-awareness and salience of the norm of helping. (Doctoral dissertation, University of Maryland, 1977). Dissertation Abstracts International 38, 6238-B, 1978

GRAUMANN, C. F.: Wahrnehmung und Beurteilung der anderen und der eigenen Person. In: Die Psychologie des 20. Jahrhunderts. Zürich: Kindler, 1979

GREENBERG, J.: Attentional focus and locus of performance causality as determinants of equity behavior. Journal of Personality and Social Psychology 38, 579–585, 1980

HAYDEN, B.: The self and possibilities for change. Journal of Personality 47, 546–556, 1979

HORMUTH, S. E.: Self-awareness, internal standards, and response dominance (Doctoral dissertation, University of Texas at Austin, 1979). Dissertation Abstracts International 40, 3, 1424-B, 1979

HULL, C. L.: Principles of behavior. New York: Appleton, 1943

HULL, G., and A. S. LEVY: The organizational functions of the self: An alternative to the Duval and Wicklund model of self-awareness. Journal of Personality and Social Psychology 37, 756–768, 1979

JAMES, W.: Psychology: The briefer course. New York: Harry Holt, 1910

LIEBLING, B. A., M. SEILER and P. SHAVER: Self-awareness and cigarettesmoking behavior. Journal of Experimental Social Psychology 10, 325–332, 1974

LIEBLING, B. A., M. SEILER and P. SHAVER: Unsolved problem for self-awareness theory: A reply to Wicklund. Journal of Experimental Social Psychology 11, 82–85, 1975

MISCHEL, W.: Personality and assessment. New York: Wiley, 1968

PALERMO, D. S., and J. J. JENKINS: Word association norms: Grade school through college. Minneapolis: University of Minnesota Press, 1964

PRYOR, J. B., F. X. GIBBONS, R. A. WICKLUND, R. H. FAZIO and R. HOOD: Self-focused attention and self-report validity. Journal of Personality 45, 513–527, 1977

RULE, B. G., A. R. NESDALE and R. DYCK: Objective self-awareness and differing standards of aggression. Representative Research in Social Psychology 6, 82–88, 1975

SCHEIER, M. F., and C. S. CARVER: Individual differences in self-concept and self-process. In: D. M. Wegner and R. R. Vallacher (Eds.), The self in social psychology. New York/Oxford: Oxford University Press, 1980 a

SCHEIER, M. F., and C. S. CARVER: Private and public self-attention, resistance to change, and dissonance reduction. Journal of Personality and Social Psychology 39, 390–405, 1980 b

SCHEIER, M. F., A. H. BUSS and D. M. BUSS: Self-consciousness, self-report of aggressiveness, and aggression. Journal of Research in Personality 12, 133–140, 1978

SCHEIER, M. F., A. FENIGSTEIN and A. H. BUSS: Self-awareness and physical aggression. Journal of Experimental Social Psychology 10, 264–273. 1974

SPENCE, K. W.: Behavior theory and conditioning. New Haven: Yale University Press, 1956

VALLACHER, R. R., and M. SOLODKY: Objective self-awareness, standards of evaluation, and moral behavior. Journal of Experimental Social Psychology 15, 254–262, 1979

WEGNER, D. M., and T. GIULIANO: Arousal induced attention to self. Journal of Personality and Social Psychology 38, 719–726, 1980

WEGNER, D. M., and D. SCHAEFER: The concentration of responsibility: An objective self-awareness analysis of group size effects in helping situations. Journal of Personality and Social Psychology 36, 147–155, 1978

WICKLUND, R. A.: Objective self-awareness. In: L. Berkowitz (Ed.), Advances in experimental social psychology. Vol. 8. New York: Academic Press, 1975 a

WICKLUND, R. A.: Discrepancy reduction or attempted distraction? A reply to Liebling, Seiler and Slaver. Journal of Experimental Social Psychology 11, 78–81, 1975 b

WICKLUND, R. A.: Objektive Selbstaufmerksamkeit: Ein theoretischer Ansatz der Persönlichkeits- und Sozialpsychologie. In: S. E. Hormuth (Ed.), Sozialpsychologie der Einstellungsänderung. Königstein, Ts.: Athenäum, Hain, Scriptor, Hanstein, 1979

WICKLUND, R. A.: Group contact and self-focused attention. In: P. B. Paulus (Ed.), Psychology of group influence. Hillsdale, N. J.: Erlbaum, 1980

WICKLUND, R. A., and S. DUVAL: Opinion change and performance facilitation as a result of objective self-awareness. Journal of Experimental Social Psychology 7, 319–342, 1971

WICKLUND, R. A., and D. FREY: Self-awareness theory: When the self makes a difference. In D. M. Wegner and R. R. Vallacher (Eds.), The self in social psychology. New York and Oxford: Oxford University Press, 1980

Analysis of Some Patterns of Normative Regulation of Child Behaviour

S. G. YAKOBSON

Normative regulation of behaviour and formation of various patterns of this regulation in children constitute part of a more general problem of moral development of the child.

Analysis of the present state of the problem of moral development shows that (1) moral development is regarded as mastering of the sphere of social norms and rules by the child and the appearance in the child of the ability to subordinate his behaviour to these norms and rules; (2) a feature common to many trends is that mastering of *different* norms and rules is regarded as the same process based on the same psychological "mechanism" (the difference between one theory and another being in the concept of this "mechanism").

In our investigation of the problem of mastering the norms of behaviour by children, we realize the methodological principle of Soviet psychology, according to which the development of the child is based on the assimilation by him of the generic experience of mankind. The psychological investigation as such in this case must be preceded by a specific logico-psychological analysis of the contents being assimilated.

Since the moral development of interest to us is based on assimilation of the ethical sphere, its psychological investigation must be preceded by analysis of this sphere. However, the question as to how such analysis should be patterned so far remains open.

Psychological investigations of moral development rather often include characteristic of the content of corresponding norms. In our opinion, however, this is not sufficient for advancing hypotheses concerning those psychological formations which ensure the observance of these norms by the individual.

In the logico-psychological analysis of the ethical sphere we draw upon the investigation of its origin, functions and structure, carried out by O. G. Drobnitsky (1974).

In our analysis we proceed from Drobnitsky's statement in which he points out a peculiar contradiction between what we shall conditionally term as individual strivings of people and possible negative consequences of the realization of part of these strivings for other people or for society as a whole.

This contradiction finds its particular expression in situations where the performing of an action corresponding to strictly individual interests incurs damage to the legitimate interests of a wider social environment. An important specific feature of these situations is that they give one objective freedom of choice between satisfaction of one's interests with prejudice to others and refusal of them in the name of the others. Such objective freedom of choice is one of the reasons for the actions of people under these conditions requiring a specific regulation on the part of society, which O. G. Drobnitsky has termed *normative* regulation.

The introduction of the concept of normative regulation makes it possible to differentiate *norms* as those cultural formations, in which the content of prescribed/prohibited behaviour is fixed with a various degree of completeness and generality, and the *process of regulation* of behaviour of people on the basis of the norms.

We consider the concept of normative regulation to be extremely fruitful for psychological investigation of the moral development of a child and of the formation of his personality. This concept allows one to put forward the statement that moral development includes not only assimilation of the content of ethical norms, but also formation of specific patterns of regulation of one's behaviour.

Of principle importance for the investigation of this regulation, of its nature and psychological mechanisms, is also the distinctions made by O. G. Drobnitsky between several patterns of the normative regulation. The formation of some of these patterns, in his opinion, presupposes the formation of the properties of a social individual, while the formation of certain other of these patterns presupposes the formation of a moral personality.

This allows one to make the suggestion that different patterns of the normative regulation are provided by different psychological "mechanisms" and require different psychological formations for their realization. One of the tasks of psychological investigation is thus to reveal the specific character of each pattern and of the respective psychological "mechanisms".

All the patterns of normative regulation are directed to the provision of norm-conforming behaviour in situations with a contradiction between the interests of an individual and those of his social environment. (At the moment we are not considering other functions of the norms, such as those emphasized by K. Otto, 1980 in his report.) Therefore the first step resides in the analysis of those contradictions in which there arises a necessity in normative regulation. These contradictions may differ as to the content of the contradicting interests, as to whether we have to deal with the interests of individual people, of social groups, of the entire strata of society, etc., and in a number of other parameters.

We shall confine ourselves to the analysis of contradictions between particular interests of individual people, since small children encounter first of all this very kind of contradiction.

An essential feature of these contradictions is the form in which the interests of other people, contradictory to the interests of the child, become manifest to him. In one case these other people (adults or children) have an opportunity to maintain and defend their interests, i.e. the latter exist in the form of real behaviour of other people.

In another case, and this difference appears to be extremely essential particularly with regard to psychology, the interests of other people are represented only in the consciousness of those individuals whose own interests they contradict. Indeed, such situations may be encountered, when people have no opportunity of effectively maintaining their interests. From this it follows that the latter can be taken into account only on condition that they are somehow represented in the consciousness of those who must take them into account. In the situations under consideration these interests must be represented in the consciousness of those very individuals whose own interests they contradict.

In the first case the contradiction of the interests of individual people may lead to an external conflict between them, in the course of which they may mutually influence the behaviour of one another. In the second case this contradiction acquires specific internal forms in the consciousness of one of the parties. In accordance with this difference (an external conflict or an internal contradiction) psychological mechanisms of the normative regulation of behaviour in these two situations must be different.

In the situation of a direct collision of the interests of several people the conflict between them may be settled, in the first place, by their exerting a direct pressure on one another, i.e. by a "force" action. In the second place, this conflict may be settled by resorting to certain general rules which regulate the behaviour of people in a conflict situation, since observance of an established rule becomes a norm obligatory for all participants of a conflict and thus presupposes normative regulation of the behaviour of those who are forced to renounce the satisfaction of their interests.

These two methods of settling conflicts differ in the forms of the action produced by the partners on each another (personal pressure or reserting to the rule which is a common denominator and in the form of control over the observance of the agreement attained.

In case of a "force" settling of a conflict the party that has gained the upper hand at the same time effects control over the observance of its superiority. In the case of normative methods being resorted to direct pressure is absent, but at least potential control is required over the observance of the rule by those people whose interests it contradicts at that time. This function, naturally, lies with those participants who are interested in the observance of this rule.

What conditions contribute to a "force" or normative settling of a conflict?

D. Thibaut and H. Kelly (1959) consider that norms which make it possible to overcome a conflict are established by people, if, while some of their interests disagree, these people are bound by mutual interests along another line. Struggle for the realization of personal partial interests constitutes a threat to the attainment of the common goal. The initial structure for the origination of such norms, which these authors assign to the category of group norms, in their opinion, is a dyad.

However, experiments with dyads has not confirmed this statement, since they showed that in the majority of cases partners do not establish norms which regulate their conflict relations (2).

We believe that the necessity in normative regulation of the conflicts under discussion arises not in a dyad, but in the case of three or more people being involved in a conflict.

In favour of this statement the following arguments can be advanced. Overcoming of a conflict in a dyad requires that one of the partners should renounce part of his interests in favour of the the the other partner. In this situation preference to "force" or normative methods is not dictated by the necessity, but is determined exclusively by the good will of the participants.

But if three and more people participate in a conflict and satisfaction of the interests of any of them requires that two or more partners should renounce their interests, the effectiveness of "force" methods principally diminishes, since each person must exert direct pressure not on one person, but on two and more persons, whose resistance becomes still more intensified due to possible mutual support. Objective reduction in the effectiveness of "force" methods contributes to the use of the normative ones.

Further, control over possible deviation from the adopted norm is effected in a dyad by one partner with regard to the other. This control can be successful in case of a relative psychological superiority of this partner. But such superiority offers him ample opportunity for using just "force" methods.

In a group of three or more persons the observance of the norm by each partner is controlled by the majority dominating over him, and this ensures effective use of normative methods.

Experimental verification of this statement resided in comparing the methods of settling conflicts in groups of 2 or 3 and 4 persons. Within the framework of the common goal adopted by all children, which was to make toys for their juniors, we created contradictions among the participants concerning the determination of that one particular toy which they could make during the day and concerning the assignment of their duties. In the first case collision of interests was created due to the possibility of choosing several toys, appealing to different children in different ways. In the second case the collision of interests was due to the radical difference in the attractiveness of the duties assigned.

The experiments were carried out with 300 groups of children from 7 to 10 years of age.

The conflicts arising under these conditions are settled both by way of direct *pressure* which takes the form of various verbal actions of the children with regard of one to another, and on the basis of certain *norms* obligatory for all. Such norms are: (1) the principle of subordination of the minority to the majority, which is used in conflicts arising in the choice of the common cause; (2) drawing lots and establishing priority of performing the disputable duty in conflicts stemming from the assignment of duties.

The use of norms for settling the contradictions between personal wishes of individual children to do this or that job and the common objectives of the group to create in the course of the joint activity a socially required product shows that in these situations we actually deal with normative regulation of the child behaviour.

However, recourse to norms and, hence, normative regulation of the behaviour was observed only in groups consisting of three and more persons and on condition that one of conflicting parties had numerical superiority over the other. We should like to emphasise this circumstance, since in a group of, say, three persons there may be a conflict between two children while the attitude of the third child is neutral.

In the case of numerical superiority at one of the poles of the conflict, recognition of the norm by this majority creates a human community, even if a minimal one, which can already demand the observance of this norm, countervail the attempts of departing from it, and realize it in general. Rather significant is the fact that out of the 60 dyads investigated in these experiments normative settling of the conflict was observed only in 1 group, wheras in the remaining 59 agreement was reached on the basis of "force" methods. At the same time, in those groups where the conflict had taken place between one and two or three children, it was settled, as a rule, on the normative basis.

In these experiments one more condition has been revealed, which influences the readiness of children in these situations to obey the norm and which, by virtue of that, determines the scope of the applicability of the norm. This condition is the degree of renunciation of personal claims, required for the observance of a given norm. Thus establishing a priority in the performance of a duty attractive to several persons, all of them get an opportunity to at least *partially* realize their wish to perform it. On the other hand, obeying the decision of the majority to do the job which is inattractive to the minority, the children comprised in this minority must completely renounce their initial claims.

This condition is of importance with regard to the age level. Thus priority is willingly and extensively used by 7–8 year olds, whereas drawing lots and subordination to the majority, which requires that some children should *completely* renounce their initial wishes, present certain difficulties even for older children.

How is the observance of such norms ensured and what psychological formations are at the basis of this kind of normative regulation?

When answering this question, it is necessary to bear in mind the following circumstances. First, such norms in general may function only in the context of group interaction, outside of which their observance is actually impossible (one cannot observe priority when being all alone). This guarantees constant external control over the observance of the norm. Second, within the described kind of normative regulation of behaviour norms came out as *means*, and their observance as *methods* for overcoming and preventing conflicts, i.e. they perform a purely instrumental function in the organization and subsequent carrying out of joint activity.

All this has allowed us to suppose that the functionally adequate normative regulation of the type described is possible without internal adoption of the norm by each participant and without readiness to follow it in the absence of external necessity.

Experiments with groups composed of children none of whom regarded the norm of priority to be obligatory for himself, have confirmed this hypothesis.

The conflict provoked by the duty most attractive to all was always settled by establishing priority in performing it. In repeated experiments children resorted to priority at once and without any conflict, as to the self-evident method for distributing interesting and uninteresting jobs. However in control experiments with shams who laid no claims to the given duty these children realized their initial wish to perform it personally. In other words, observing the norm of priority to avoid conflict, they departed from the norm at the very first opportunity. Thus, if the logic of the norms as such guarantees external control over their observation, adequate functioning of the latter is possible without internal adoption of these norms by the individual.

What psychological formations lie at the basis of observance of such norms? The aim of their establishment is carrying out joint activities, and, more broadly, *co-operation*. Therefore we suppose that among such formations is a *general positive attitude* of children towards *co-operation* with other children. Another such formation should be a certain degree of voluntariness of behaviour, since subordination to the norm requires that one renounces his initial intentions and wishes. Further, since this range of norms regulates the interrelations of children in the co-operative activities *independently* organized and carried out by them, it presupposes a certain level of the development of the activity as such. In so far as co-operative activities of children reach this level at the lower school age, extensive use of such norms in "children's society" begins after the age of 7 to 8.

The source of translation of such norms to each individual child and of his initiation into this kind of normative regulation is "children's society". An optimum method of controlling these processes by adults resides in creating special conditions for cooperative activities of children.

The next pattern of normative regulation which we shall discuss is moral regulation of behaviour. An important feature of this regulation is that the interests of other people don't appear before an individual in the form of defence of their own interests by other people, i.e. not as specific behaviour of the latter. They are specified in the form of positive ethical appraisal of actions directed towards the good of other people. Ethical appraisal of such actions is of particular importance, since in some cases people cannot maintain their interests at a given moment by themselves, and thus they are found to be in directly dependent on the actions of their partners and on the extent to which these actions are regulated by moral norms.

Actions which, while answering the interests of one person, infringe the interests of other people and are detrimental to the society, its future, etc., are disapproved on moral grounds. However, refusal to undertake such actions, motivated by their renunciation in the name of other people, is approved.

Thus, the contradiction between the interests of several people acquires the form of contradiction between one's self-interest in a certain action and the ethical value of this action.

From this it follows that if the actions of an individual may be detrimental to other people, such actions must be qualified not only with regard to the self-interests of this individual, but also from the standpoint of their ethical value, which, in this case, represents the interests of other people. The ethical value of such actions will contradict one's personal interest in them.

Further, it is known that a moral act is characterized by the so-called freedom of choice. In view of the above-stated feature of the moral act, this means that a person, when performing this act may choose one of the alternative actions which differ (1) in the extent of his self-interest in them; (2) in their ethical value which contradicts this self-interest.

This may be represented in the following manner:

| ETHICAL VALUE OF THE ACTION | + | − |
| PERSONAL INTEREST IN UNDERTAKING THE ACTION | − | + |

Thus, the moral act is the one which requires that a person should renounce some of his interests. What may induce a person to choose a moral act only?

Since such preference is possible on the grounds of ethical merits of this act, a prerequisite for an ethically correct choice is, evidently, ethical appraisal of both actions. Such an appraisal, in contradistinction to personal interests with which everyone is endowed directly, requires a comparison with some criteria. Moreover, an ethical appraisal must be made for two acts, opposite in their ethical value. This particular circumstance has induced us to suggest that criteria of ethical appraisal exist in a quite specific form, namely, in the form of polar but mutually related standards. The integrity and polarity of the ethical appraisal standards correspond to the polarity of the two main ethical categories of good and evil, the standards being a particular ambodiment thereof. This integrity and polarity of the ethical appraisal standards we regard as being the main specific feature of a moral act, which constitutes its principle distinction from any object-action: when specifying a model of an objectaction, we never specify an obligatory, matching anti-model. There is no model of how one should *not* drive in nails.

The next question is *who* compares alternative actions with standards and makes an ethical appraisal of these actions.

It is generally accepted that a truly moral act is one which is made without any external control or pressure. This means that such comparison must be made by the person himself. But in such a case the polar ethical appraisals of both acts given by the person himself must become the factor which will motivate him to make the ethically correct choice.

It is well known, however, that such appraisals, as a rule, do not noticeably effect behaviour.

We suggested that in order to acquire the real forcing influence, such appraisal must stir some significant personal patterns which may countervail one's self-interests.

We suppose that such a significant personal pattern is a positive image of oneself.

The idea of an image of oneself and one's self-respect closely related to it playing an important role in the regulation of moral behaviour is not new. However, this idea has not been the subject of experimental investigation in child psychology.

How can the image of oneself influence the choice of an ethically valuable act? Evidently, this may be the case if this image is included into comparison with the ethical standards. This becomes possible if not only acts but also the person who acts are compared with the standards. Then the preference of an ethically evil deed will result in the negative appraisal of oneself. This already undermines the positive image which one has of oneself. Self-interest in an ethically negative action now starts contradicting not only its objective ethical value, but also the preservation of one's positive image of oneself. As a result, the choice between a wrong though attractive action and an ethically valuable action turns into the choice between the attractive action and the preservation of one's positive image of oneself. One's urge to preserve one's positive image may countervail one's direct interests and ensure the ethically correct choice. It should also be emphasized that its resemblance to the negative standard may affect the image the child has of himself only if this negative standard is personally unpleasant and unacceptable to him and not because it is merely considered to be bad. Therefore the introduction of the image of one's self and its comparison with the ethical standards brings forth one more new and essential moment: personal, emotional attitude towards the standards as such, a desire to correspond to definite standards and, on the contrary, to differ from certain other standards.

As a result we may say that free ethically correct choice presupposes: (1) the presence of two polar standards which embody the categories of "good" and "evil" in some concrete form; (2) comparison of not only separate actions of a person, but of one's whole personality with these standards; (3) comparison of oneself and of one's acts with the standards must necessarily be performed by the person himself; (4) one should develop one's personal adequate attitude towards both standards.

The last statement gives rise to a new and relatively autonomous question about the source of such adequate, i.e. polar attitude to both standards and about the form in which they should be prescribed to children.

The main requirement we can formulate with regard to the standards is that they must be prescribed to children in a form which can be correlated with the image the child can have of himself. Such a form may be descriptions of people or those of characters of literary compositions.

When do such descriptions arouse in children polar emotional attitude and desire to resemble some particular characters and, on the contrary, not to resemble other characters?

This is possible, in the first place, of one of these characters is endowed with such properties which appeal to the child, while the properties of another character cause his disapproval. In the second place, it is known that a powerful source for the origin of an actually polar attitude is the emotional response of children to the situations with, and actions of, literary heroes. If between a positive hero and the negative one there develop sufficiently dynamic antagonistic relations, this practically always ensures a polar attitude of children towards them.

Proceeding from these considerations, we decided to verify the effectiveness of using, in the function of standards for the ethical appraisal: (1) the heroes of popular fairy-tales (buratino and Carabas), (2) descriptions good/bad boy and girl (these children-characters were represented in pictures, were given fictitious names and polar characteristics), (3) in a new series of experiments the same children-characters became heroes of the experimental stories composed by us, in which the good child was fighting for a just cause against the bad child and after several adventures came out victor. (In this way these children were involved in antagonistic relations similar to those of polar heroes of fairy-tales), (4) appraisals "good" and "bad".

An experimental study was done with 62 children aged from 6 to 7. The study was conducted as a transformational experiment. Subjected to the experiment were children with stable patterns of ethically wrong behaviour; by applying appropriate influence, we tried to attain transformation of this behaviour under controlled experimental conditions.

We studied such misbehaviour as manifestations of greediness and unfairness. The initial situation was that a certain number of rather attractive toys had to be distributed by a child among two other children and himself. In the case of boys we gave various machines, in the case of girls, doll's garments.

The experiments were conducted as games, in the course of which we pretended to check how well the children knew the names of various objects to be distributed, the purpose these objects served, etc. None of these tasks required a greater number of toys than the other and didn't provoke, therefore, unfair distribution. Each child had to divide and then send on special machines lots of toys in succession, for example, 6 planes, 5 racing cars, 7 ships, etc. From 24 to 30 objects were sent in such a way during one experiment. All the participants were isolated by screens, so that two children who were to receive the toys could not see how many toys the child who distributed had left for himself. The experimenter remained always benevolent and discussed only the abovementioned knowledge and skills. This situation sharply differentiates the children and reveals those who constantly send 1 toy and rarely 2 toys from each group of the same toys leaving all the rest (for instance 4 toys out of 6) for themselves. These children became the main subjects of our transformational experiment.

The scheme of the experiment was as follows.

Diagnostic test (two distributions of different toys).

Influence aimed at transformation of ethically wrong behaviour.

Diagnostic test with new toys.

Another influence.

Diagnostic test with new toys, etc.

As regards influences, we first checked those, which, in our belief, were less effective. This allowed us, on the one hand, to learn the comparative effectiveness of different influences on the same children and, on the other hand, to get additional proof of the stability of misbehaviour of these children and, hence, of the non-fortuitous character of the occurring transformation.

The experimentally tested factors were as follows.

1. Comparison of the child, taken as a personality, with a negative standard, this comparison being made first by other children and then by the child himself. 2. Comparison (made by the child himself) of his negative action with the negative standard and then, in the next experiment, his negative self-appraisal. 3. Comparison of the child's own self with standards which differ in the extent of the possible attitude of the child towards them.

The standards employed were appraisals "good" and "bad", portrayals of well-behaving and mis-behaving children, polar characters of fairy tales.

Our experiments have shown that ethically wrong behaviour does not change, if: (1) the child's resemblance to the negative standard is asserted by other people; (2) the child qualifies only his given particular action, and not his own self; (3) the child has not assumed personal polar attitude towards the standards as such.

However, the same children instantly and steadily changed their behaviour for the ethically correct one, if: (1) the resemblance of the child to the negative standard was established by the child himself; (2) the child qualified not only his particular action, but his own self; (3) the child had assumed personal polar attitude to both standards.

We have also revealed one essential additional condition for the correction of the studied misbehaviour. It is desirable that after the negative self-appraisal made by the child, other people should express their confidence in that, nevertheless, this child, on the whole, conforms to the positive standard. Thus, disapproval comes from the child himself, while belief in a better principle in him comes from other people.

It should also be especially emphasized that a correlation of one's own self with the negative standard is established by children not of their own accord, but in the context of confidential communication with an adult, who, by putting various questions to the child and asking him in a benevolent manner, gets the required acquisition on the part of the child.

Now we shall try to analyse the psychological significance of inclusion of the child as a personality into the process of comparison with the ethical standards.

First, due to such inclusion, the ethical standard which objectively exists outside becomes, as it were, internally subjectively embodied in the integral of the child (in the image of his own self), thus becoming internally mediated. The role of this mediating link is played by the image of one's own self as of a specific integrity corresponding to the positive ethical standard. Secondly, due to the appearance of this image which is a subjective embodiment of the objective ethical standard, the discrepancy between the ethical value of one's action and one's self-interest becomes transformed into a discrepancy between the ethical appraisal of one's own self viewed as a whole and one's self-interest. This means that the external contradiction between the ethical value and individual interest becomes transformed into the internal contradiction between the image of one's own self viewed as a whole and one's own, though particular (and in this sense partial) interest.

The inconsistency of this image of one's self, manifested (in the situation of making an ethical choice) in the contradiction between the positive image of one's self as a definite integrity and the negative one of oneself while acting ethically wrong lies at the basis of ethical regulation of behaviour. The psychological mechanism of such regulation consists in the elimination of this contradiction by the individual's overcoming the negative patterns of his own behaviour.

The individually psychological patterns lying at the basis of the moral regulation are: the image of one's self as being identical with the positive ethical standard; the action of correlating certain deeds a person undertakes with the negative ethical standard; the ability to realize the contradiction between the image of himself as a whole and his particular action.

The revealing of the function of the image of one's self in the regulation of moral behaviour of children offers promise for uniting moral development and the development of personality in one theoretical model. Being an essential component of personality and of the structure of moral action the image of one's self is the key link which may make it possible to connect in one model these two most important subjects of psychological research.

It should also be noted that specific relations of children with adults are the source of the development of moral regulation. It is the adult who shapes in the child an image of himself as corresponding to the positive standard and at the same time patterns the action of correlating certain deeds with the negative standard.

References

Drobnitsky, O. G.: Concept of moral. Moscow 1974 (Russian)
Murdoch, P., and D. Rosen: Norm formation in an interdependent dyad. Sociometry 3, 7, 264–275, 1970
Otto, K.: Soziale Normen und deren innere Repräsentation als Faktoren der Verhaltensregulation. Abstracts des XXII ICP Leipzig 1980
Thibaut, J. M., and H. H. Kelley: The Social Psychology of Groups. N. J. 1959

Situational Effects in Empirical Personality Research

David Magnusson

For decades, researchers from very different perspectives – behaviorists, personologists, trait psychologists, field theorists etc. – have stressed the evident fact that behavior cannot be understood in isolation from the situational conditions under which it occurs, and have advocated that situations and situational conditions must be considered in any effective model of personality. However, such formulations have only recently, and slowly at that, led to the two obvious consequences in empirical research: (a) systematic analyses of the lawfulness of person by situation interactions, and (b) systematic analysis of the situations, in which behavior is observed (Magnusson, 1976).

When, in the middle of the sixties, I explored the literature to see which situational factors to vary systematically in studies of person situation interactions, I found almost nothing. In connection with the renewed interest in the old topic of personality consistency and the research on person situation interactions during the seventies, the need for systematic analyses of situations has been further emphasized.

Awareness of the importance of the role of situations in models of behavior in general and in personality research naturally suggests a need for systematic knowledge about situations and how they influence actual behavior. For understanding *the individual in the situation* we need a) knowledge about the effective person variables and their interrelations, a recurrent theme during the history of personality and differential psychology, b) knowledge about the effective situation variables and their interrelations, and c) knowledge about the interplay between these two networks of factors (Magnusson, 1980a). In the past most resources in the field of personality have been devoted to theorizing and research on the person side of the personsituation system. There is an obvious need at the present time for a psychology of situations.

My purpose here is to draw attention to the potential of systematic studies on situations, and to the importance of incorporating knowledge about situations and situational conditions in research in the field of personality. I will do that by discussing two empirical studies performed in my research group in Stockholm in cooperation with Håkan Stattin and Bertil Törestad. In discussing these studies I want to emphasize that my main purpose is not to present conclusive or decisive results, but rather to illustrate the systematic and lawful nature of the relation between person factors and situational characteristics and to underline the consequences of such results for further theorizing and empirical research.

Sex differences in reactions to anxiety provoking situations

The first study is concerned with sex differences in reactions to anxiety provoking situations.

The existence of important sex by situation interactions has often been demonstrated in empirical research. From our own department I can refer to studies by Frankenhaeuser (1980), Bergman & Magnusson (1978) and Lundberg (1980), who have studied sex differences in physiological reactions in psychosocial, stressful situations.

The present study was planned to investigate such interactions by a systematic variation of the character of the situations (Magnusson & Törestad, 1980), using data for state anxiety reactions, obtained in different types of anxiety provoking situations.

Situations. The situations were chosen to represent four different categories of anxiety provoking situations found to form distinct categories in earlier empirical research. In addition, neutral situations were included. Thus, five a priori groupings of situations were used. Each category was represented by four situations.

1. *Innocuous, nonprovocative situations*

These situations were included in order to determine whether there is a tendency for one sex to score higher than the other on anxiety in the absence of situational threat.

2. *Achievement-demanding situations*

Situations one is supposed to adapt to by accomplishing a goal or where one is to be evaluated along with peers and thus runs the risk of failure.

3. *Threat of punishment situations*

Situations involving a threat of punishment from someone higher in status or power, as a consequence of breaking norms.

4. *Physical danger situations*

Two situations ("Injection by doctor", and "In the dentist's waiting room") were supposed to induce anticipation of pain, and two situations ("Approached by a gang" and "Car accident") were supposed to involve anticipation of physical injury and destruction (violence).

5. *Inanimate situations*

Situations involving an undefined, possible danger (darkness, loneliness, fantasies, etc.).

Each of the twenty situations was presented to the subjects in the form of a drawing. The situations are shortly described in Tab. 1.

Subjects. The subjects were 15 year old boys and girls randomly drawn from a school within the undifferentiated, compulsory school system.

Data. Reactions to the situations were measured by IRS 2 – an inventory for state anxiety containing ten subscales covering feelings of psychic and somatic arousal ("I feel nervous" – "My stomach gets upset").

Tab. 1: *Brief descriptions of situations within the five types of situations*

Inanimate threat	*Threat of punishment*
Thunder in woods	Taken by police
Fire at home	Cheat at test
Something at the window	Late home
Lost in woods	Store detective

Physical threat	*Achievement-demanding*
Injection by doctor	Speech before class
Approached by a gang	Report card
In dentist's waiting-room	Math test
Car accident	School kitchen

Innocuous
On the phone
Read a book
Bike ride
Listening to music

Results and conclusions. Means and standard deviations of reported anxiety reactions for each type of situation are reported in Tab. 2. Fig. 1 gives a summary picture of the results. It is based on mean reactions of boys and girls for types of situations, and the situation categories are ordered on the basis of their anxiety provocation, expressed in total means of reactions.

Tab. 2: *Means and standard deviations for each type of situations. Sex difference scores*

| | Boys | | Girls | | |
	M	s	M	s	Diff.
Inanimate	107.2	20.3	140.7	23.5	33.5*
Threat of punishment	112.4	26.2	130.3	32.7	17.9
Physical threat	104.6	29.5	116.5	27.1	11.9
Achievement-demanding	97.3	32.3	95.5	28.8	−1.8
Innocuous	43.7	6.1	45.3	8.1	1.6

* $p < .02$

Fig. 1 shows the two main results of interest here. *First*, there is a significant sex by situation type interaction in anxiety reactions ($p < .01$). *Second*, the interaction takes the general form of an increasing sex difference with increasing level of mean anxiety reactions. The systematic relationship between anxiety provocation in situations and the size of sex difference in anxiety reaction is clearly visible for single situations. The correlation between the rank order of single situations on the basis of mean anxiety reactions, on the one hand, and the rank order of sex differences in anxiety reaction for single situations, on the other is 0.76.

Fig. 1 also reveals another interesting feature. For boys, mean reactions vary insignificantly and unsystematically across anxiety provoking situation types. For girls, in contrast, a one way analysis of variance for the differences between mean reaction in types of situations gave a significant result ($p < .02$).

The exact form of the curve in Fig. 1, representing intensity of anxiety reactions as a function of type of situation, should not be exaggerated. All inanimate situations do not provoke higher anxiety reactions than all other situations and so on. This means that the form of the curve will be dependent, to some extent, upon the sampling of situations to represent each category. However, the main result of a sex by situation interaction and that it takes the form summarized above has been demonstrated in two other studies in the project, one based on a reanalysis of data from an earlier study and one study that is a replication of the study presented here.

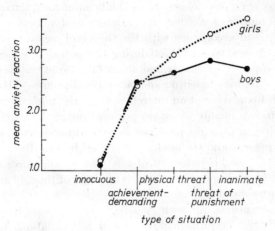

Fig. 1: Mean anxiety reactions as a function of type of situation.

As stated above, the existence of sex by situation interactions has been demonstrated earlier. However, the systematic nature of this interaction, in the form that is showed in the present study, was not predicted. The result emphasizes the necessity of incorporating the character of the situations – in which behavior is observed – in planning, carrying through and evaluating the results in personality research. However, this cannot be done effectively without knowledge about situations in relevant terms, obtained in systematic research. Such knowledge is sorely needed, so that situational conditions can be considered in a known, predictable and controlled way.

Age differences in perception of anxiety provoking situations

The second study is concerned with developmental trends in the perception and interpretation of anxiety provoking situations (Stattin, 1980). In a recent study boys and girls for each of the age groups 12, 15, and 18 were asked to describe the three most anxiety provoking situations that came to their mind. For each of the situations they then described *what* in the situation made them anxious and *why* it did. In the analyses of the youngsters' motives for anxiety a rather obvious age difference appeared. The preadolescent youngsters often referred to physical properties of the situations, to external bodily consequences and possible external sanctions; by contrast older teenagers referred to psychological consequences such as anticipated shame, guilt, separation, lack of personal integrity, etc. Where the young subjects spoke about spatially and temporally close sanctions, older ones referred to anticipated consequences in the future, in professional life, in marriage, etc. The preadolescent boys and girls even showed difficulties in conceptualizing the consequences for themselves. A preadolescent explanation in response to the described situation, "I am afraid when I ski down a steep hill" was "Because the hill is so steep" and did not refer to the possible physical injury that would be a common explanation given by older subjects.

The difference between preadolescents and older subjects with respect to experienced and expressed motives for situationally determined anxiety as indicated in the description above, is in accordance with the theory of cognitive development suggested by Piaget. According to Piaget during the period of concrete operations a child acquires the capacity to classify and interrelate objects in the environment and to give causal explanations based on spatialtemporal premises. However, the logic of the child is still mainly based on inferences from the immediately present situations, and relations are mainly based on physical properties of the objects. When formal operations begin, thought processes become progressively more independent of the immediate present and the adolescent can go beyond the physical properties of the situation and base his judgment of relations on inferences and more subtle inherent qualities. There is a continuous "decentering" of thought processes from the given perceptual stimulus field.

Based on our observations, and with Piaget's theory on cognitive development as a background a study was performed to investigate age variations in perceptions and interpretations of anxiety provoking situations, from pre- to postadolescence.

The basic assumption was that preadolescents would see relations between situations in terms of manifest physical characteristics, while older subjects would conceptualize resemblances between situations more and more in terms of latent psychological anticipated consequences.

Method. Data were obtained for three age groups, 11–12, 14–15 and 17–18, with about 60 boys and 60 girls for each age level. (For the age level 17–18 the number of boys was only 29.)

From a sample of nearly one thousand descriptions of anxiety provoking situations given by youngsters in the same age groups, eleven were selected for the present study. The criterion for the selection of situations was that they were reported by youngsters at all three age levels.

Our hypothesis was tested by the use of similarity ratings (Magnusson, 1971). For studying our hypothesis this method was particularly adequate since, besides yielding quantitative, direct measures of subjective similarity between situations, it does not require verbal ability (which varies systematically with age).

All possible combinations of the eleven situations were rated on a four point scale.

Ratings of similarity between two situations were possible on two different grounds. According to the first principle, situations could be judged as similar with reference to a common central object or person which was clearly visible and salient in the situations. In this respect, situations could have one of the following four elements in common; Classmate, Brother, Relative and Dog. They can be designated Manifest characteristics.

According to the second principle, similarity could be judged on the basis of common anticipated consequences. Four types of consequences were used; Physical injury, Separation, Guilt and Shame. They will be designated *Latent characteristics*.

The categories were taken from content analysis of adolescents' own explanations of why they were anxious in various types of anxiety-provoking situations. The categories discriminated satisfactorily between consequences of this type.

An example will illustrate the way this procedure works. Two situations were described as follows: "An angry dog nips at you when you are out walking" and "Your dog is sick and has to be taken to the veterinary". According to the main hypothesis these two situations will be judged as similar among preadolescents because of the common element Dog, but as different by postadolescents since the anticipated consequences are different (Physical injury and Separation).

Mean ratings of similarity for situations *without* common manifest and latent characteristics were used as the basis for testing the significance of similarity ratings based on manifest and latent characteristics, respectively.

Results and Conclusions. The overall results are presented. in Tab. 3 and Fig. 2.

Tab. 3.: *Difference scores for ratings of similarity based on Manifest and Latent characteristics, respectively*

| | Boys | | | Girls | | |
	12ys	15ys	18ys	12ys	15ys	18ys
Manifest charasteristics	.164***	.149***	.080	.160***	.119*	.095
Latent characteristics	.179***	.277***	.421***	.189***	.342***	.436***

* $p < .05$
*** $p < .001$

The results are clearly in line with the hypothesis for both boys and girls. With increasing age, there is a gradual decrease in similarity ratings based on Manifest characteristics, and a corresponding increase in similarity ratings based on Latent characteristics.

The results thus support the assumption that the perception and interpretation of environmental threats change in nature from pre- to postadolescence.

This is not the place to go into a detailed discussion and analysis of the results. (For a discussion see Stattin, 1980.) Let me only point out one implication, which is of more general interest for theory and research in the field of personality. During the seventies, the problem of personality consistence – both in a cross-situational and in a longitudinal perspective – has been a central and controversial theme. As summarized above, our results indicated a clear change in the perception and interpretation of anxiety-provoking situations from pre- to postadolescence. To the extent that behavior is a function of how we perceive and construe the outer world as we encounter it in actual situations, the environmental conditions that determine cross-situational stability in actual behavior vary with age, i.e. what constitutes a stable environment as a prerequisite for behavioral consistency varies with age. For preadolescents a stable environment is characterized by similarity in physical, external properties. For postadolescents, on the other hand, it is characterized by situations that are similar with respect to psychological, latent qualities. Age differences in the perception and interpretation of anxiety-provoking situations can also be assumed to imply age differences in actual behavior in the same kind of situations. These speculations open up a series of important and fruitful problems for systematic research in the field of personality as a whole.

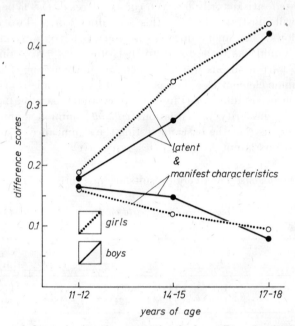

Fig. 2: Developmental change in situation perception for boys (B) and girls (G), respectively.

Final comment

The results presented here show the systematic character of the interaction between person variables such as sex and type of anxiety-provoking situations. In a broader perspective, this demonstrates the systematic nature of the interaction between person and situation characteristics as emphasized especially by those advocating an interactional model of behavior. Again, this underlines the need for systematic research on situations. Systematic knowledge about situations is a prerequisite for more effective theory and empirical research in the field of personality.

What seems to be a basis for confusion, when one looks at the diversity of empirical results , is actually often lawfulness, that has to be detected and understood. The lawfulness of the person-situation interactions cannot be effectively investigated if we do not devote resources to the systematic study of the situation side of the person-situation system, as we have done on the person side for the hundred years that have gone since Wundt founded his laboratory (Magnusson, 1980a, b). Descriptions and classifications of situations in relevant terms are needed to enable us to understand and explain human behavior in its environmental context.

References

BERGMAN, L. R., and MAGNUSSON, D.: Overachievement and catecholamine excretion in an achievement demanding situation. Psychosomatic Medicine 41, 191–188, 1979

FRANKENHAEUSER, M.: Psychoneuroendocrine approaches to the study of stressful person-environment transaction. In: H. Selye (Ed.), Selye's Guide to Stress Research. New York: Van Nostrand Reinhold Company, Vol. 1, 1980

LUNDBERG, U.: Catecholamine and cortisol excretion patterns in three year old children and their parents. Department of Psychology, University of Stockholm, 1980. (Manuscript)

MAGNUSSON, D.: An analysis of situational dimensions. Perceptual and Motor Skills 32, 851–867, 1971

MAGNUSSON, D.: The person and the situation in an interactional model of behavior. Scandinavian Journal of Psychology, 17, 253–271, 1976

MAGNUSSON, D.: Wanted: A psychology of situations. In: D. Magnusson (Ed.), Toward a Psychology of Situations: An Interactional Perspective. Hillsdale, N. J.: Lawrence Erlbaum Associates, 1980 a

MAGNUSSON, D.: Personality in an interactional paradigm of research. Zeitschrift für Differentielle und Diagnostische Psychologie 1, 17–34, 1980 b

MAGNUSSON, D., and TÖRESTAD, B.: Situational influences on sex differences in anxiety reactions. Reports from the Department of Psychology, University of Stockholm, No. 559, 1980

STATTIN, H.: The appraisal of relations between emotionally threatening situations: A developmental study. Reports from the Department of Psychology, University of Stockholm, 1980

On Importance of Cognitive Styles Structuralization for Personality Research

C. S. NOSAL

Problem

From the structural point of view, the concept of personality is usually defined as hierarchy of individual experience, i.e. a set of cognitive codes (descriptive, operational, evaluative) or cognitive networks) e.g. semantic representation) by which any person can control his directive behaviour (Obuchowski, 1970). Is this framework the term "individual experience" refers to a level of deep structure representing the basic structure of personality. Many cognitive approaches to the personality description or explanation strongly correspond to the above mentioned paradigm. But in this context we have an unsolved problem concerned with the interpretation of surface structures of personality. This problem can be presented as a problem of a gap between deep and surface structure of personality. It seems this gap is concerned with functional interpretation of personality.

From the functional viewpoint the concept of personality can be defined only if we take into account some facts and descriptions connected with the psychology of cognitive styles. Generally, functional sections of personality can be defined as a relatively stable organization of set of styles (i.e. cognitive, emotional, interpersonal) manifested by behavioral traits and action indices.

However, many researchers will agree that styles phenomena are a good functional description of personality, they will also point at the absence of attempts to cognitive styles index (CSI) structuralisation.

General assumption

The functional view of the personality requires a new approach to the analysis of CSI widely known in psychological literature (cf. Messick, 1976, Royce, 1973). The existing CSI that includes 18–20 items can be reduced on the basis of general theory of the human information processing system (HIPS). It seems this basis creates new possibilities for the redefinition of traits, abilities and cognitive styles typically analyzed by psychologists as isolated aspects of the human intellect and personality. The abovementioned HIPS theory plays the role of a metatheory in relation to:

1. detailed descriptions of specific cognitive processes such as attention, perception, memory etc.;

2. informational interpretation of any "stylistic" phenomena as a stable type of HIPS organization;

3. cognitive interpretation of personality as any type of "processing system".

124

A tentative version of the general theory of HIPS functioning is presented in another work (cf. Nosal, 1979). For our purposes we will present this proposal in a sketch form only.

Tentative solution for CSI structuralization

Let us start our analysis with the description of some CSI containing basic cognitive dimensions as they are presented in Tab. 1.

Tab. 1: *Basic dimensions enumerated*
in the cognitive style indexes (CSI)

No	Dimension content
1	field dependence – independence
2	perceptual field articulation
3	breadth of conceptualization
4	equivalence range
5	conceptual structures articulation
6	tolerance for unrealistic experiences
7	levelling – sharpening
8	epistemic global style
9	extensiveness of scanning
10	reflection – impulsivity
11	rigidity – flexibility
12	locus of control

Items in Tab. 1 can be structured in another form and described in more detail if we assume that the above style dimensions are sections (functional representations) of four basic levels (L_i) of personality viewed as an information processing system:

L_1, dividing, searching for and perceiving of any field containing unstructured, primary data; first level environment representation by short-time percepts;

L_2, formation and ordering of any conceptual representation of environment in the form of different structures (symbolic, semantic, semiotic);

L_3, actualizing, changing and organizing of personal experience on the basis of environment models ("theories", "constructs", "visions" etc.);

L_4, goal-directed activity based on personal programming and strategies of decision-making; on this level we have observed long-term behaviour (consistences in so-called preferends, life styles and value hierarchies).

The four levels of information processing as noted above can be described from different viewpoints, terms and paradigms. It must be stressed that items of CSI represent only one possibility of such description. For example, ability theories give us another solution for understanding (L_i) but, of course, cognitive styles vs. abilities represent complementary aspects of HIPS. As it has been noted by many researchers (cf. Messick, 1976, Royce, 1973, 1978, Witkin, 1977), this complementariness concerns an opposition: a form of cognitive organization vs. content of cognitive task.

The CSI, as presented in Tab. 1, can be redistributed according to L_i specifity as it is shown in Tab. 2.

Tab. 2: *Cognitive style dimensions as the descriptors of four levels (L) of human information processing system (HIPS)*

Level/descriptor	Some aspects of processing
L_1. Characteristics of HIPS input concerned with dividing, searching for and perceiving of any primary-external data:	
DIMENSION 1 field dependence – independence	global vs. articulated perceptual activity; "distance" to data field informational autonomy; reinforcement procedure.
DIMENSION 2 field articulation	frequency of field scanning; changes in perceptual patterns; direction of orientation: intro- vs. extraorientation; learning strategies: step by step vs. insight.
L_2. Processing characteristics of HIPS concerned with formation and ordering of any environment representations in the form of symbolic, semantic, and semiotic units:	
DIMENSION 3 breadth of conceptualization	broad inclusiveness vs. narrow exclusiveness; reductional power of conceptual units/systems; ascendancy of similarities vs. differences as the representation center (focus).
DIMENSION 4 equivalence range	number of conceptual units on the equivalence scale; conceptual control of environmental changes
DIMENSION 5 articulation of conceptual structures	conceptual integration vs. compartmentalization; complexity-simplicity; semantic dimensions vs. semantic categories; types of conceptualizing: relational, analytic-descriptive, categorial-inferential.
L_3. Processing characteristics of HIPS concerned with actualizing, redefining and organizing of individual experience:	
DIMENSION 6 tolerance of unrealistic experiences	primary and secondary suggestibility; distribution of vigilance states; sensitivity to cognitive conflicts; lability-stability of cognitive criteria.
DIMENSION 7 leveling – sharpening	memorization type; influence of new darta; durability of short-term memory units; locus of criteria for comparisons (STM vs. LTM)
DIMENSION 8 epistemic profile: empirical, rational, metaphorical	hierarchical index of discriminands concerned with epistemic subscales
L_4. Characteristics of HIPS concerned with cognitive control, programming, and output activity for different space-time sections:	
DIMENSION 9 extensiveness of scanning	cognitive control on the elementary (short-time) level; parameters of scanning activity: direction, frequency, size, depth.

Tab. 2.: *Cognitive style dimensions as the descriptors of four levels (L) of human information processing system (HIPS)*

Level/descriptor	Some aspects of processing
DIMENSION 10 reflection – impulsivity	types of informational basis for control: anticipation vs. retrospection; fast vs. slow behavior; caution vs. risk taking; differences in the decision making strategies.
DIMENSION 11 rigidity – flexibility of control programs	changes in the hierarchy of control units/scales; balance between feed back and feed fore trials; perceived degree of behavioral freedom.
DIMENSION 12 locus of control (processing)	dominant basis of data or processing criteria: external vs. internal; dominant source of reinforcement; displacement of processing (control) locus.

On the basis of Tab. 2 we may conclude that the CSI items existing in psychologica literature are concerned with incomplete, different and arbitrarily selected aspects of human cognitive organization. For this reason, attempts at CSI structuralization by localization of stylistic dimensions in the context of HIPS theory play an important role. As we know from contemporary literature (cf. Goldstein and Blackman, 1978, Royce, 1973, 1978, Pinson, 1978) only the authors quoted have any proposal for the solution of the mentioned problem.

The first proposal is based on the description of CSI items as some manifestations of personality. Goldstein and Blackman start with a good review of literature and select the following five basic dimensions: authoritarianism, dominance, personal construct-cognitive complexity, cognitive integrity and field dependence-independence. This book-review is important and interesting but not clear in its theoretical (integrative) background.

Royce's approach to CSI structuralization is based on the theory of individual experience (ways of knowing). In another terminology this approach concerns empiricism, rationalism and metaphorism as the basic or dominant way towards knowledge. Starting from this general assumption, Royce has developed the theory of the hierarchical structure of CSI. However, it seems to the author of this article that the observed indices of cognitive style depend on many classes of determinants. This point of view is more clearly depicted in Fig. 1.

An interesting proposal for CSI structuralization is presented by Pinson (1978). The author also stresses the statement that style dimension represents permanent differences in individuals' manner of processing information. Pinson distinguishes between two classes of cognitive styles dealing with: (1) information processing complexity on a conceptual level, (2) accommodative or control function of cognitive models by which a person tends to consolidate a state of cognitive balance. In the terms of our proposal (see Tab. 2), the two classes of style listed above refer to certain aspects of L_2 and L_4.

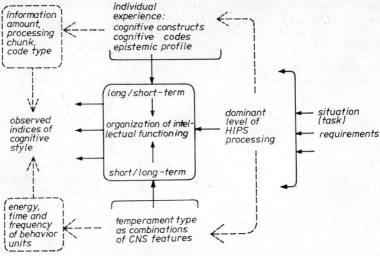

Fig. 1: Basic set of cognitive style determinants (interrupted lines signify any reasoning fields amitted in the psychological analysis of styles).

As Fig. 1 depicts, the observed indices of cognitive style depend on: (1) dominant level of HIPS involved in the solution of a task, (2) CNS features constitute the temperament type, (3) profile of individual experience. From this we can assert that a stylistic aspect is any section of intellectual (informational) functioning; any style represents an invariant (module) of psychological organization by which a subject can balance his individuality as bio-psychological structure, based on CNS features and profile of experience, with situational requirements.

Now we can develop a tentative solution of CSI structuralization (as it is shown in Tab. 2) according to the assumptions below: (1) definition of style essence as an organizational fact, (2) assumption on the HIPS structure presented by the four levels (L_i) of processing.

In this context the style phenomena can be examined for each separate L_i. It is

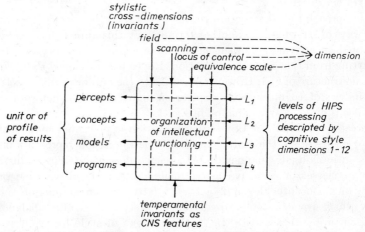

Fig. 2: The stylistic cross-dimensions in relation to the levels of HIPS processing.

interesting and important for our analysis to pay attention that each L_i can be intersected by any set of stylistic cross-dimensions (invariants); see Fig. 2.

Fig. 2 confronts our previous CSI redistribution among L_i with the new statement that between CSI items there exists an inner structure described as the four cross-dimensions. Of course, to understand the cross-dimensions nature properly, we must give the following definitions:

(1) *field cross-dimensions* represents a bipolar tendency to perceive any set of influences at any time as separate-unseparate from the rest part of environmental stimulation or individual experience unit; field cross-dimension produces a type of operational area which changes step by step during information processing.

(2) *scanning cross-dimension* represents a two-vectorised (directed + random) procedure for searching for and comparing elements of field data; dominance of the directed or random scanning component produces such stylistic phenomena as, for example, functional fixation vs. chaotic behavior.

(3) *locus of processing center* (or locus of control) as cross-dimension represents a bipolar tendency to locate any metacriteria of processing at the internal vs. external center (basis of control: field of data, sources of reinforcement etc.).

(4) *equivalence range* as cross-dimension represents a two-vectorised procedure (compartmentalization + integration) of recognition, understanding and projecting the models of the environment; dominance of the mentioned component of the equivalence procedure can be manifested by superiority of sequential vs. simultanic processing.

When taking into consideration the above-listed definitions of the cognitive style cross-dimensions, we are able to describe a structural basis of bipolarity as the fundamental aspect of cognitive style. As we know from psychological literature, all authors emphasize these aspects of style, but without an explanation of causal mechanism which generate two qualitatively different polarities and the middle region of a cognitive style dimension.

In the last step of our analysis, according to the mapping manner presented in Fig. 2, we can locate the CSI items in a new framework (see Fig. 3).

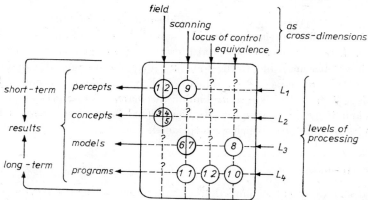

Fig. 3: Some gaps in the tentative location of CSI items (number of CSI items; see Tab. 1).

On the basis of Fig. 3, we can detect some gaps in the area of cognitive style research. For example, dimension number 12 (Rotter's locus of control) is mainly studied on the global level L_4; this research direction concerns the use of inventory scales to measure dominant direction for locus of control. Another example concerns widely-known field dimension (Witkin's theory) which is mostly studied on the basis of a perceptual task.

Basic results of our reasoning can also be presented in a functional form based on the important assumption as follows: the distinguished four cross-dimensions constitute a *module of information processing program*. This functional module starts with field limitation as an unstructured unit, includes scanning procedure as a form of elementary processing, is controlled by differently located centers, and is finished by equivalence procedure. A simple form of four-fold module (field – scanning – locus – equivalence) is depicted in Fig. 4.

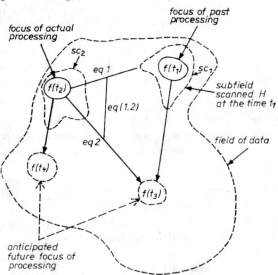

Fig. 4: The module of any information processing program based on four cognitive style cross-dimensions (invariants): field dimension scanning dimension (sc), locus of processing (control) dimension, equivalence dimension (eq).

It seems that the theoretical content validity of the described module confirms our attempt at CSI structuralization. We can find much information concerning empirical confirmations in psychological literature, if we agree that empirical facts have double-valence according to the dominant level of processing (L_i), and the type of cognitive style treated as a cross-dimension. For example, we do not understand why field dependence or locus of control implicates many consequences for personality and behaviour if we do not respect any hierarchical (hidden) structure of the concepts of Witkin and Rotter which we mentioned.

General conclusions

We started our analysis by completing a CSI and separating its items among four levels of information processing, according to the theory of HIPS (see Tab. 1 and 2).

130

The next step of our analysis was concerned with the attempt to describe generally stylistic phenomena as a for of organizational invariant determined by many factors (see Fig. 1). Then we defined four types of stylistic cross-dimensions and demonstrated that the important CSI analysed in the literature can be significantly redefined and redistributed according to two-dimensional criteria; i.e. level of processing and type of stylistic cross-dimensions (see Fig. 2 and 3).

It must be emphasized that the proposed CSI structuralization corresponds very much to many cognitive theories of personality based on different terms such as codes, constructs, networks, discriminants, preferends, attitudes, and activity programs etc. Our analysis also confirms the possibility that some style dimensions (e.g. field dimension) have a hierarchical structure and can be more adequately described as cross-dimensions. It seems that the type of correspondence mentioned plays an important role for the integration of our knowledge of personality because different style measurements can be utilized for functional interpretation of personality.

References

GOLDSTEIN, K. M., and S. BLACKMAN: Cognitive style: five approaches and relevant research. New York: Wiley, 1978

MESSICK, S. (Ed.): Individuality in learning, San Francisco: Jossey-Bass Publ., 1976

NOSAL, C. S.: Mechanizmy funkcjonowania intelektu: zdolności, style poznawcze, przetwarzanie informacji (Mechanisms of intellectual functioning: abilities, cognitive styles, information processing). Wrocław: Technical University Press, 1979

OBUCHOWSKI, K.: Kody orientacji i struktura procesów emocjonalnych (Codes of orientation and structure of emotional processes). Warszawa: PWN, 1970

PINSON, C.: Consumer cognitive style: review and implications for marketers. In: E. Topritzhofer (Ed.), Marketing. Wiesbaden: Gabler 1978.

ROYCE, J. R. (Ed.): Multivariate analysis and psychological theory. New York: Academic Press, 1973

ROYCE, J. R. et al.: Toward a multi-factor theory of styles and their relationships to cognition and effect; Res. Report the Center for Advanced Study in Theoretical Psychology, University of Alberta, 1978; mimeo.

WITKIN, H. A. et al.: Field dependence revisited. Princeton, Educ. Testing Service, Res. Bull., 77–16, 1977; mimeo.

Experimental Questionnaires – a New Approach to Personality Research[1]

GEORG LIND

The concept of Experimental Questionnaires is an attempt to facilitate new, adequate means for assessing dynamic-structural traits. In this paper I shall give, as briefly as possible, an account of the rationale, the design and the utility of the concept.

1. Introduction

Traits and dispositions of individual persons are the genuine object of personality research. Contrary to Differential Psychology which embarks upon the assessment of any difference between persons, for personality research the assumption of behavior organizing traits is constitutive (Mischel, 1977, p. 248.).

But, in spite of the simplicity of this insight, it remains a rather difficult task to translate the notion of traits into an unanimously accepted scientific concept. Hitherto, the empirical evidence pertaining to this issue has been ambiguous and has served both, those who believe in the reality of traits and those who deny it, While in some fields of personality research (test-) behavior is strikingly consistent, consistency is disappointingly low or absent in others.

How can this persisting crisis be overcome? How can we cope with the stagnation in personality research? For a considerable time we believed, maybe with a few exceptions, that the crisis was due to a lack of either theoretical or methodological sophistication. We have witnessed a flood of new theoretical speculations and of new research strategies that are triggered by the failure of personality psychology to account for its perplexing findings. Doubtlessly, these endeavors have enriched personality research, yet we must admit that the "slow progress of soft psychology" (Meehl, 1978) is still among the few facts on which psychologists would most easily agree.

If the stagnation of personality research cannot be overcome by the improvement of either theory or method, the problem may be more fundamental. In fact it may be located in the *relation* between theory and method. As early as 1951, Travers pointed

[1] I would like to thank my colleaques of the 'Forschungsgruppe Hochschulsozialisation' at the University of Konstanz (Sonderforschungsbereich 23), T. Bargel, B. Dippelhofer-Stiem, G. Framhein, H. Peisert (director), J.-U. Sandberger and H. G. Walter for their critical support in developing and applying the concept of Experimental Questionnaires.

I am also very grateful to a number of colleagues outside our research unit for their co-operativeness and their sincere encouragements, especially to G. Kanig, W. Kempf, M. Lieberman, P. Meehl, W. Perry and R. Wakenhut. Their comments on this concept have helped to sharpen this paper on several points. For remaining soft spots I take sole responsibility.

to the importance of theory-guided construction of personality tests for the enhancement of psychological knowledge. Recently, Fiske (1970) mentioned again the "problem of coordinating the measure and the concept" (p. 51). The programs of "construct validation" (Cronbach & Meehl 1955) and of "substantial validation" (Loevinger, 1957) have also this problem in mind, but unfortunately reduce it to the problem of optimizing the correlation between 'similar' measures.

The cleavage between theory and method in personality research has lead to two major ‚solutions'. Some eminent researchers have turned completely away from psychometrics and formed methods of their own, the so-called clinical methods (e.g. Freud, Piaget). The clinical interview method is doubtlessly theory-related and deserves to be considered further on. Yet the lack of transparency and testability forces us, in addition, to search for more "objektive" methods. (The expectional method of G. A. Kelly is somewhere in the middle and would need to be treated in a larger paper.)

Most others apparently have adopted a dualistic view that conceives of theory and method as two somehow related yet not strictly connectable realms of research. This way, it is believed, one could escape the reproach of positivism and still take advantage of „objective" methods. Allport (1951), one of the prominent advocates of this approach, admits however, that as a consequence "we must rest content with mere approximations to the structure of personality" (p. 442). So the latter approach is not satisfactory either.

As Block (1968) sharply stated, "if a science of personality is to be formed, the responsibility of coupling concept and measure must be met" (p. 30). For that we cannot borrow methods from elsewhere; "the task itself must create the method that is appropriate for it"! (Dilthey)

Yet the problem of coordinating theory and method, in fact, is difficult to achieve particularly in the field of personality research. Koffka (1934): "nowhere is it easier to miss the point, and run either into the Scylla of blind statistical investigations of trait, or the Charybdis of ultimately unscientific abstract discussions" (p. 677).

Moreover, the solution of this problem cannot be confined to the construction of a 'valid' and 'reliable' assessment method but must also comprise a re-thinking of the methodological criteria for test construction. We must be aware of the fact that concepts like 'validity' and 'reliability' may be inadequate themselves.

Validity: Given that research methods are not ends in themselves but are always means for executing and testing a theoretical proposition, the validity problem is twofold: (a) *How empirically valid* is the theoretical proposition? And (b) how theoretically valid (adequate) is the assessment method? In 1957 Loevinger pointed out the necessity of making this distinction, but unfortunately did not recognize the profundity of its implications for her cause and for psychometric methods in general. Such an epistemological point of view challenges the meaningfulness of the current practice of speaking of 'the impirical validity of tests'. Accordingly a test cannot be empirically validated, at least not directly. One may *conclude* that if a test has been successfully employed for validating a theory it must have possessed theoretical validity. Note, however, that this conclusion is a-symmetric: A failure to produce supporting findings may be *either* due to lack of empirical validity of the theory or to the lack of theoretical validity of the method *or* to both. Hence theories are falsified by empirical findings if and only if the method was theoretically valid (Lokatos' objection to crude falsificationism). So, in order to prevent confusion, I rather prefer to speak of the test's *utility* than of its (empirical) validity, when the test helped to produce 'good' results.

Reliability: Lumsden (1974) has made a strong case for regarding the reliability problem also as a problem of a test's validity. In fact the necessity of doing so is obvious since (a) classical test theory has advanced a substantial theory of inconsistencies of test behavior, namely error theory, and (b) this theory is testable, for it entails the assumption that this error is solely due to the test (and not to the properties of the individuals tested). When this objection is disregarded psychology runs the risk of carrying along hidden "anthropological assumptions" (Hilke, 1980) which are at odds with the very theory involved.

So "the study of measurement must begin within discussion and analysis of such matters as the nature of traits and the mode of representation of the total personality" (Cattel, 1946, p. 4).

2. Problems of translating personality theory into an adequate research methodology (Theory of trait assessment)

Experimental Questionnaires (EQs) are designed to fit the intentions of dynamic-structural theories of personality (e.g. Warren & Carmichael, 1930, Lewin, 1961, Allport, 1961, Kohlberg, 1969, but also many of the theoretical propositions of Stern, 1911, Hartshorne & May, 1928, Cattel, 1946). According to these theories,

Personality is the dynamic organization of the individual's mind that determines (or better: that is) his, or her characteristic interaction with the social environment at a particular level of development.

This is not the place to discuss in depth the problems that result from translating this definition of personality into an adequate research methodology. But a condensed account of the following ten problems of personality research may help to understand the rationale of the concept of Experimental Questionnaires and some of its implications. As far as I can see, these problems are, by and large, those which other researchers in this field also encounter frequently:

(1) the problem of conceptualizing traits, (2) the problem of infering traits from behavioral acts, (3) the problem of functional ambiguity of acts, (4) the problem of separating the dynamic and structural components of a trait, (5) the problem of conceptualizing person-situation interaction, (6) the problem of assessing meaningful behavior, (7) the problem of determining the experimental unit, (8) the problem of defining behavioral consistency, (9) the problem of locating the source of inconsistency, and (10) the problem of representativity.

For the purpose of this paper these problems need not, and cannot, be extensively treated. It will suffice to make explicit the set of tentative solutions which constitute the rationale of EQs.

(1) Graumann (1960) juxtaposed two scientific concepts of trait: One is the "statistical", which "is nothing else but a labelling of any frequent coincidence of particular, consistent, (behavioral) signs for the sake of better communication". The other is the "hypothetical construct" concept of trait, which comprises only those correlations signs that "can be interpreted through recourse to a hypothesized common

instance, i.e. through reference to a substruction, as meaningful associations" (p. 147; translation mine).

Resorting to a dynamic (teleological, organismic) definition of personality brings us, of course, closer to the latter, Internal-Structure (Allport), rather than to the former, Positivist, concept of a trait. Yet, since the latter definition seems to contain a moment of unwarranted speculation we prefer not to distinguish between 'real' behavior and 'hypothetical' traits. Surely, traits are different and need to be assessed in a different way. But this does not necessarily entail that they are less real, or more hypothetical, than acts (cf. Loevinger's, 1957, p. 642, critique of Cronbach and Meehl's understanding of "hypothetical constructs"; also Hempel's, 1958, discussion of "theoretical entities"). According to our conception, traits are not an instance 'behind' the behavioral acts, nor are they a 'cause' of acts but must be regarded as the combined whole of (a) dynamic goals (values, orientations), (b) instrumental acts, and (c) the relational structure between acts and goals (Lind et al., 1980).

We conceive of the formal ground-structure of dynamic-structural traits as being a little more complex than Miller et al.'s (1960) T–O–T–E model in so far as we regard the multiple determination of acts as being of great importance for theory (e.g. for conceptualizing 'conflict') and for research into personality (see below). But it is still rather simple so that the difference to other trait concepts can be seen easily (cf. the following graph):

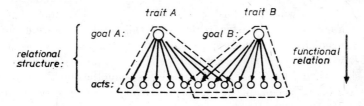

(2) This model has a direct bearing upon the problem of inferring traits from behavioral acts. First, the relation between acts and dispositions should be conceived of neither as *unknown*, nor as stochastic nor as mediated by an *intervening variable* but as being of logical inclusion: Acts are constitutive parts of a trait. Second, the relation of acts to the two components of a trait, the dynamic and the structural, is well defined and can be reconstructed empirically if that particular trait really exists.

(3) Viewing acts as being multiply determined implies that when interpreting a single act we have to cope with its *functional ambguity* (Kempf, 1978, p. 12, Nunner-Winkler, 1978, p. 352). Since there is no one-to-one relationship the problem of making inferences about a trait from a single observation is a substantial one. For example (cf. Lind, 1978), a person may agree to an argument of mine in defence of someone's decision

– because it fits nicely into his opinion about the matter which he, or she, already held before (opinion agreement),

– because the person feels, the argument is referring to a good reason (quality or level of reasoning),

– or because it is me who has forwarded the argument (acquiescence).

The index in parantheses alludes to the diversity of traits that may be involved, either alone or in combination, in producing a single behavior and that is of so great

135

annoyance to the psychometrician who attempts to design a uni-dimensional test. This problem seems to be ubiquitous, as it is encountered in the research into moral attitudes (Nunner-Winkler, 1978) as well as in intelligence testing (Kempf, 1978, Loevinger, 1957, p. 647).[2]

(4) A further problem pertains to the conceptual relation between the dynamic (valuing, motivational) component and the structural (cognitive) component of a trait, i.e. between the *Richtungs-* and *Rüstungs-*component (W. Stern) of a disposition. According to the concept adopted both components are clearly *distinguishable* but not *separable*. We, therefore, do not speak of different 'dispositions' or 'faculties of mind' but of different components of one and the same trait. The theorem of unseparability entails also that neither component can be defined without reference to the other. While purely formal relations are empty, unrelated acts and values remain meaningless. This problem is, in my opinion, of great relevance for the prevailing discussions about (a) the 'content-specifity' of cognitive structure (complexity, style, etc.) and (b) the 'cognitive turn' of motivation and attitude research. In both instances, the superficial separation of the two components of traits apparently has resulted in severed difficulties with regard to conceptualization and measurement of personality variables.

(5) Another perplexing conceptual problem arises from the notion of *person-situation interaction*. In fact it seems as if we are even moving away from some promising attempts of early personality research. Though many refer today to the well-known formula of Lewin: $V = f (P \& U)$ (behavior is a function of person *and* environment interaction) only a few realize that this formula does not imply that, as 'modern' interactionism surmises, person and environment can be empirically separated. Lewin (1961) did not mean that we should conceive of separate entities but emphasized their *interaction*, i.e. 'life-space', as being the objekt of psychological research. Accordingly, personality *is* the way a person perceives, evaluates, and reacts to a situation (Helm, 1960). Hence "in concrete experiments both cannot be separated" (Olweus, 1976, p. 65). Maybe, that our language is responsible for some of the prevailing bewilderment as it does not distinguish between a separating and a combining '*and*'.[3]

(6) Personality research is not concerned with the mere physical properties of human behavior – physiology and other branches of science take care of this – but with meaningful behavior. Verbal behavior is not the only kind of meaningful behavior but it may reasonably be considered its most preferred medium. Verbal behavior, however, alone does not suffice to represent meaning. In addition we neep to ascertain its functional and structural properties with regard to the '*totality*' of a trait.

[2] There are similar problems in natural sciences. As Piaget (1973) observes, also in physics, chemistry and biology" at the outset the problem is always to isolate the components out of the bewildering mass of phenomena" (36; translation mine). See also Popper (1979).

[3] Again this problem is not unique for psychology. Also in the natural sciences the "Observable is only result of an interaction between experiment and reality" (Piaget, 1973, p. 52). Hence the scientist's major task is to disentangle the nature of the observation (i.e. the observation mediating processes) and the nature of the observed. This is, even in physics, less trivial than might be assumed. Heisenberg, for example, interpreted his indeterminancy principle for a long time as pertaining to the measurement process while it was only eventually realized that it pertained to the nature of a quantum (cf. Popper, 1979, p. 305).

(7) Nothing seems to be more obvious than that the unit of personality research is the individual. In theory, we almost exclusively refer to the individual personality. There seems to be no meaningful way of setting the 'personality of a sample of persons' equal to the individual personality structure. In practice, however, it is often implicitly or explicitly assumed that traits are commonly organized. Since such a notion does not take into account the individuality of traits, Allport (1961) has aptly called this the External-Effect definition of traits. Persons are judged merely according to some external, socially defined standards of conduct and achievement. This is an approach in its own right but it does not accord with our concept of personality.

(8) In many text-books one can find the statement that personality development means both integration and differentiation. In empirical research this often is translated as: Behavior becomes more and also less consistent. An obvious contradition! In fact research has produced supporting evidence for both propositions. A closer look shows that at the heart of this problem there is an *insufficient definition* of '*consistency*'. If 'consistency' means "holding to the same principle or practice" (Webster's New World Dictionary), a proposition which does not specify the 'principle' or 'practice' is incomplete. In this context 'consistency' is a relational concept. A behavior cannot be consistent per se, but only 'consistent with regard to something', in our case: 'with regard to the function it is to serve'. So behavior may become more consistent with regard to function A and, at the same time, become less consistent with regard to function B. Besides such simple processes of integration and dis-integration there may also be a superposition of traits, whereby the superposed trait does not become disintegrated but 'differentiated' with regard to another 'qualifying' trait.

The problem of defining consistency also has a bearing upon the distinction between the External-Effect and the Internal-Structure model of trait (Allport). While the former assumes that behavior must be, if at all, consistent with regard to some external standard, the latter assumes the reality of internal standards to which behavior may, or may not, accord.

(9) One way to save the External-Effect (common trait) model in the face of an overwhelming number of discrepant facts is to assume that the measurement process introduces random error, i.e. that inconsistency of behavior with regard to a hypothesized common trait is due to a property of the assessment method. This assumption, advanced by classical psychometrics (Spearman, Gulliksen, Guilford etc.), raises the problem of attributing inconsistency. While 'error theory' attributes inconsistency to the 'reliability' of the method, the theory of dynamic-structural personality conceives of it as an attribute of trait organization. This is an empirically testable question! In fact, research into personality and personality development has produced ample evidence that inconsistency of behavior varies systematically with the kind of trait measured and with the phase or stage of personality development (see, for example, Hartshorne & May, 1928, Kohlberg, 1969, Loevinger, 1976, Lind, 1978). In sum, I think, we should not rule out the assumption of random error (unreliability). This precisely defined concept (Kempf, 1978), which is to be distinguished clearly from the trivial explanation of 'unknown factors', may, however, come in as the last, and not as the first, explanation for observed inconsistencies.

(10) Finally we need to provide a tentative solution for the problem of represen-

tativity. Brunswik (1955), as many psychologists after him, has invoked the concept of ecological validity which means that the experimental stimuli should be distributively representative. But what population of stimuli should we refer to when designing an experiment? There are uncountable possibilities, some of which are unassessable in principle (e.g. the distribution of events over time). So how to chose? I believe that this problem is spurious with respect to theory-guided research. Generalizations can never be based merely on a single experiment but are always based on the comprehensive experience comprised in a scientific theory. In order to test the empirical validity of a hypothesis we need rather to ascertain *categorial representativity*. Only this guarantees that the research instrument tests what it is supposed to test. I, therefore, believe that many objections against systematic experimental design are truely directed at the positivist spirit in which they are often used. Like Lewin (1963) I think that "experiments become superficial only if just one or the other condition is operationalized but not the essential structure" (p. 200). What is "essential" must, of course, be determined by a theory. It is noteworthy that Brunswik (1955) has not only introduced the concept of 'ecological validity' but also shown very convincing causes for the epistemological utility of systematic research designs (the "diacritical method").

For the choice of a theoretically valid research strategy our previous assertions have three basic implications. First we must conceive of the research situation as being part of the personality investigated. Adequate research methods need not eschew interaction with the subjects but may rather profitably make use of "those individual and concrete person-environment constellations which conspicuously expose their dynamic characteristics" (Helm, 1960, p. 374).

Second, according to the dynamic-structural trait concept "the task of psychometrics is to isolate, to identify and, so far as possible, to measure separately (though not as separate objects!) the important components of (behavioral) variance" (Loevinger, 1957, p. 649; parantheses added). We would add: The task is to translate a particular personality theory into an adequate research situation which allows the researcher to infer the structural and the dynamic component of the hypothesized traits, i.e. their behavioral relevance ('cognitive anchoring') and their directional value (attitude, orientation).

Third, the problem of multiple determination of acts, and the resulting functional ambiguity of acts, should not be viewed as being insolvable in principle ('indeterminism') but can be coped with through applying the 'diacritical method' (Brunswik). I believe this hermeneutic device is well suited to sort out to which of several functional unities (traits) an act belongs. It requires that a *pattern of responses to a systematically (orthogonally) designed pattern of probing questions* is analyzed as to which trait, or set of traits, account for that particular person-situation *interaction*.

With regard to these three points, I think, the question of whether trait assesment is executed by a skillful clinician through personal interview or by a survey researcher though carefully prepared questionnaires is of minor importance (Lind & Wakenhut, 1980). The variation of theoretical validity within each approach seems to be greater than between them.

There are, however, some good reasons why personality research cannot rest solely on highly elaborate and extensive clinical interviews. The lack of sufficient transparancy and systematics, which makes it all too easy for uninformative circularities and trivial explanations to creep in, is not the least important reason for attempting a new, complementary, approach to personality research.

3. The design of Experimental Questionnaires

At the first sight this method appears to be a contradiction in itself Experimental Questionnaires (EQs) neither fit into usual methodological categories, e.g. Cattel's distinction of L-, Q-, and T-techniques, nor are they a new way of utilizing questionnaire methods within experiments. This method rather combines, maybe in a surprising way, the meaningfulness and economy of the questionnaire technique with the epistemological advantages of systematic, multifactorial design.

Unlike self-report questionnaires, EQs are conceptualized as "objective tests" in Loevinger's (1957) sense, namely in the sense "of structured tests viewed behavioristically" (p. 648). The behaviorism of EQs, however, is not a Watsonian or a Skinnerian one but more like the "subjektive behaviorism" of Miller et al. (1960) and the "social behaviorism" of G. H. Mead (1968/1934). EQs are viewed "subjectively" because they are designed to penetrate through the surface of unrelated behavioral acts and to assess the dynamic trait structure of individuals EQs are, nevertheless, also social in so far as their scientifically construed categories are bound to the sociality of communication.

EQs are used nomothetically (i.e. they seek systematic regularities of human behavior), but, at the same time, they possess idiographic sensibility.[4]

EQs are designed to answer two questions of measurement in this order:

1. To what degree does a hypothesized trait account for an observed pattern of responses of an individual? and

2. in which direction does this factor influence to test response? While the first question aims at the assessment of the cognitivestructural component of a particular trait, the second question aims at a trait's dynamic-motivational component (Lind, 1980a).

In addition, EQs may be designed as a multi-factorial experiment so that more than one dynamic trait can be incorporated in order to study a more complex system of traits. This way EQs also facilitate means to cope with the problem of functional ambiguity. Through multifactorially designed EQs it becomes possible to find out which of several traits functions alone, or in combination with other traits, as a frame of reference for a particular person-situation interaction. In principle, an unlimited number of traits can be analysed diacritically by EQs, although in practice the rule of parsimony (Ockham's razor) may be applied which entails starting always with as few hypothesized traits on possible.

As an example for EQs, the three-factorial design of the "Moralisches-Urteil-Test" (m-u-t; Lind 1978) is depicted in Tab. 1. The aim of this is to assess the cognitive and the evaluative component of an individual's moral consciousness. The m-u-t has been developed on the basis of Kohlberg's theory of moral-cognitive development

[4] Unfortunately 'nomothetic science' is sometimes misunderstood as postulating a priori the lawfulness of any behavior. This is, of course, not the case. Nomothetic sciences are rather law-seeking. They critically test the question to which extent the hypotheses of lawfilness is empirically valid. This implies also that sciences have to be aware of idiosyncracies.

(Kohlberg, 1969, Rest, 1973, Lind, 1978, 1980a), and on a theory of response behavior which contains three tentative assumptions derived from recent moral judgment research (Keasey, 1974, Lind, 1977):

These assumptions assert (1) that an individual's evaluation of moral arguments for and against a particular moral decision is determined by the quality of the moral argument, i.e. by the individual's attention to the Stage-type of moral reasoning exhibited by the arguments (according to Kohlberg, 1969);

(2) that the statements may be also evaluated with regard to their agreement or disagreement with one's own opinion about the moral dilemma; and

(3) that inconsistency of judgment behavior may not just indicate a lack of moral development but a greater differentiation; it may indicate (a) the successful coordination of the moral consciousness factor and the opinion agreement factor ('mature moral commitment'; Perry, 1970); and (b) the differentiation of the preferences for a particular level of moral reasoning according to the situation context in which the moral decision is made ('contextual relativism').

The test-version depicted in Tab. 1 contains two subtests (Theft and Mercy Killing). Each is introduced by a brief description of a dilemma of action and by a subsequent question as to how "wrong" or "right" the respondent judges the solution chosen by the protagonist. Thereafter six pro-arguments and six con-arguments are presented, each at random order.

Tab. 1: *Experimental questionnaire: The design of the "Moralisches-Urteil-Test"* (m-u-t)

Independent variables (factors)			Dependent variable
1. Story (dilemma)	2. Stage of reasoning	3. Pro-Con (opinion-agreement)	Judgment of acceptability
– A	–I –II –III –IV –V –VI	Pro Con	completely unacceptable completely acceptable −4 −3 −2 −1 0 +1 +2 +3 +4
– B	–I –II –III –IV –V –VI	Pro Con	

For scoring the m-u-t we have surveyed several computational procedures (Lind et al., 1976, Lind, 1980a). Hitherto the analysis of variance components proved to be one of the most adequate and fruitful methods. It enables the psychologist to quantify the degree to which a certain hypothesized trait, alone or in conjunction with others, determines an individual's pattern of response behavior (the structural-cognitive component). The evaluative component is scored as usual by summated ratings (average response).

4. Some concluding remarks on the empirical utility of Experimental Questionnaires

We have argued that prevailing standards of test evaluation do not apply to assessment methods like Experimental Questionnaires. But this does not mean that there are no other ways to ascertain the goodness of a research method. I can see at least two possibilities: One is concerned with the *theoretical validity* of the assessment technique. Since we have 'deduced' the concept of Experimental Questionnaires from a theoretical proposition this method may legitimately be evaluated with regard to that claim. The other criterion involves both theory and method. The choice of the dynamic-structural definition of traits entails that a test based on this definition is an *empirically useful* device for personality research in so far as it widens the 'categorial overlap' (Campbell, 1963) between the researcher and his, or her, subjects. The greater this categorial overlap is, the better, we can say, we understand a particular person-situation interaction. I believe that both criteria provide good means for criticizing the method of Experimental Questionnaires, and thus foster the progress of personality research.

Theoretical validity, of course, cannot be quantified but must be established on the grounds of conceptual analysis and theoretical reflection. A profound explication of the respective theory as well as some kind of expert-rating of the resulting test are the major devices for securing theoretical validity. This has been done in the case of the m-u-t. So for the time being we shall assume that it is theoretical valid.[5]

With respect to the categorial overlap of Experimental Questionnaires there is some quantitative evidence available. The m-u-t which is based on the EQ-methodology has been employed recently in a number of studies comprising several hundred of subjects. One of the most important results is that some propositions of Kohlberg's (1969) theory of cognitive-moral development were rather well corroborated (Lind, 1980b). A second important result is that it may suffice to take into account only a few dynamic-structural traits in order to understand a person's judgment behavior in a moral situation. This is of relevance for the utility criterion.

Ideally the hypothesized trait-structure of moral consciousness should account completely for the variance of the individual response behavior in the experimental situation. This does not necessarily imply that behavior is completely predictable, but that we can comprehend it as meaningful given the knowledge of a particular trait structure.

Past personality research has shown that such a complete overlap between theory and reality is far from being reached. Hartshorne and May's (1928) Studies in the Nature of Character revealed only minimal categorial overlap; the squared inter-correlations of children's behavior across different 'moral' situations, which was

[5] Note that EQs always require the existence of an explicit substantial theory (which is more than a statistical account of singular investigations or a mathematical model). Otherwise there is no reason for employing EQs. On the other hand a theoretically valid EQ can be regarded as the explication of a theoretical concept and, therefore, constitute the meaning of the concept. If there was non concept from the outset, such an "operational" definition would be meaningless.

141

taken as an indicator for this, was as low as .05. This is even below the .10 which Mischel (1968) has identified as a barrier to past personality research.

G. Allport criticized this study for being a typical representative of the External-Effect definition of traits. Children may not behave consistently with some socially defined criteria and still be consistent with regard to their own motives. Bem and Allen (1974) showed, though with regard to another topic, that consistency increases up to .20 when the individual's awareness of trait consistency is taken into account.

Since EQs represent a new approach which claims greater adequacy with regard to the dynamic-structural trait concept we should expect a better agreement between the hypothetical model and the reality of an individual's reasoning in a moral situation. In fact, in a study of German high school graduates ($N = 516$) one trait – moral consciousness – already accounts on average (median) for .27 of the individual's behavior variance. There is also evidence that this number varies with the level of moral development; the less people are developed the less they apply moral dimensions in their judgment behavior (Keasey, 1974, Lind, 1980a).

Tab. 2: 'Categorial overlap' in three approaches to personality research: a tentative comparison

Approach (-example)	Categorial overlap* r^2
1. Common trait, external-effect definition	
– Hartshorne & May (1928)	.05
– Mischel (1968)	
2. Restricted common trait definition	
– Bem & Allen (1974)	.20
3. Internal-structure definition, dynamic-structural traits	
– Lind et al. (1980)	.27

* Squared correlational coefficient, i.e. proportion of variance of judgment accounted for by moral consciousness and personality traits, respectively.

But this can also be looked at from another angle. Usually a trait is assessed, regardless of whether there is a large, medium or no categorial overlap between the researcher and the particular subject. If the consistency of test-behavior across a sample of persons is not perfect, according to most textbooks, this can be coped with by enlarging the number of items, unless reliability is zero.

Besides the frequent experience that more items often add more 'heterogeneity' to the assessment device and thus, in practice, often do not improve it, this strategy is basically problematic as noted above. In many cases we 'measure' traits that do not exist in subjects and *do not even notice it*. Someone who does not 'have' the particular trait measured gets the same score as the person who exhibits a medium (or neutral) 'amount' of this trait. E.g. a person who is as much introvert as extravert in his responses to individual items of a scale receives the same, average, score as a person who responds consistently medium extrovert, or medium intravert.

In assessing the degree to which a hypothesized dynamic component organizes instrumental acts into a functional whole, Experimental Questionnaires avoid this pitfall. This method provides a measure for ascertaining the degree of categorial overlap between an individual person and the researcher before the respective category is applied for classifying this person. The person is thus not forced into a descriptive system which actually does not tally with his, or her, way of perceiving the world. The measure of 'cognitive anchoring' of a trait thus gives us also an opportunity of becoming aware of the descriptive adequacy or inadequacy of the theory on which the assessment technique is based. It tells us something about the ability of a psychological theory to understand particular persons and persons in general. (I am deliberately not speaking of the psychologist's ability to understand since this may deviate greatly from the common knowledge as codified in a theory. Certainly, and hopefully, many psychologists also make successful use of other sources of knowledge).

References

ALLPORT, G.: Pattern and growth in personality. New York: Holt, 1961

BEM, D. J., and A. ALLEN: On predicting some of the people some of the time. Psychological Review 81, 506–520, 1974

BLOCK, J.: Personality measurement. Overview. In: International Enzyclopedia of the Social Sciences, Vol. 12, 30–36, 1968

BRUNSWIK, E.: Representative design and propabilistic theory in a functional psychology. Psychological Review 62, 193–217, 1955

CATTELL, R. B.: The description and measurement of personality. New York: World Book, 1946

CAMPBELL, D. T.: Social attitudes and other acquired behavioral dispositions. In: S. Koch (Ed.) Psychology: A study of a science, Vol. 3. New York: McGraw-Hill, 94–172, 1963

CRONBACH, L., and P. MEEHL: Construct validity in psychological tests. Psychological Bulletin 52, 281–301, 1955

FISKE, D., and P. H. PEARSON: Theory and Techniques of Personality measurement. Annual Review 49–86, 1970

GRAUMANN, C. F.: Eigenschaften als Problem der Persönlichkeitsforschung. In: Ph. Lersch and H. Thomae (Eds.), Handbuch der Psychologie, 4. Bd., Persönlichkeitsforschung und Persönlichkeitstheorie. Göttingen: Hogrefe 87–154, 1960

HARTSHORNE, H., and M. A. MAY: Studies in the nature of character. Vol. 1. Studies in deceit. New York: Macmillan, 1928

HELM, J.: Über Gestalttheorie und Persönlichkeitspsychologie. In: Ph. Lersch and H. Thomae (Eds.), Handbuch der Psychologie, 4. Bd., Persönlichkeitsforschung und Persönlichkeitstheorie. Göttingen: Hogrefe, 1960

HEMPEL, C. G.: The theoretician's dilemma: A study in the logic of theory construction. In: H. Feigl, M. Scriven and G. Maxwell (Eds.), Minnesota studies in the philosophy of science. Vol. II. Minneapolis: University of Minnesota Press, 37–98, 1958

HILKE, R.: Zu den impliziten „anthropologischen" Voraussetzungen der klassischen Testtheorie. Diagnostica XXVI, 99–111, 1980

KEASEY, Ch.-B.: The influence of opinion-agreement and qualitativ supportive reasoning in the evaluation of moral judgments. Journal of Personality and Sociel Psychology 30, 477–482, 1974

KEMPF, W.: Kritische Bemerkungen zu impliziten Voraussetzungen psychologischer Testtheorie und -praxis und ihre Angemessenheit zur Erfüllung der Aufgaben curricularer Evaluation. Vortrag zum Symposium „Aspekten von Leerplanevaluatie", Veldhoven (Holland)

KOHLBERG, K.: Feldtheorie in den Sozialwissenschaften. Bern/Stuttgart: Huber 1963 (Original: Field theory in social sciences. New York: Harper, 1951)

LIND, G.: Wie mißt man moralisches Urteil? Probleme und alternative Möglichkeiten der Messung eines komplexen Konstrukts. In: G. Portele (Ed.), Sozialisation und Moral. Weinheim: Beltz, 1978, S. 171–201

LIND, G.: Zur Bestimmung des Entwicklungsstandes der moralischen Urteilskompetenz beim Übergang vom Gymnasium auf die Universität. In: J. Domnick (Ed.), Aspekte grundlagenorientierter Bildungsforschung. Forschungsberichte 18, Zentrum I Bildungsforschung, Universität Konstanz 1980 a

LIND, G.: Toward an evaluation of the impact of university on students' moral development. In: E. v. Trotsenburg (Ed.), Higher Education – A Field of Study. Vol. 5. Frankfurt: Lang, 1980 b

LIND, G., A. NIELSEN and U. SCHMIDT: Moralisches Urteil und Hochschulsozialisation – Materialien, Beiträge. Arbeitsunterlage 40, Forschungsgruppe Hochschulsozialisation. Universität Konstanz 1976

LIND, G., J.-U. SANDBERGER and T. BARGEL: Moral judgment, egostrength and democratic orientations – Some theoretical contiguities and empirical findings. Arbeitsunterlage 64, Forschungsgruppe Hochschulsozialisation. Universität Konstanz 1980

LOEVINGER, J.: Objective tests as instruments of psychological theory. Psychological Reports 9, 635–694, 1957

LOEVINGER, J.: Ego Development. San Francisco: Jossey-Bass, 1976

LUMSDEN, J.: Test theory. Annual Review of Psychology 27, 251–280, 1976

MEAD, G. H.: Geist, Identität und Gesellschaft. Frankfurt: Suhrkamp, 1968 (Originally published: 1934)

MEEHL, P. E.: Theoretical risks and tabular asterisks. Sir Karl, Sir Ronald, and the slow progress of soft Psychology. Journal of consulting and clinical Psychology 46, 806–834, 1978

MILLER, G. A., E. GALANTER and K. H. PRIBRAM: Plans and the structure of behavior. New York: Holt, 1960

MISCHEL, W.: Personality and assessment. New York: Wiley, 1968

MISCHEL, W.: On the future of personality measurement. American psychologist 246–254, 1977

NUNNER-WINKLER, G.: Probleme bei der Messung des moralischen Urteils mit standardisierten Verfahren. In: L. H. Eckensberger (Ed.), Entwicklung des moralischen Urteilens. Universität des Saarlandes. Saarbrücken: Universitätsdruck, 1978

OLWEUS, D.: Der moderne Interaktionismus von Person und Situation und seine varianzanalytische Sackgasse. Zeitschrift für Entwicklungspsychologie und pädagogische Psychologie 8, 171–185, 1976

PERRY, W. G.: Forms of intellectual and ethical development in the college years. New York: Holt, 1970

PIAGET, J.: Erkenntnistheorie der Wissenschaft vom Menschen. Frankfurt: Ullstein 1973 (Original: 1970)

POPPER, K.: Objective Knowledge. An evolutionary approach. Oxford: At the Clarendon Press (Revised Edition), 1979

REST, J. R.: The hierarchical pattern of moral judgment: a study of pattern of comprehension and preference of moral stages. Journal of Personality 41, 86–109, 1973

STERN, W.: Die Differentielle Psychologie in ihren methodischen Grundlagen. Leipzig: Barth 1911

TRAVERS, R. M.: Rational hypotheses in the construction of tests. Educational and psychological Measurement 11, 128–137, 1951

WARREN, H. C., and L. CARMICHAEL: Elements of human psychology. Boston: Houghton Mufflin (Revised edition), 1930

Investigations into the Personality Assessment of Young Children

URSULA SYDOW

An early diagnosis of disorders in the personality development of children requires not only the description of the behavior disorders and symptoms from the parents' and educationists' viewpoint. Moreover, it is of importance to know the children's self-assessment and their own experiences. Diagnostic interviews with young children in these areas are always concerned with two problems:
1. the ability of the children to report on themselves and
2. the usefulness of the questions to obtain information for psychiodiagnosis and for the choice of therapeutic measures.

Whenever we try to discover the personality traits of the child the question arises as to whose reports will provide more useful information about the characteristic qualities of the child – the reports of the mothers' or the children's self-reports? A further question is what should one do, for example, if mothers' and children's reports differ? Most of the investigators incline to rely more on the mothers' statements. However, this inclination is not supported by empirical studies, testing whether children's reports are indeed less useful than those of their educators.

The present paper deals with these problems. We are going to report on an investigation which can be regarded as a first approach to this issue.

Methods of investigation

The persons questioned in our study were 24 normally developed first-grade children and their mothers. The objective of the investigation was to compare the children's and mothers' reports in dealing with the same questions of a child personality inventory. In the first stage of this work we dealt with the requirements for item formulation in the questionnaire. By relying on some empirical findings on language understanding and laguage aquisition (cp. Sydow and Hagendorf, 1979) we wanted to guarantee that the children had the same cognitive prerequisites in order to understand and interpret the questions in the questionnaire as the respective mothers had. The following criteria were applied to the selection of the items:

1. The child has to be able to comprehend the intended content of the items and to reflect on it.

2. The child has to be able to understand the specific meaning of the words used in the questions.

3. The child has to be able to respond properly to the pertinent question according to his main reaction tendencies.

4. The child has to be able to distinguish between his own wishes and facts.

5. Furthermore, we have to take into account the children's particular strategies in dealing with the syntactic structure of statements.

In this study we applied a modified version of the Early School Personality Questionnaire (ESPQ) of Cattell (1966). The questionnaire was revised according to the five criteria mentioned above (cp. Sydow and Hagendorf, 1979).

The ESPQ consists of two parts, each of them with a number of 80 items. The questionnaire was developed for application to children at the age of 6–8 years. In our investigation the mothers were confronted with the same questionnaire and asked to answer the questions according to the caracteristic traits and intentions of their children.

The content of the ESPQ was determined with reference to the "16 PF-Questionnaire" of Cattel for adults. The wide range of items was related to various behavior intentions of the children. A large amount of these questions dealt with social behavior intentions. Moreover, the items referred to predilections and aversions, emotional reaction tendencies of the child, evaluations which the child registers from the persons of his environment and – last but not least – his tendency to respect orders and prohibitions.

In addition to their statements in the ESPQ the mothers were asked to describe the predominant (*observable*) behavior tendencies of their children in the Stern-Behavior Questionnaire. This is a behavior-rating questionnaire which consists of 100 items, concentrating mainly on social behavior, the observance of orders and behavior standards and behavior in performance situations.

Results and discussion

1. *Frequency of mother-child differences dependent on the item contents*

By a comparison of mothers' and children's ESPQ-statements we obtained the following results. In many questions the mothers' reports coincided with the children's reports. However, differences appeared more frequently in a number of items. We found a striking difference between mothers and children that seems to be due to the particular content-domain of items. The mother-child differences did not indicate any regularities dependent on the personality dimensions to which the items were assigned (by factor analysis) by Cattell. Therefore we applied a data analysis dependent on the content of the items. They were connected, for reasons to be explained in detail in the discussion of results, to the following domains: 1. social behavior toward other children, 2. preferred spare-time activities and 3. observance of orders and prohibitions.

The striking dependency of mother-child differences on the content-domain of items led to the conclusion that differences in the mother-child reports are not only dependent on developmentally determined response strategies of the children. In this case we would expect nearly the same differences independent of the particular thematic domain in question. Thus, on the contrary, we assume that the cause of divergent reports has something to do with divergent opinions of mothers and children about the same subjects.

The comparison of the relative frequencies of mother-child differences showed that the most striking differences occured in the domain "social behavior towards other children".

Some examples of the items characterized by a relatively large number of mother-child differences were:

146

1. If your friends were not in the playground, would you also play with strange children?
   (Contrary to their children, most mothers hold that their sons and daughters would play with strange children.)
2. Imagine that your class-mate tells you that he has trouble at home. Are you sorry for him or are you not?
   (Contrary to their children, mothers always think that they will be sorry for their class-mates. The children, however, often attach their readiness for compassion to certain pre-conditions, e. g. that their class-mate has trouble through no fault of his or her own or he has trouble because of a minor offence.)

The relative frequencies of mother-child differences in the various content-domains (social behavior, preferred activities and the observance of orders and prohibitions) were compared and statistically proved by the sci-square method.

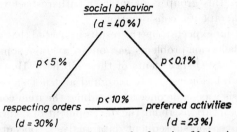

Fig. 1: Mother-child differences (d) dependent on the domain of behavior.

It could be shown that in the domain of social behavior there were significantly more mother-child differences than in the domain of observing orders and prohibitions ($p < 5\%$). That means that the differences in the domain of social behavior were considerably greater than could be expexted for reasons of social desirability. This interpretation can be supported by the fact that the statements of the mothers and children in the domain "social behavior" are distributed among both the alternative answers, so that the discrepancies cannot be reduced to a unilateral tendency in answers of one of the persons questioned.

Furthermore, the relative frequency of agreement in the domain "preferred activities" was much more greater than in the domain "social behavior towards other children" ($p < 0,1\%$). This can be explained by the fact that the mothers in general have only limited impressions of their children's behavior outside family life. Therefore we assume that the mothers' reports in the domain "preferred activities" are more valid than their reports in the domain "social behavior towards other children".

2. *Relations between mother-child differences and the children's tendency to display behavior disorders*

In the next stage of the data-analysis we tried to discover causes of the mother-child discrepancies in the ESPQ-statements. Therefore we tried to establish relations between the tendency of the children to display behavior disorders (according to the descriptions by the mothers in the Stern-Behavior Questionnaire) and the frequency of the mother-child differences in the ESPQ-statements. For this purpose the group of children was split according to the degree of the various types of behavioral deviations. Corresponding to the main scales of the Stern-Behavior Questionnaire the children were divided into the respective two sub-groups according to the following criteria:

1. the degree of "behavioral problems" (aggressiveness, egotism and disobedience),
2. the degree of "social inhibition" and
3. the degree of what Stern calls "socialization" (a factor analytically defined scale which is characterized by performance behavior and the observance of moral norms for behavior).

Analyzing the data of the Stern-Behavior Questionnaire we found that the difference between the C-values were as a rule not greater than 3 points and that they were spread around the mean values of the corresponding age norms for behavior. That means the following conclusions about the relations between behavior qualities (Stern-questionnaire) and the various statements about the children's intentions (ESPQ) will be drawn only for children without considerable behavior problems. Psychodiagnostically, this group is of interest with respect to psychoprophylactic rather than psychotherapeutic considerations.

In agreement with our expectations the results indicated that children with stronger tendencies towards behavior problems had on an average some more differences in comparison with the ESPQ-statements of their mothers. However, contrary to our expectations, the correlation was only marginal and not significant. Therefore the following data analysis was made once again taking the item content into account.

Considering the observations about the development of neurotic disorders and our results described above, the subsequent data analysis concentrated on the domain "social behavior towards other children". There we pooled the items with comparable contents and obtained two larger groups he first item group concerned the intentions of the children towards sociable versus unsociable (i.e. isolative) behavior. The second one applied to their dominance, i.e. the intentions of the children to realise their wishes and needs in interaction with other children. We obtained the following results:

Tab. 1.: *Answer tendencies of mothers and children in the domains "sociability" and "dominance" (n = the frequency of statements of the 24 children and their mothers)*

Sociability			Dominance		
Statements	yes	no	Statements	yes	no
Children	63% (n=121)	37% (n=71)	Children	47% (n=67)	53% (n=77)
Mothers	77% (n=148)	23% (n=44)	Mothers	60% (n=87)	40% (n=57)

I. Comparison of mother-child differences in the various groupings of children

1. Mothers generally seem to underestimate the need of the children to be alone sometimes to withdraw from other children, or to avoid contacts with strange children. These differences between the respective tendencies in answers could be shown as statistically significant ($p < 2,5\%$) by the sci-square method.

2. Furthermore, the mothers tend to overestimate their children's intentions to realise their wishes and needs in interaction with other children. The differences between the respective tendencies in answers could also be shown as statistically significant ($p < 1\%$) by the sci-square method.

148

3. In all groupings of children, which – according to the descriptions in the Stern-Behavior Questionnaire – incline more to behavior problems (more behavior disorders and stronger social inhibition, lower "socialization"), the above-mentioned differences between the mothers' and children's answer tendencies were greater and sttatistically significant. On the other hand, in all groupings of children with lower inclination to behavior problems these differences were smaller and statistically insignificant.

II. The relation between mothers ESPQ-statements and the behavior qualities of children

We found no striking differences between the mothers' descriptions of their children's intentions in their social interaction, which can be brought in relation to the predominant behavior tendencies (or behavior problems) of the children. Thus, we assume that the mothers have a relatively unspecific idea of the children's needs and intentions in their social interaction with other children, and that they therefore underestimate the individual characteristics of their children.

III. The relation between childrens' ESPQ-statements and their behavior qualities

1. Remarkable, statistically significant differences, which are related to the inclination of the children to behavior problems, occurred in the children's self-descriptions about their intentions in social interaction.

Tab. 2: *The relation between the intentions of children in their social interaction and their inclination to behavior disorders (n = the frequency of statements)*

Sociability

Statements of the children	yes	no
Fewer behavior disorders	72% ($n = 69$)	28% ($n = 27$)
More behavior disorders	54% ($n = 52$)	46% ($n = 44$)

Children with relatively stronger tendencies to behavior disorders had considerably lower needs for social communication with other children, and respectively more requirements for being sometimes alone.

It is interesting that besides the statistical relations between the needs for social communication and behavior disorders there is also a logical relation, which is connected with immediately therapeutic consequences. Thus, it is an important question for the choice of methods of therapeutic intervention, whether the behavior disorders of a child occur in connection with a strong need for social contact, or whether the behavior disorders are connected with a tendency towards indifference to social integration within a group. This fact was already pointed out by Slavson (1956) in his description of indicative criteria for a group therapy.

2. Contrary to our expectations we could not find any relations between the social inhibition of the children (according to their mothers' descriptions in the Stern-Behavior Questionnaire) and their intentions to realise (or not to realise) their wishes and needs in social interaction with other children. Educational processes, which are determined by individually given and societydetermined circumstances, should not

be undervalued in their responsibility for this results. However, the interviews with the children indicated that the statements about the intentions of realising their own wishes and needs in social interaction with others are much more determined by situational conditions than by personality traits. For example, whether a child realises his initial wishes at play within a social group, depends – according to the children's statements – to a large extent on the imagination at play of the other children, on the fact as to whose ideas at play are better, how strong the emotional relationships are within the group, how big the differences are in age or physical superiority compared with other children, etc.

Finally, we want to emphasize once again that these results were obtained with children whose behavior qualities did not show any larger deviations from the statistical age norms and that the assumptions based on the results obtained should be confirmed to a corresponding population.

Conclusions

We have to point out that our investigation is only a first approach in dealing with developmentally determined validity problems of child personality diagnostics. Thus, the results achieved should primarily provide a guidance for subsequent empirical studies, and the conclusions we have drawn should be regarded as hypotheses for further research.

1. The results indicate that the statements of first-grade children about their intentions in social interaction are of remarkably diagnostic importance, and in cases of doubt could be considered more significant than the respective statements of their mothers.

2. A description of children's personality by their mothers is to be completed in every case by interviews of the child. This principle has consequences not only for the application of free explorations but also implicates the aim of promoting the development of standardized personality questionnaires for younger children, which up to now has been neglected. In this context the ESPQ by Cattell can be regarded as a first important approach to this domain.

3. The results of our investigation have shown that the intentions of children in social interaction with others indicate not only personality traits but also individual characteristics of the corresponding social partners or the composition of the social group. Thus, there is evidence for the empirical relevance of the principles of dialectic-materialistic determinism for personality diagnostic research (cp. Schmidt, 1970), which should be increasingly taken into account in further approaches of the personality assessment of young children.

References

CATTEL, R. B.: Guidebook for the Early School Personality Questionnaire "ESPQ". Institute of Personality and Ability Testing, Champaign, Illinois, USA, 1966

HÖCK, K., H. HESS and E. SCHWARZ: Der Beschwerdenfragebogen für Kinder. Berlin, 1978

SCHMIDT, H.-D.: Persönlichkeitsdiagnostik und Persönlichkeitstheorie. In: Rösler, H.-D., H. D. Schmidt, H.-D. Szewczyk (Eds.), Persönlichkeitsdiagnostik. Berlin, 1970

SLAVSON, S. R.: Einführung in die Gruppentherapie. Göttingen, 1956

STERN, K.: Der Verhaltensfragebogen. Paper presented at the symposium „Forschungen zur Diagnostik und Therapie psychischer Fehlentwicklungen", Berlin 1979

SYDOW, U., and H. HAGENDORF: Zur Entwicklung von Persönlichkeitsbefragungen von Kindern. Paper presented at the symposium „Forschungen zur Diagnostik und Therapie psychischer Fehlentwicklungen", Berlin 1979

Diagnosing Social Behaviour in Neurotics, Psychotics and Abusers

EDITH KASIELKE, KLAUS HÄNSGEN, HEIDEMARIE HUGLER
and FREYA KNISPEL

Disturbed interpersonal relations and maladapted social behaviour are main characteristics of neurotic patients as well as of other psychopathological groups. They
determine the course of the illness and are relevant for prognosis too (Bodalew, 1970,
Weise, 1971, Seidel et al., 1978). Therefore it is very important for clinical psychologists to diagnose the social behaviour and social feelings of their patients. Psycho-
and sociotherapists are engaged in the modification of abnormal social behaviour not
only of neurotics but also of psychotics, alcoholics and drug-addicts and other psychopathological groups. But they can be successful only if they are able to assess differently the abilities of patients to communicate with other persons, to empathize
their emotions, to correct their own behaviour dependent on the assessment by
others.

In recent years we have been dealing with the problem of diagnosing such abilities in
patients (Helm et al., 1974, Kasielke, 1981). Traditionally we began by using methods
of self-judgement as questionnaires and Q-sort-methods (Q-data sensu Cattell).
Researching only neurotics we could use these methods very effectively and economi-
cally. We were able to find out four socially related personality-dimensions, which are
suitable for discrimination between special forms of neurosis. Cluster- and discrim-
inantanalytic studies have shown socially-relevant attributes of patients being very
sensitive to modification by psychotherapy, especially client-centered therapy (as
developed by Rogers, 1973, Tausch, 1973, Helm, 1978).

But this kind of psychodiagnostic is one-sided, it is concentrated only on the
patient's characteristics, while the problems both of neurotics and other abnormals
in their relations with other persons include difficulties in communication. Therefore
we have to diagnose these disturbances too, so as to be able to help the patients correct their behaviour.

Unfortunately there are no suitable instruments available for this task. Using the
Grid-method of Kelly (1955), Hugler (1979) developed a factoranalytic-based four-
scaled instrument in order to fill the gap. This instrument makes possible the diagnosis of characteristics of the patient by self-judgement (self-concept), judgement by
other persons (rater-concept) and by the expectation the patient has as to how he is
judged by others ("social self" sensu Wylie 1961 or expectation-concept). Here an
example:

Tab. 1

	very- a little-	
The patient judges himself: I am active		not active
		self-concept

His co-patients' judgement: he is active .... not active
rater-concept

The patient says: I think

My co-patient judges that I am active .... not active
expectation-concept

By comparing the self-concept, the rater-concept and the expectationconcept, we will find out to what extent the patient is able: 1. to judge himself, 2. to agree with his partner and 3. to know how he will be judged by his partner.

In two series we tested both a group of neurotics and a controlgroup of healthy persons (Hugler, 1979); both a group of schizophrenics and a control-group of students by a short form of the test (Hallensleben, 1980). The neurotics were at the beginning of psychotherapy, the schizophrenics were not in an acute phase, but in a phase of of rehabilitation.

It was necessary to explore groups of patients and controls. Each of them had to act both as reference person and as rater for his co-patients. Because of the low motivation of some psychotics a very complicated experimental design was used.

In order to test the ability to differentiate between persons, the schizophrenics had to judge persons who were popular and those who were unpopular in their groups (divided according to the ratings made by medical staff and by patients using the social-distance-profile by Feldes (1976). The neurotics and the control-group judged only popular persons.

We will analyze only some of the results of these studies.

To make some tendencies clearer, we combined the data of the two different studies in one graph. In the following figures the self-concepts (SC), rater-concepts (RC) and expectation-concepts (EC) of the three groups: neurotics, psychotics and normals are given. Along the abcisses, the scales of the test:

1. social activity (similar extraversion)
2. mental abilities and achievement motivation
3. emotional stability and
4. social flexibility, social adjustment.

High standard points (C-scale) refer to a healthy personality, low values to disturbances.

Self-concepts (Fig. 1a)

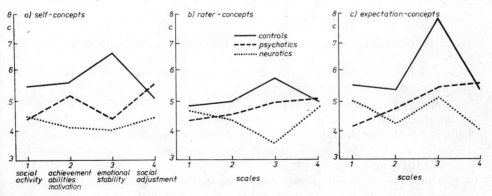

Fig. 1 a–c): Different assessment-concepts within 3 Person groups.

As expected the control group describe themselves as being most socially active, efficient and highly motivated, very stable and sufficiently adjusted.

Neurotics rate themselves as being more introverted, not so efficient, emotionally unstable and moderately adjusted.

Schizophrenics state that they are introverted too, but more efficient and motivated and nearly as unstable as neurotics. Though they have many problems in social adaptation, they describe themselves as being well adjusted.

Here we are confronted with a well-known problem: the tendency of psychotics to describe themselves as very positive. But contrary to other findings which say that schizophrenics deny especially their symptoms and topics relevant to neuroticism (for example by Behrends and Decker, 1977, Steinmeyer, 1975, Pfotenhauer and Wellhöfer, 1975) the distortion of self-evaluation in our findings is especially large in scale four – social adjustment.

Rater -concepts (Fig. 1b)

The ratings given by co-patients about the reference patients show the same tendencies, but they are not so marked as in the self-ratings.

Expectation-concepts (Fig. 1c)

The controls expect to be assessed as very stable, socially active and efficient and well adjusted.

It a interesting to note the expectation-profile of the neurotics: contrary to the self-concepts, they expect to be rated more socially active and more emotionally stable by others than they think to be themselves (see also Fig. 2)

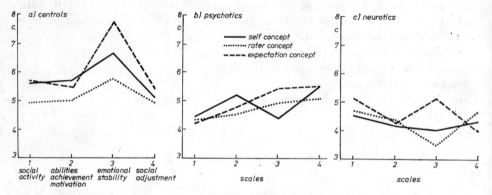

Fig. 2a–c): Different assessment-concepts and relations within and between some person groups.

Comparison of self-concepts, rater-concepts and expectation-concepts in controls, psychotics and neurotics (Fig. 2a–c)

Comparing the three groups of profiles according to the level of assessment scores, a high similarity between the three concepts in all groups is striking – the controls naturally with the highest levels, the neurotics as known from other studies the lowest levels, but the most disturbed psychotics evaluated themselves as more normal than neurotics do.

But there are some interesting differences within the groups, too. The controls expect to be rated more stable and socially adjusted than they pretend to be. They tend to rate other persons more critically (RC is significant lower). This tendency is not so marked in the patient groups. The differences between psychotics and neurotics in scale 4 are interesting: neurotics rated other persons more socially adjusted than themselves, but psychotics do the contrary; obviously they are more able to see social problems of their co-patients than their own, self-concept as well as expectation-concept are unrealistically high.

Analyzing the stability-scores, neurotics recognize their own emotional lability, they rate other neurotics as being to a higher degree unstable than they think to be themselves, but they expect that their co-patients are not able to recognize their emotional problems. So the relevance of the scales (scale 4 for psychotics, scale 3 for neurotics) is taken into account, too, in evaluation of the diagnostic possibilities of self-assessments.

These and the other results here not mentioned suggest that neurotics as well as normals are sufficiently able:
1. to give reliable and valied self-evaluations
2. to judge co-patients and other reference-persons realistically,
3. to know how they are rated by others.

Schizophrenics not only deny their symptoms, they are even not able to evaluate their own social abilities.

They realize the characteristics of other persons a little bit better, but not sufficiently enough; and they have difficulties in recongizing how they are perceived by others.

Are these tendencies typical of all schizophrenics or do they depend especially on the patient's position within their group?

The following figures contain the results of *self-concepts, rater-concepts and expectation-concepts of popular and unpopular patients* (Fig. 3a, b)

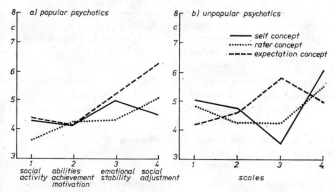

Fig. 3: Different assessment-concepts for popular and unpopular psychotics

Comparing the rater-concepts, we can state that the unpopular patients are rated as being more socially active (extraverted) than popular patients, there are no significant differences in the other three scales. The relations between self-concepts and expectation-concepts in scales 3 and 4 are very interesting regarding emotional stability, the popular patients expect to be rated as they evaluate themselves, whereas the unpopular patients think themselves to be emotional unstable, but expect to be rated by other patients very stable. The most relevant scale of social adjustment shows the problem very distinctly: Though the popular patients expect to be evaluated as well adjusted ("popular") they rate themselves only moderately adjusted ("self-critical''), but the unpopular patients rate themselves as being very socially adjusted and expect to be rated by other to a lesser extent but well enough adjusted.

So, disturbances in person perception seem to be more distinct in unpopular patients, in those schizophrenics who face many problems in social communication, in those patients who need sociotherapy more than others. But the dilemma is that they cannot supply us with reliable informations to diagnose their social abilities.

What can be done?

We want to make only a few remarks about one of our studies (carried out by Knispel), in which we *compared different methods of diagnosing the social behaviour of patients and normals.*

A group of patients (schizophrenics, neurotics, alcoholics and drugaddicts) and a control-group were tested in a standard co-operation-situation, from which several diagnostic criteria were derived, for instance "social dependency" and "social flexibility".

Before playing this game with a fictive partner, the patients had to judge themselves with regard to the same behaviour-characteristics.

Using an adapted form of the PSE-scales, an interviewer evaluated the patients. The only information the interviewer had at his disposal was a standardized interview with the patient.

In addition patients had been judged by their therapist, who had observed them for many weeks.

A personality questionnaire including control-scales made it possible for us to divide the patients into those who had valid self-ratings, those who were diminishers or dissimulators and those who were aggravators or simulators.

Tab. 2: *Compared social-diagnostic methods in the study of* KNISPEL

Method		Population	Aim of research
self-ratings given by patients and controls	personality-questionnaire including control-scales	neurotics, psychotics, abusers and controls	dividing patients into valid, aggravators and diminishers
	revised PSE-scales global ratings of social behaviour	neurotics, psychotics, abusers and controls	diagnosis of social abilities (f.i. social dependency, social flexibility)
interviewer ratings	standardized interviews and ratings given by the interviewer on revised PSE-scales	neurotics, psychotics, abusers	diagnosis of social abilities
therapist ratings	ratings given by therapists after a long-term-observation on revised PSE-scales	neurotics, psychotics, abusers	diagnosis of social abilities
co-operation-situation	standardized strategy-game with a fictive partner, revised form of the technique of MAIWALD 1979	neurotics, psychotics, abusers, controls	diagnosis of social abilities

Fig. 4 shows the results we obtained during this study only for criteria "dependency" (a high score means a high degree of dependency on others).

According to the self-ratings as well as to the co-operation-situation-scores, the control-group behaves significantly more independently than the patient groups ($SR_{c/p} t = 4,85$, $\alpha < 0,05$; $Coop._{c/p} t = 3.58$, $\alpha < 0,01$).

Comparing the self-ratings and the behaviour in the real situation, the scores of patients with valid control-scale-scores are not significantly different, but aggravating and diminishing tendencies in self-ratings are distinct.

Is the interviever or the therapist able to correct these tendencies? Obviously, they are not sufficiently able to do this. Both the interviewers and the therapists diminish and aggravate too, the therapists doing it to a lesser extent than the interviewers.

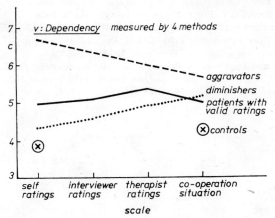

Fig. 4: Comparing methods.

From these results the following *conclusions* can be drawn:

1. For diagnosing social abilities or disabilities in psychotics, self-ratings must be completed by other psychodiagnostic methods.

2. Ratings by diagnosticians which are based only on a standard interview are not sufficient; ratings given by therapists including a long-term-observation of the patient give more correct information about social characteristics of patients, but,

3. it will be best to combine ratings and testing the patient in real situations. Further research is necessary to develop and standardize such diagnostic situations which will make it possible to get extensive and correct information about social disturbances of psychotic patients and indication for special forms of sociotherapy.

References

BEHRENDS, A., and U. DECKER: Überprüfung der Anwendbarkeit psychodiagnostischer Verfahren im psychiatrischen Feld. Dipl.arb. HU Berlin 1977 (unveröff.)

BODALEW, A. A.: Ausbildung von Wissen über die Persönlichkeit anderer Menschen. Leningrad 1970 (russ.)

FELDES, D.: Standardisierung von Schätzskalen für den sozialen Raum und ihre Anwendung als soziometrisches Verfahren bei Gruppenstrukturanalysen in psychiatrischen Krankenhäusern. In: Bach, O., D. Feldes, A. Thom und K. Weise (Hrsg.): Sozialpsychiatrische Forschung und Praxis. Leipzig 1976

HALLENSLEBEN, H.: Die Personeinschätzung schizophrener Patienten. Dipl.arb. HU Berlin 1980 (unveröff.)

HELM, J.: Gesprächspsychotherapie. Berlin 1978

HELM, J., E. KASIELKE und J. MEHL (Hrsg.): Neurosendiagnostik. Berlin 1974

HUGLER, H.: Die Personeinschätzung neurotischer Patienten. Diss. Humboldt-Universität zu Berlin 1979

KASIELKE, E.: Neurosenklassifikation. Berlin 1982

KELLY, G. A.: The psychology of personal constructs. New York 1955

MAIWALD, E., und D. MAIWALD: Zur Analyse von Persönlichkeitsvariablen sozialer Inkompetenz bei Patienten der Psychotherapie. Diss. KMU Leipzig 1979

PFOTENHAUER, P., und B. WELLHÖFER: Kriterienvalidierung und faktorielle Validierung einer Kurzform des MMPI (PPKV). Dipl.arb. HU Berlin 1975 (unveröff.)

ROGERS, C. R.: Die klient-bezogene Gesprächstherapie. München 1973

SEIDEL, K., und H. SZEWCZYK (Eds.): Psychopathologie. Berlin 1978

STEINMEYER, E. M.: Zur internen Validität von Selbstbeurteilungsskalen hinsichtlich Forschung und Diagnostik im psychiatrischen Feld. Z. klin. Psychol. 1975

TAUSCH, R.: Gesprächspsychotherapie. Göttingen 1973

WEISE, K.: Stellung und Funktion der Psychopathologie. In: Schwarz, B., K. Weise und A. Thom (Hrsg.): Sozialpsychiatrie in der sozialistischen Gesellschaft. Leipzig 1971

WYLIE, R. C.: The self concept. Lincoln 1961

Testing Stability of Suggested Behaviour by Means of a "Forcing" System

VLADIMIR GHEORGHIU

A group of hyposuggestible and one of hypersuggestible subjects, each comprising 22 Ss (students between 16 and 12 years of age), were selected by means of a sensorial suggestibility scale, according to the median. Six to eight months later both groups were subjected to the same suggestibility scale with the difference that by use of a "forcing" system an attempt was made to diminish hypersuggestible subjects' scores and to increase those of hyposuggestible ones. A certain change was obtained in hyposuggestibles only. Although after a second test, the global score of this group proved to be higher than the score on the first test, this score was significantly lower than the global one obtained by hypersuggestible subjects on the second test. In general, hypo- as well as hypersuggestible belonged to the same category as previously (hypo- of hypersuggestible) even after the "forcing" system had been applied.

Introduction

Studies on the particularities of suggestibility in the waking state have been recorded from the end of the last century (Scripture, 1893, Seashore, 1895, Binet, 1900). Testing procedures different from those used in the studies of hypnotizability, had an indirect character. In this way the dissimulation of the real goal of investigation was assured. The most appropriate was the field of sensoriality, where according to each sensorial modality, experiments with a wide range of objective or only simulated stimuli could be designed.

Today, there are frequently-used tests originating from old procedures (see Eysenck, 1943, Stukat, 1958, Duke, 1964 etc.). Many studies of correlative purposes emphasized that the variety of procedures used in the field of sensoriality does not permit a rigorous classification (see Duke, 1964 and Evans, 1967).

The difference between a "primary" suggestibility (based on direct motor tests) and a "secondary" one (based on indirect sensorial tests) suggested by Eysenck and Furneaux (1945), and still widespread today, could not be confirmed in general by later studies (see Evans, 1967).

Starting from the analyses of those contradictory results, we tried to underline a few short-comings of research into suggestibility in general and into the field of sensory suggestibility in particular (Gheorghiu, 1972, 1973, Gheorghiu, Hodapp and Ludwig, 1975 etc.). In close connection with our research strategy, which will be presented in this paper too, we considered it necessary to refer to a certain deficiency in traditional research.

Suggested behaviour which could be produced at the sensorial level is usually indicated by the following: (A) a sequence of stimuli which directly "suggest" the way to be followed without any other explanation (the typical example is Binet's progressive lines test). At first, segments successively longer are presented to suggest that the following segments, which in fact are equal in size, would be (eventually) progressively longer; (B) by simulation of an objective stimulation with stimuli generators: the suggestive influence is performed by devices previously verified from a functional point of view or by special explanations delivered by the experimenter (the typical example is Scripture's heat illusion test. Drugs could be used instead of devices (placebos) in order to induce the occurrence as well as modifications in sensorio-perceptual reactivity). (C) By manipulating "prestige" factors, e.g. value judgements, suggestive questions, group pressure, involving allies in experiments as co-judges from Sherif's, Asch's, Stukat's experiments etc.

In all these examples a state of expectancy is developed from which, according to real life experience, a reaction congruent to the suggested direction (should emerge).

It might be that the foreseen effect is not perceived by the subject, but he reacts in the suggested way because "the logic of the situation" convinced him that everything followed as forecast; but he could not concentrate enough in the given situation, because he did not want to contradict the experimenter or because the procedures used did not supply plausible enough explanations to justify his non-perceiving of the stimuli.

Since the subject's declaration concerning the perceiving or not of the announced stimuli, continues to be the indication of the occurrence of suggestion effects, the problem as to whether we had an actual "perception" or a rather conformist tendency or other reaction of this kind remains open. Ivo Kohler notices that, in general, it is a question of the influence of "internal factors" upon perception. In stressing situations such as those in which the individual supervised by several observers is asked to estimate some segments (the majority being previously instructed to make false estimations) it is difficult to assess whether the uninstructed subjects perceive the segments otherwise than they really are, or if they simply go along with the assessments of the majority (Kohler, 1952, p. 95).

By a special procedure we tried to conteract this danger. The procedure was applied only in the study of suggestibility which was based on stimulation of sensorial stimuli. We named it the indirect-direct procedure, starting from the idea that it comprises characteristics of both indirect and direct suggestive procedure. The indirect character, which is predominant, consists of the fact that the real aim of the research (testing the suggestibility) is never uncovered. The direct characteristic consists of the fact that the subject is openly told that the announced stimuli could never be presented, but the experimenter would stimulate its administration. To a certain extent, the system of influencing is disclosed, the manipulations of the devices which the experimenter could use being revealed. What subjects never know previously is the fact that in none of these experimental situations will an objective stimuli be presented and that "perception" of "stimulus" in this condition is due to the subject's receptivity to suggestion. It is expected that by obliging the subject to be more cautions, to be more self-controlled, the indirect-direct procedure would provoke a restriction of the subject's tendency to compliance. His decision, anyway, will be less dependent on his desire to please the experimenter, simply because the experimental design itself does not reveal precisely the experimenter's wish. If, in spite of solicitation not to confound an objective stimuli with a fictive one, the subject would react, it could be supposed that his reaction would be less marked by experimenter – subject relationships.

The sensorial suggestibility scale initially elaborated by us in an indirect variant (Gheorghiu, Hodapp and Ludwig, 1975, Gheorghiu, Grimm and Hodapp, 1978) was meanwhile applied in an indirect-direct form. The twelve items of the scale are based on an experimental process. They test the "perceptions" conditioned by expectant attention system in tactile auditory and visual fields. The global score of the indirect-direct variant proved to be significantly lower than the global score resulting from the application of the same scale in an indirect variant. This result supports our supposition that by means of an indirect-direct variant a reduction of conformist and compliance tendencies takes place.

Research purpose

We intended to verify whether the indirect-direct procedure offers special conditions for testing the suggested behavior stability. Our particular problem was to see whether based on the indirect-direct procedure, a forcing system by which hyper-suggestible would be converted to hyposuggestible and vice-versa could be elaborated. The main purpose was in this way, to test to what extent the resistence towards such a forcing system could be considered as an indicator of suggested behavior consistency.

Experimental design[1]

The already mentioned scale was applied in a shortened form (see Tab. 1). Each of the four selected items was administered three times on each part of the sensorial receptor (first on the right part, then on the left one). The total number of administrations was 24 (three applications twice-right-left – for each of the four items).

The total number of administrations in the complete form of the scale was twenty-four, too; twelve items, twice, right-left.

The subjects were told that the aim of the experiment was to test their sensorial thresholds under difficult conditions.

Subjects were told that the announced stimuli could never be administred, the administration being simulated only, but if presented they would be of low intensity. In order to stress the real difficulties, it was emphasized at the same time that on respective receptors there would be applied obstacles: proofing materials on hands, earphones and half-translucid glasses.

The use of these obstacles was intended to accomplished several objectives: a) to level experimental conditions in a way in which by simple application of obstacles the concentration of attention was reduced; b) to offer some extraplausible explana-tions for the situation in which the announced stimuli eventually were not perceived; in this way the extracted program and the obstacles as well could be considered responsible for their failure in perceiving; c) to increase the degree of uncertainity of perception; the obstacles themselves limit the efficiency of self-control supplying, in this way, a favourable condition for suggestion.

Before the subject was seated in front of the apparatus, he was asked to extract from a pile a program which he was supposed to give immediately to the experimenter,

[1] We wish to thank Nadia Lia for her substantial help during experiments.

without looking at it. He was told that he might be confronted with the following situations. The stimuli will be presented: a) in all the experimental situations (tests); b) fairly frequently; c) seldom; d) not at all. The subject was instructed to concentrate in such a way as to be able to distinguish a real stimulus from a fictive one. In none of the experimental situations was a real stimulus presented. The experimenter behaved as if he had administrated the stimulus each time. Before each test he explained and demonstrated the way the apparatus functioned and how the effect which might accur would be signaled. Each test, as already mentioned, was applied six times, (three times on the right and three times on the left part of the sensorial receptor), the presentation order being always the same. By this means the subject was told that the purpose of the experiment was the determination of sensorial thresholds; that the next stimulation would not be in the same place or from the same direction (see Tab. 1). In this way each repetition was like a new stimulation, and we were assured the least concentration for each new stimulation.

Tab. 1: *4 tests from 12 tests of suggestibility scale used in our research*

	Items	Stimulation Schedule	The test	The charecteristics of repetitions (3 × 2 right-left)
1	Tactile 2	Simulation of a sensorial stimulation by previous objective stimulation	Subject introduces his hand in a box of a display designed for touch sense testing. By means of a windlass 3 weights, each progressively lighter, are succesively moved downwards only two of them actually, touching the subject's hand. The third one is discreetly directed aside. The hand is covered by a cotton bandage	Three different zones in which stimulation follows to be applied are delimitated.
2	Auditory 1	Simulation of stimulus intensification	Throught earphones connected to a sound generator a sound is presented. Some intensification is simulated. Between the earphones and the ear, a piece of sponge is introduced	The next administration to each ear uses the same sound of the same intensity but of different frequency
3	Auditory 4	Simulation of a simultaneous bilateral stimulation	Two chronometers, only one functioning are put to subject's ear. The ear by which the apparent functioning chronometer is brought, was covered by an earphone	Chronometers are put to ears each time from three different directions
4	Visual 3	Simulation of a sensorial stimulation without previous objective stimulation	A black disk is moved toward subject's eye. He is told that in the middle of the disk there might be a green spot. The subject looks to the stimulus throught half translucid spectacles	The disk is brought toward eyes from three different directions each time

Experiments took place in two sessions. In the first one, 64 subjects were involved. This sample was divided into two groups. One of these groups consisted of hyposuggestibles (individual scores between 0–6 below the median value of the entire sample global score), the other one comprising hypersuggestibles (individual scores between 7–20). Each group contained 22 subjects, 11 girls and 11 boys between the ages of 16–17, all college students in Bucharest.

The second experimental session with both groups took place 6–8 months after the first one. The difference between the two experimental sessions consisted in introducing the following explanation, corresponding to the essence of the forcing system we have referred to in the first part of this paper.

The "hyposuggestibles" were told: *"The way in which you reacted in the first test was compared to the program you had selected. In this manner we establish that in several opportunities you did not react, although the stimuli were objectivly presented."*

The "hypersuggestibles" were told: "By comparing *the modality in which you reacted to the first test with the program you had extracted, it was established that in several cases you reacted even when we did not present any actual stimulus."*

Both categories of subjects were told then that they would be tested, again with the same tests, the whole experiment following exactly the same conditions as in the first variant.

The fact was stressed again that the sensorial stimuli administration could not be foreseen and when presented the proportion of stimulation would also be random. Subjects were told that the purpose of this second test was to verify whether the established disparity between stimulation and perception was due to insufficient concentration or to environmental distractions.

Each subject was asked to choose a new program and the whole experimental procedure was the same as that of the first variant.

The main experimental target was to verify to what extent the suggested behavior of the two groups of subjects was modified in the direction suggested by the forcing system and what level would be reached by this modification.

Results

The hystogram shows: a) an increase of hyposuggestibles global score; the difference proved to be statistically significant ($\bar{x} = 2,23$ vs. $\bar{x} = 5,09$); b) no relevant modification in hypersuggestibles global score was obtained ($\bar{x} = 11,09$ vs. $\bar{x} = 11,00$); c) the higher score of hyposuggestibles after the second variant proved further lower statistically than that of hypersuggestibles after this second experiment; d) between the first and the second variant no correlation of hyposuggestibles was obtained. But correlation between the two variants of hypersuggestible was positive and significant ($r\ .70,\ p < .05$).

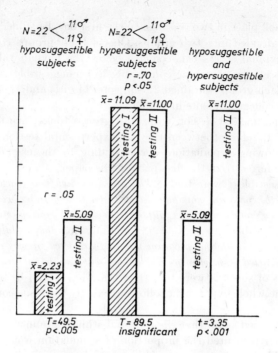

Fig. 1

Discussion

The main result of this research consists without doubt in the fact that the second experiment did not produced any important modification.

The stability of suggested behavior could be testified as a general fact in the situation in which a forcing system was used in order to "convert" hypo- and hypersuggestible subjects. As a group the hyposuggestibles consistently obtained a relatively low score and the hypersuggestibles a higher one.

But there occurred interindividual differences which somehow qualify this result. From a total number of 22 subjects in the hyposuggestible group after the forcing system, 7 obtained a score above median value; in the case of hypersuggestibles, 5 subjects from 22 subjects after forcing obtained a score below median value. Taking into account the correlations and numerical values of global score differences as well, the suggested behavior of hyposuggestible subjects appears less consistent compared to the suggested behavior of hypersuggestibles. When a repetition on a similar sample was performed under habitual conditions, i.e., without a forcing system and without dividing the sample into hypo- and hypersuggestible groups, a reliability coefficient test-retest of r .70 was obtained (Gheorghiu and Albu, 1977).

The general result of the research supports our hypothesis that by application of a sensorial suggestibility scale in an indirect-direct approach an obvious limitation of conformity and compliance tendency is produced.

Otherwise a relevant modification of the behavior previously performed especially by hypersuggestibles was produced after the critique from the forcing system. The individual score of lo hypersuggestible subjects from 22, was even higher after the second variant than after the first one; in the hyposuggestible group, 17 out of 22 subjects after the second variant had a lower score, i.e. equal with that obtained after the first variant. Suggested behavior measured by the scale emphasized cognitive components of suggestibility, including those of an imaginative nature, rather than psychosocial ones.

The question is whether it would not be proper to accord more attention to forcing procedures namely to assessment of resistence to their influence, when stability manifestation is investigated.

List of Contributors

GHEORGHIU, VLADIMIR, Institute of Pedagogical and Psychological Research,
Bucarest, Str. Frumoasa 26, Rumänien

HÄNSGEN, KLAUS, Department of Psychology, Humboldt-University,
1020 Berlin, Oranienburger Straße 18, GDR

HAUTAMÄKI, AIRI, Institute of Behavioral Sciences, University of Joensuu,
80101 Joensuu 10, Finland

HOLMGREN, ALLAN, Department of Psychology, Northwestern University,
Evanston IL 60201, USA

HUGLER, HEIDEMARIE, Department of Psychology, Humboldt-University,
1020 Berlin, Oranienburger Straße 18, GDR

KASIELKE, EDITH, Department of Psychology, Humboldt-University,
1020 Berlin, Oranienburger Straße 18, GDR

KNISPEL, FREYA, Department of Psychology, Humboldt-University,
1020 Berlin, Oranienburger Straße 18, GDR

KOSSAKOWSKI, ADOLF, Institute of Pedagogical Psychology, Academy of Pedagogical
Sciences, 1035 Berlin, Böcklinstraße 1–5, GDR

LIND, G., University of Konstanz, Sonderforschungsbereich 23,
D-7750 Konstanz, FRG

MAGNUSSON, DAVID, Department of Psychology, University of Stockholm,
S-11385 Stockholm, Sweden

NOSAL, C., Polytechnical University of Wroclaw,
53-622 Wroclaw, ul. Zachodnia 38/10, Poland

OBUCHOWSKI, KASIMIERZ, Polish Academy of Sciences, Department of Psychology,
60-814 Poznan, ul. Zwierzyniecka 20, Poland

OTTO, KARLHEINZ, Pädagogische Hochschule Erfurt/Mühlhausen, Institut für
Unterstufenmethodik, 5010 Erfurt, Am Hügel 1, GDR

PALUCHOWSKI, WLADYSLAW, Polish Academy of Sciences, Department of Psychology,
60-814 Poznan, ul. Zwierzyniecka 20, Poland

PETERMANN, HARALD, Department of Psychology, Karl-Marx-University,
7030 Leipzig, Tieckstraße 2, GDR

SHAMES, C., Berkeley, California 94709, 1305 Oxford Street, USA

SCHRÖDER, HARRY, Department of Psychology, Karl-Marx-University,
7030 Leipzig, Tieckstraße 2, GDR

SCHOROCHOWA, E. W., Academy of Sciences of the USSR, Institute of Psychology,
129366 Moscow, ul. Jaroslawskaja 13, USSR

SIGEL, IRVING, E., Educational Testing Service, Psychological Development Research Division, Princeton, New Jersey 08541, USA

SYDOW, URSULA, Humboldt-University, Bereich Medizin (Charité) Kinderklinik,
  1040 Berlin, Schumannstraße 20/21, GDR
THOMAE, HANS, Institute of Psychology, University Bonn,
  D-5300 Bonn 1, An der Schloßkirche 1, FRG
YAKOBSON, S. G., Institute of General and Pedagogical Psychology,
  Moscow, Marx-Prospekt 18, USSR